W9-AFG-830

Multicultural Feminist Therapy

Multicultural Feminist Therapy

Helping Adolescent Girls of Color to Thrive

Edited by
Thema Bryant-Davis

Foreword by **Jessica Henderson Daniel**

AMERICAN PSYCHOLOGICAL ASSOCIATION
Washington, DC

Published by
American Psychological Association
750 First Street, NE
Washington, DC 20002
https://www.apa.org

Order Department
https://www.apa.org/pubs/books
order@apa.org

In the U.K., Europe, Africa, and the Middle East, copies may be ordered from Eurospan
https://www.eurospanbookstore.com/apa
info@eurospangroup.com

Typeset in Charter by Circle Graphics, Inc., Reisterstown, MD

Printer: Sheridan Books, Chelsea, MI
Cover Designer: Gwen J. Grafft, Minneapolis, MN

Library of Congress Cataloging-in-Publication Data

Names: Bryant-Davis, Thema, editor.
Title: Multicultural feminist therapy : helping adolescent girls of color to
   thrive / edited by Thema Bryant-Davis.
Description: Washington, DC : American Psychological Association, [2019] |
   Includes bibliographical references and index.
Identifiers: LCCN 2018059462 (print) | LCCN 2019005886 (ebook) | ISBN
   9781433830686 (eBook) | ISBN 143383068X (eBook) | ISBN 9781433830679
   (hardcover) | ISBN 1433830671 (hardcover)
Subjects: LCSH: Feminist therapy. | Cross-cultural counseling. | BISAC:
   PSYCHOLOGY / Clinical Psychology. | SOCIAL SCIENCE / Feminism & Feminist
   Theory. | PSYCHOLOGY / Psychotherapy / Child & Adolescent.
Classification: LCC RC489.F45 (ebook) | LCC RC489.F45 M85 2019 (print) | DDC
   616.8900835/2—dc23
LC record available at https://lccn.loc.gov/2018059462

http://dx.doi.org/10.1037/0000140-000

Printed in the United States of America

10 9 8 7 6 5 4 3 2 1

*To my daughter Ife Ingoma Davis, may you thrive
and always be at home within yourself.
May you remain mindful of your rich faith,
community, roots, and wings.
You are worthy of respect, love,
and authentic peace.*

*Special thanks to my Pepperdine University
graduate research assistants,
Ana Flora Arounian and Bemi Fasalojo.
I appreciate your dedication, intellect,
compassion, and spirit.
I feel honored to journey with you.*

Contents

Contributors

Thema Bryant-Davis, PhD, Graduate School of Education and Psychology, Pepperdine University, Los Angeles, CA

Monique Clinton-Sherrod, PhD, U.S. Navy, Clemmons, NC

Lillian Comas-Díaz, PhD, Department of Psychiatry and Behavioral Sciences, George Washington University, Washington, DC

Jessica Henderson Daniel, PhD, Harvard Medical School and Children's Hospital, Boston, MA

Jacqueline S. Gray, PhD, Center for Rural Health, University of North Dakota, Grand Forks

Stephanie Hawkins, PhD, Youth Violence Prevention & Community Justice Program, RTI International, Research Triangle Park, NC

Devon S. Isaacs, BA, Department of Psychology, Utah State University, Logan

Shavonne J. Moore-Lobban, PhD, Massachusetts Mental Health Center, Boston

Indhushree Rajan, PhD, Project Satori, Los Angeles, CA

Tiffany G. Townsend, PhD, American Psychological Association, Washington, DC

Pratyusha Tummala-Narra, PhD, Department of Counseling, Developmental and Educational Psychology, Boston College, Chestnut Hill, MA

Melissa J. Wheeler, MA, Department of Educational Psychology, Northern Arizona University, Flagstaff

Eun Jeong Yang, MA, Children's Charter Trauma Clinic, Waltham, MA

Foreword

Every great woman in leadership, in the field of psychology and beyond, started as a girl with great potential who was protected, inspired, mentored, and given the opportunity to flourish. I can attest that my development into the American Psychological Association's first African American female president began with those who emotionally, academically, and spiritually invested in me while I was still a girl. While there is much attention in our field given to children, less focus has been given to adolescents, particularly girls of color.

Preceding my career and throughout my career as a psychologist, I have held a deep commitment to improving the lives of adolescent girls. I am keenly aware of their great potential and strengths, as well as the challenges they face to their full and healthy development. Early in my career, I sought to publish a book that focused on the mental health needs of ethnic minority girls. I faced multiple roadblocks from people who did not see the value of or need for such a book. On my election to the presidency, I knew it was time to revisit my vision for this book because I now had the influence and experience to bring the vision to fruition.

A great part of my work has been dedicated to the practice of working with ethnic minority girls and women. I have seen the devastating impact of stress, trauma, and oppression. These consequences show up as panic, distrust, depression, phobias, body image dissatisfaction, eating disorders, anger, and surrendered dreams and potential. The realities of racism and sexism, as well as discrimination based on disability, sexual orientation, and migration status, negatively impact the lives of the individual girl, as well as her family and entire community. I have held onto my hope despite these realities by seeing the continued benefits of cultural strengths, spirituality, social support, activism, education, community building, and leadership development.

As a result of my long-standing commitment to the ideals of multicultural feminist psychology, I have been especially focused on the work done by APA's Society for the Psychology of Women. Integrating multicultural feminist psychology with the provision of care for adolescent girls of color is a pathway for healing and empowerment that I would like to highlight. I have seen its effectiveness in my practice and the research of many of my colleagues and mentees.

A major element in the negligent care provided to adolescent girls of color is a lack of knowledge of their cultural context and of multicultural feminist therapy approaches. By combining both areas of knowledge in this resource, this book will benefit adolescent girls of color by providing a rich practical resource to you, their providers. Providing education on both cultural context and specific therapeutic frameworks will aid in the therapeutic engagement and effectiveness with adolescent girls of color.

As I began my presidential year and started requesting the assistance of various colleagues, I was grateful that my career-long commitment to mentorship has produced a number of emerging leaders in the field. I asked one of my mentees, Thema Bryant-Davis, whom I have mentored for the past 20 years, to take on the project of this book. I am glad she agreed and assembled great scholars in the field of multicultural feminist psychology to contribute to this text. I believe you will find this book, as I have, a welcome and much-needed resource and timely contribution to our field. Most important, I hope you will apply the knowledge within these pages to enhance your service to adolescent girls of color. They are worthy of our time, attention, and care. Their lives and their mental health matter.

Jessica Henderson Daniel

Multicultural
Feminist Therapy

INTRODUCTION

An Upbeat Song for Girls of Color

THEMA BRYANT-DAVIS

Who will sing an upbeat Black girl's song?

We will sing it for ourselves and the world will marvel at how long we hold our notes.

—Thema Bryant-Davis

As a multicultural feminist psychologist and a womanist psychologist, I strive to attend to the marginalized voices in our field and the larger society. Multicultural feminist psychology centers on women of color, whom many psychologists have historically glossed over or painted in muted tones. In addition, psychologists—including feminist and multicultural psychologists—have often sidelined the voices and experiences of girls of color. Minimal work exists on the application of empirical studies for cultivating treatment approaches and strategies that centralize the concerns, strengths, and well-being of adolescent girls of color. Multicultural feminist psychology recognizes the need for the creation of practical

I gratefully acknowledge the assistance of Shavonne J. Moore-Lobban in writing this chapter.

http://dx.doi.org/10.1037/0000140-001
Multicultural Feminist Therapy: Helping Adolescent Girls of Color to Thrive,
T. Bryant-Davis (Editor)

interventions that celebrate and empower girls of color while attending to historical and contemporary manifestations of oppression and injustice.

I am honored and appreciative that one of my mentors in the field, Dr. Jessica Henderson Daniel, requested that I serve as editor of this book, which was one of her initiatives as president of the American Psychological Association (APA). As scholars, practitioners, and educators, Dr. Henderson Daniel and I approached this book project with a shared commitment to multicultural feminist practice and the empowerment of racially and ethnically marginalized youth. This book is primarily for practitioners who serve adolescent girls of color and who are interested in enhancing their awareness, knowledge, and skills and in providing more effective and empowering treatment. The secondary audience for this book is students who have a desire to build a deeper foundation as they prepare to work with diverse populations, including or with a special focus on adolescent girls of color.

Adolescent girls of color have numerous emotional, cognitive, and social strengths that can be cultivated through healthy community engagement, family practices, internal reflection, and psychotherapy interventions. The needs, goals, relationships, and health of racially and ethnically diverse girls matter. APA has advocated for the protection and preservation of the rights of youth and against many forms of violence and oppression that compromise the development and well-being of children and adolescents. The APA Commission on Violence and Youth (1993) issued a report highlighting the psychological harm of violence against adolescents, the social and cultural factors that impact adolescents of color, and the multisystem-level efforts that are needed for intervening. APA's Working Group on Child Maltreatment Prevention in Community Health Centers also issued a report of multifaceted approaches to prevent child maltreatment by increasing practices that are geared toward youth's overall development and well-being (APA, 2009). APA's Violence Prevention Office (APA, 2010) also developed a national training program, "Effective Providers for Child Victims of Violence," which aims to increase mental health providers' clinical skills for working with children and adolescents who are impacted by violence and victimization. Further, psychologists have developed guidelines related to both the therapeutic treatment of racial and ethnic minorities (APA, 1993; Council of National Psychological Associations for the Advancement of Ethnic Minority Interest, 2003; Root, 1985), as well as psychological services for women and girls (APA, 1978, 2007a; Enns, Rice, & Nutt, 2015).

In late 2017, APA's Board of Professional Affairs sought guidance on an updated working draft of the *Guidelines for Psychological Practice With Girls and Women* (APA Practice Organization, 2017). According to their call for public and member comments, they intend that the guidelines provide practice recommendations that address considerations such as intersectional identities, challenges over the life span, strengths of girls and women, and many other areas (APA Practice Organization, 2017). In addition, the National Association of Social Workers has also developed standards for the practice of social work with adolescents, which focus on important issues of adolescent development and clinician cultural competence (Bailey, 2003). There are still, however, few resources that centralize training for the provision of culturally congruent care for adolescent girls of color. *Multicultural Feminist Therapy: Helping Adolescent Girls of Color to Thrive* seeks to fill in this gap using the framework of multicultural feminist therapy.

After Dr. Henderson Daniel requested that I edit this book, I invited multicultural feminist psychologists to shape and contribute to the project. I selected these scholars on the basis of their demonstrated expertise with the particular cultural group and their lived experience of being gender- and race-conscious women of color. Through conference calls, e-mails, in-person meetings, and a peer-reviewed convention symposium, we explored the need for this book and the focus areas we would cover. The project benefits clinicians and trainees by (a) equipping them with an understanding of the sociopolitical history and contemporary context of adolescent girls of color; (b) providing them with a gendered, culturally affirming frame for assessment, diagnosis, rapport development, goal setting, and therapeutic strategy application; and (c) outlining specific intervention approaches through case studies and a multicultural feminist group model.

NEED FOR THIS RESOURCE

Cultural and social factors play a role in increased mental health concerns in communities of color (Pascoe & Smart Richman, 2009; Williams & Mohammed, 2009; Williams, Neighbors, & Jackson, 2003). The Office of the Surgeon General (U.S. Department of Health and Human Services, 2001) noted that ethnic and racial minorities are confronted with environments of racism, discrimination, inequality, poverty, and violence, all of which take a toll on their mental health. In their Conference on Children's Mental Health (U.S. Public Health Service, 2000), they noted a specific concern for issues related to mental health needs of ethnic minority youth. They discussed the higher rates of suicide for Latino youth, higher rates of referrals for conduct problems and juvenile justice interventions (vs. mental health treatment) for African American youth, and overall higher levels of unmet mental health needs for all youth of color.

All populations have a need for mental health services, yet services remain underutilized within communities of color. Communities of color are less likely to seek psychotherapy (Abe-Kim et al., 2007; Harris, Edlund, &

Larson, 2005; Neighbors et al., 2007), and those who do engage in psychotherapy are more likely to terminate prematurely (Fortuna, Alegria, & Gao, 2010; Kearney, Draper, & Barón, 2005). There are well-documented barriers prohibiting some cultural groups from engaging in treatment, such as financial, cultural, familial, and psychological (Scheppers, van Dongen, Dekker, Geertzen, & Dekker, 2006). Scheppers and colleagues (2006) conducted a literature review to better understand barriers to health services (including mental health services). They analyzed studies from different countries, with sample populations of various ethnic minority groups, and found that barriers exist at three levels: patient, provider, and system. At the patient level, they found barriers in the areas of education, knowledge of health services, socioeconomic status, health insurance, culture, acculturation, language, and values. They stated, "Although the decision to use health services is stated to be an individual choice, we imagine that these choices are mostly framed in the social context through cultural social and family ties; especially for ethnic minorities" (p. 326). Additional barriers for racial and ethnic minorities include distrust of the mental health system (Suite, LaBril, Primm, & Harrison-Ross, 2007), seeking help and support within (vs. outside) the family system (Alvidrez, 1999; Cauce et al., 2002), and concern about mental health stigma (Alvidrez, 1999; Carpenter-Song et al., 2010; Ward, Clark, & Heidrich, 2009). Limited time for therapy due to work and family demands and limited transportation or childcare are additional barriers to consider (U.S. Department of Health and Human Services, 2001). McKay, Lynn, and Bannon (2005) conducted a study to understand the mental health needs of inner-city youth, mostly youth of color, who were referred and accepted to mental health treatment. An alarming result of their findings showed that over one fourth of the youth accepted for services in their study were not seen for their initial appointment and therefore did not receive treatment even when they had significant levels of trauma exposure. McKay and her colleagues provided multiple accounts of adolescent girls who were referred for services with presenting concerns such as trauma symptoms, low self-esteem, and other complex psychological needs but for myriad reasons remained unseen in treatment and without an intentional effort to engage them on the part of the mental health clinic. Although adolescents of color and their families may at times be unaware of the mental health services that are available to them (Ward et al., 2009), they may also believe that services they are aware of do not fit their cultural needs and values. As a result, these families may be reluctant to bring their youth to mental health services (Cauce et al., 2002).

Adolescents of color and their families value wellness and holistic health and may hope that spiritual practices and determination will address mental health issues. Although these positive beliefs and values may serve to buffer and protect youth of color (APA Commission on Violence and Youth, 1993), they also have the potential for disconnecting youth of color from seeking and participating in treatment. To better address these challenges and provide culturally congruent and effective care, psychologists have to adopt the ethical code outlined by APA (2016), which states that ethical care attends to cultural identity and context. Psychologists should also use resources such as APA's (2017) "Addressing the Mental Health Needs of Racial and Ethnic Minority Youth: A Guide for Practitioners," which highlights that mental health providers should demonstrate culturally competent practice with youth by showing respect, acceptance, sensitivity, commitment to equity, openness, humility, and flexibility. Additional resources that lay the groundwork for prioritizing the mental health and well-being of adolescent girls of color include the APA Resolution Against Racism (APA, 2001) and the Report of the APA Task Force on the Sexualization of Girls (APA, 2007b).

Although many adolescent girls of color demonstrate intrapersonal and interpersonal strengths, they also face numerous challenges and barriers to their emotional, cognitive, and social development that include (but are not limited to) discrimination, oppression, trauma, and poverty. For example, adolescent girls of color may have developed strength, resilience, and a sense of cultural pride in the wake of being confronted with prejudice and discrimination throughout their lives, but such prejudice and discrimination still have negative implications for important aspects of their growth and development. In a 3-year longitudinal study of correlates of perceived discrimination, Green, Way, and Pahl (2006) found that peer discrimination was associated with increased depression and decreased self-esteem among Black, Latino, and Asian American high school students. Although the exploration of racial identity and cultural pride can be a strength for many adolescents, it can also result in their pain being minimized and overlooked by mental health care providers. As Pahl and Way (2006) found in studying Black and Latino adolescents from low-income families, and as Goodluck and Willeto (2009) summarized from literature looking at Native American families from different tribal groups, the trajectory of ethnic identity exploration, pride, strength, and resilience can be developed in the face of challenging adversity. Lack of awareness of these factors, as well as a dearth of literature on culturally congruent paths to well-being, development, and thriving, can result in mental health professionals being ill-equipped to serve adolescent girls of color. The purpose of this book is to provide mental health care providers with the tools needed to build on the strengths of adolescent girls of color and to cultivate healthy contexts and schemas among this often-underserved population.

STRUCTURE OF THE BOOK: PROVIDING THE ROAD MAP FORWARD

This clinical resource provides thought-provoking considerations to enhance therapeutic services to adolescent girls of color. The contributors to this resource have outlined a number of both unique and overlapping recommendations to inform mental health professionals as they seek to empower adolescent girls of color to thrive. On the basis of contributors' work, this book's concluding chapter presents integrative suggestions for individual or group interventions centering on racially and ethnically marginalized adolescent girls. These suggestions are evidence informed and combine cultural modifications and culturally emergent strategies that are born out of the traditions of ethnically diverse girls of color.

Multicultural feminist psychology centralizes both theory and application, as evidenced in quantitative and qualitative research. Womanist, *mujerista,* and multicultural feminist psychologies have a great appreciation for the voices of women of color, and as a result, the chapters include the reflections of both clients and practitioners of color. From meta-analyses to case studies, this project animates the dynamics of therapeutic engagement with adolescent girls of color. Multicultural feminist psychology honors other ways of knowing, and as such, the contributors provide chapters that are rooted in theory, empirical knowledge, clinical experience, and personal wisdom. The book begins with a chapter describing the theory, tenets, and practical application of multicultural feminist psychology with girls of color. The next four chapters of the book focus on the primary racial (American Indian, Black, Asian) and ethnic (Latina) girls within the United States. Each of these four chapters provides information on the sociohistorical context of the racial or ethnic group of focus, then discusses the specific challenges and resources (both internal and external) of the girls of that community, and finally outlines multicultural feminist practice with the focus group. The practice section includes considerations for rapport building, goal setting, diagnosis, strategies, and at least one case study to illuminate the application.[1] The authors conclude by highlighting the contributions that psychologists have made and recognizing the work that remains to be done. The concluding chapter of the book presents an integrative model of multicultural feminist therapy with adolescent girls of color that builds on the knowledge provided in the prior chapters.

---

[1] Client descriptions have been anonymized to protect confidentiality.

WHO ARE ADOLESCENT GIRLS OF COLOR?

For the purposes of this book, adolescent girls can broadly be defined as 13 to 19 years of age. Recognizing the important role of culture in self-definition, however, the contributing authors were free to define the adolescent years in the ways that were meaningful for them. Some cultural groups may perceive adolescence as including the preteen years, and some may consider it to last until the youth has fully launched into independence or their early 20s. When working with adolescent girls, it is important for multicultural feminist psychologists to determine how the girl, her family, her community, and the larger society views her developmentally. The interplay of these varying perspectives will have some influence on the girl's daily life and well-being. In terms of gender, self-definition for girlhood and culture are important areas for therapists to explore before selecting an intervention. A component of this work is facilitating adolescent girls of color to appreciate their identity in terms of gender and culture. Being respectful of self-definition, the interventions described focus on clients who identify as girls and who are from racially and ethnically marginalized communities. Therapists for gender nonconforming adolescent clients may consider multicultural gender-queer or gender nonconforming affirmative interventions.

The current U.S. census categorizes people racially as White, Black, American Indian, and Asian and ethnically as Latino or non-Latino. The decision to focus this book on Black, American Indian, Asian, and Latina adolescent girls is due to both the U.S. census categories and the availability of research on adolescent girls of the particular race or ethnicity. Instead of having an independent chapter on biracial or multiracial adolescent girls of color, many of the chapter authors address biracial and multiracial adolescent girls within their discourse. Future editions of this book will benefit from including chapters on Alaskan Native, African immigrant, Caribbean immigrant, and Arab American and Middle Eastern adolescent girls.

It is important to note the movement to shift the categorization of Middle Easterners and Arab Americans from White people to people of color. Years ago, members of these groups in the United States advocated for being included within the White racial category; these efforts resulted from their observation that people of color were treated at a secondary level. The term *White* came with privilege, yet Middle Easterners and Arab Americans—particularly those whose features and/or names are culturally recognizable—have not fully benefited from White privilege but instead have faced stigma and stereotypes as people who are terrorists, dangerous, and un-American. Although we hope that future editions of this book will have the body of literature and possibly the U.S. categorization to have a full chapter about

Middle Eastern and Arab American adolescent girls, for now, we emphasize that culturally congruent counseling with Arab American and Middle Eastern adolescent girls should attend to religion, values, family life, socialization, gender roles, perception and manifestation of mental illness, the challenges of navigating two cultures, the impact of stigma and stereotype, and the importance of honor (Ajrouch, 2004; Ganim, 2001).

Family plays an important role in the development and well-being of Arab American and Middle Eastern American adolescent girls. For Arab American Muslim adolescent girls, quality of maternal relationship mitigates the relationship between stress and behavior (Aroian, Templin, Hough, Ramaswamy, & Katz, 2011). The gender identity of Middle Eastern Muslim girls living in the United States is shaped by identification with their culture, engagement with religious practices, and exposure to foreign cultural values (Abu-Ali & Reisen, 1999). Specifically, those who have been in the United States longer endorse more masculine traits than those who have been here for shorter durations. Those who have higher engagement with their culture and religion endorse more feminine traits and more conservative views of sexuality than those who report less engagement (Abu-Ali, 2004). Multicultural feminist therapists working with Middle Eastern and Arab American adolescent girls should explore the socializing agents in their lives as well as the messages about their identity that they receive, reject, and/or modify. Arab and Middle Eastern American adolescent girls encounter children and youth who hold assumptions about them and their families. Non-Arab American youth endorse the stereotype that Arab Muslim American boys and men are hostile and un-American and the stereotype that Arab Muslim American girls and women are culturally and religiously oppressed (Brown, Ali, Stone, & Jewell, 2017). Along with identifying stressors, multicultural feminist therapists should also attend to and celebrate strengths. In comparison to adolescents in Lebanon, Arab American adolescents endorse a higher self-concept on subscales for physical ability, physical appearance, peer relations, reading, general school performance, and general self-concept; these strengths are consistent with scholarship on the benefits of biculturalism (Alkhateeb, 2010).

CONCLUSION

Envisioned and authored by multicultural feminist psychologists, this groundbreaking book provides a needed resource for mental health professionals working with adolescent girls of color. Some of the highlights the readers will discover in this text include the therapeutic use of crafts and scents with Native American adolescent girls, religion and music with African American adolescent girls, mindfulness and youth advocacy groups with Asian adolescent girls, and spoken word and activism with Latina adolescents. This resource equips psychologists to better serve adolescent girls of color through cultural humility, a gender-conscious knowledge of their rich and diverse cultural histories and contemporary realities, and practice strategies to heal and empower their clients to thrive.

In addition, throughout this text, readers will note the focus on healing, which is broader than but inclusive of trauma-informed work. Healing-centered engagement is broader than trauma-informed care because it (a) centers on the strengths of clients versus centering on the deficits created by trauma; (b) enthusiastically embraces the holistic, multidimensional identity of clients, including their culture, gender, and spirituality; (c) conceptualizes and addresses trauma as a collective experience and not simply an individual experience; and (d) identifies the appropriate response to family, institutional, and societal violation as not just psychological but political (Ginwright, 2018). Multicultural feminist psychology calls for the healing, celebration, and empowerment of adolescent girls of color so they may fully grow and thrive; therapeutic, healing engagement is one of the vehicles that animates this ongoing journey to wellness, fulfillment, and wholeness.

REFERENCES

Abe Kim, J., Takeuchi, D. T., Hong, S., Zane, N., Sue, S., Spencer, M. S., . . . Alegría, M. (2007). Use of mental health-related services among immigrant and US-born Asian Americans: Results from the National Latino and Asian American study. *American Journal of Public Health, 97*, 91–98. http://dx.doi.org/10.2105/AJPH.2006.098541

Abu-Ali, A. (2004). *Ethnic identity and religiosity as predictors of sexual attitudes among Muslim adolescent girls* (Doctoral dissertation). Available from ProQuest Dissertations and Theses database. (Accession Order No. AAI 3114114)

Abu-Ali, A., & Reisen, C. A. (1999). Gender role identity among adolescent Muslim girls living in the US. *Current Psychology: A Journal for Diverse Perspectives on Diverse Psychological Issues, 18*, 185–192.

Ajrouch, K. J. (2004). Gender, race, and symbolic boundaries: Contested spaces of identity among Arab American adolescents. *Sociological Perspectives, 47*, 371–391. http://dx.doi.org/10.1525/sop.2004.47.4.371

Alkhateeb, H. M. (2010). Self-concept in Lebanese and Arab-American pre-adolescents. *Psychological Reports, 106*, 435–447. http://dx.doi.org/10.2466/pr0.106.2.435-447

Alvidrez, J. (1999). Ethnic variations in mental health attitudes and service use among low-income African American, Latina, and European American young women. *Community Mental Health Journal, 35*, 515–530.

American Psychological Association. (1978). Guidelines for therapy with women: Task Force on Sex Bias and Sex Role Stereotyping in Psychotherapeutic Practice. *American Psychologist, 33*, 1122–1123.

American Psychological Association. (1993). Guidelines for providers of psychological services to ethnic, linguistic, and culturally diverse populations. *American Psychologist, 48*, 45–48.

American Psychological Association. (2001). *Resolution against racism and in support of the goals of the 2001 UN World Conference Against Racism, Racial Discrimination, Xenophobia, and Related Intolerance.* Retrieved from https://www.apa.org/about/policy/racism.aspx

American Psychological Association. (2007a). Guidelines for psychological practice with girls and women. *American Psychologist, 62*, 949–979. http://dx.doi.org/10.1037/0003-066X.62.9.949

American Psychological Association. (2007b). *Report of the APA Task Force on the Sexualization of Girls.* Retrieved from https://www.apa.org/pi/women/programs/girls/report.aspx

American Psychological Association. (2009). *Effective strategies to support positive parenting in community health centers.* Retrieved from http://www.apa.org/pi/prevent-violence/resources/positive-parenting.pdf

American Psychological Association. (2016). Revision of Ethical Standard 3.04 of the "Ethical Principles of Psychologists and Code of Conduct" (2002, as amended 2010). *American Psychologist, 71*(9), 900.

American Psychological Association. (2017). *Addressing the mental health needs of racial and ethnic minority youth: A guide for practitioners.* Retrieved from https://www.apa.org/pi/families/resources/mental-health-needs.pdf

American Psychological Association's Violence Prevention Office. (2010). *Effective providers for child victims of violence.* Retrieved from http://www.apa.org/pi/prevent-violence/programs/child-victims.aspx

APA Commission on Violence and Youth. (1993). *Violence & youth.* Retrieved from http://www.apa.org/pi/prevent-violence/resources/violence-youth.pdf

APA Practice Organization. (2017). Call for comments on proposed guidelines for psychological practice with girls and women. Retrieved from http://www.apapracticecentral.org/update/2017/09-21/girls-women-guidelines.aspx

Aroian, K. J., Templin, T. N., Hough, E. E., Ramaswamy, V., & Katz, A. (2011). A longitudinal family-level model of Arab Muslim adolescent behavior problems. *Journal of Youth and Adolescence, 40*, 996–1011. http://dx.doi.org/10.1007/s10964-010-9615-5

Bailey, G. (2003). *NASW standards for the practice of social work with adolescents.* Washington, DC: National Association of Social Workers.

Brown, C. S., Ali, H., Stone, E. A., & Jewell, J. A. (2017). US children's stereotypes and prejudicial attitudes toward Arab Muslims. *Analyses of Social Issues and Public Policy, 17*(1), 60–83.

Carpenter-Song, E., Chu, E., Drake, R. E., Ritsema, M., Smith, B., & Alverson, H. (2010). Ethno-cultural variations in the experience and meaning of mental illness and treatment: Implications for access and utilization. *Transcultural Psychiatry, 47*, 224–251. http://dx.doi.org/10.1177/1363461510368906

Cauce, A. M., Domenech-Rodríguez, M., Paradise, M., Cochran, B. N., Shea, J. M., Srebnik, D., & Baydar, N. (2002). Cultural and contextual influences in mental health help seeking: A focus on ethnic minority youth. *Journal of Consulting and Clinical Psychology, 70*, 44–55. http://dx.doi.org/10.1037/0022-006X.70.1.44

Council of National Psychological Associations for the Advancement of Ethnic Minority Interest. (2003). *Psychological treatment of ethnic minority populations*. Retrieved from https://www.apa.org/pi/oema/resources/brochures/treatment-minority.pdf

Enns, C. Z., Rice, J. K., & Nutt, R. L. (Eds.). (2015). *Psychological practice with women: Guidelines, diversity, empowerment*. Washington, DC: American Psychological Association.

Fortuna, L. R., Alegria, M., & Gao, S. (2010). Retention in depression treatment among ethnic and racial minority groups in the United States. *Depression and Anxiety, 27*, 485–494. http://dx.doi.org/10.1002/da.20685

Ganim, H. E. (2001, September). *A resource for clinicians: Understanding Lebanese American adolescent girls and their families* (Doctoral dissertation). Retrieved from https://lib.pepperdine.edu/login?url=https://search.ebscohost.com/login.aspx?direct=true&db=psyh&AN=2001-95018-274&login.asp?custid=s8480238&site=ehost-live&scope=site

Ginwright, S. (2018). The future of healing: Shifting from trauma informed care to healing centered engagement. *Medium*. Retrieved from https://medium.com/@ginwright/the-future-of-healing-shifting-from-trauma-informed-care-to-healing-centered-engagement-634f557ce69c

Goodluck, C., & Willeto, A. A. A. (2009). *Seeing the protective rainbow: How families survive and thrive in the Native American and Alaska Native community*. Retrieved from https://www.aecf.org/m/resourcedoc/aecf-howfamiliessurviveindianandalaskan-2009.pdf

Greene, M. L., Way, N., & Pahl, K. (2006). Trajectories of perceived adult and peer discrimination among Black, Latino, and Asian American adolescents: Patterns and psychological correlates. *Developmental Psychology, 42*, 218–236. http://dx.doi.org/10.1037/0012-1649.42.2.218

Harris, K. M., Edlund, M. J., & Larson, S. (2005). Racial and ethnic differences in the mental health problems and use of mental health care. *Medical Care, 43*, 775–784. http://dx.doi.org/10.1097/01.mlr.0000170405.66264.23

Kearney, L. K., Draper, M., & Barón, A. (2005). Counseling utilization by ethnic minority college students. *Cultural Diversity and Ethnic Minority Psychology, 11*, 272–285. http://dx.doi.org/10.1037/1099-9809.11.3.272

McKay, M. M., Lynn, C. J., & Bannon, W. M. (2005). Understanding inner city child mental health need and trauma exposure: Implications for preparing urban service providers. *American Journal of Orthopsychiatry, 75*, 201–210. http://dx.doi.org/10.1037/0002-9432.75.2.201

Neighbors, H. W., Caldwell, C., Williams, D. R., Nesse, R., Taylor, . . . Jackson, J. S. (2007). Race, ethnicity, and the use of services for mental disorders: Results from the National Survey of American Life. *Archives of General Psychiatry, 64*, 485–494. http://dx.doi.org/10.1001/archpsyc.64.4.485

Pahl, K., & Way, N. (2006). Longitudinal trajectories of ethnic identity among urban Black and Latino adolescents. *Child Development, 77*, 1403–1415. http://dx.doi.org/10.1111/j.1467-8624.2006.00943.x

Pascoe, E. A., & Smart Richman, L. (2009). Perceived discrimination and health: A meta-analytic review. *Psychological Bulletin, 135*, 531–554. http://dx.doi.org/10.1037/a0016059

Root, M. P. (1985). Guidelines for facilitating therapy with Asian-American clients. *Psychotherapy: Theory, Research, Practice, Training, 22*, 349–356. http://dx.doi.org/10.1037/h0085514

Scheppers, E., van Dongen, E., Dekker, J., Geertzen, J., & Dekker, J. (2006). Potential barriers to the use of health services among ethnic minorities: A review. *Family Practice, 23*, 325–348. http://dx.doi.org/10.1093/fampra/cmi113

Suite, D. H., La Bril, R., Primm, A., & Harrison-Ross, P. (2007). Beyond misdiagnosis, misunderstanding and mistrust: Relevance of the historical perspective in the medical and mental health treatment of people of color. *Journal of the National Medical Association, 99*, 879–885.

U.S. Department of Health and Human Services. (2001). *Mental health: Culture, race and ethnicity.* Rockville, MD: U.S. Department of Health and Human Services, Substance Abuse and Mental Health Services Administration, Center for Mental Health Services.

U.S. Public Health Service. (2000). *Report of the Surgeon General's Conference on Children's Mental Health: A national action agenda* (Stock No. 017-024-01659-4). Washington, DC: Department of Health and Human Services.

Ward, E. C., Clark, L. O., & Heidrich, S. (2009). African American women's beliefs, coping behaviors, and barriers to seeking mental health services. *Qualitative Health Research, 19*, 1589–1601. http://dx.doi.org/10.1177/1049732309350686

Williams, D. R., & Mohammed, S. A. (2009). Discrimination and racial disparities in health: Evidence and needed research. *Journal of Behavioral Medicine, 32*, 20–47. http://dx.doi.org/10.1007/s10865-008-9185-0

Williams, D. R., Neighbors, H. W., & Jackson, J. S. (2003). Racial/ethnic discrimination and health: Findings from community studies. *American Journal of Public Health, 93*, 200–208. http://dx.doi.org/10.2105/AJPH.93.2.200

1

A FOUNDATION FOR MULTICULTURAL FEMINIST THERAPY WITH ADOLESCENT GIRLS OF COLOR

THEMA BRYANT-DAVIS AND SHAVONNE J. MOORE-LOBBAN

Survival is necessary. Thriving is elegant.

—Dr. Maya Angelou

In a society with pervasive oppression, discrimination, and gendered racism, the wellness and empowerment of adolescent girls of color represent an act of defiance. Multicultural feminist psychologists defy the institutionalized, systemic, and individual efforts to marginalize and silence girls and women of color. This work of healing and justice is the foundation of multicultural feminist psychology. In this chapter, we provide readers with the foundation of multicultural feminist theory and therapies and give attention to gaps in the field that can be addressed using this approach. We describe the context in which multicultural feminist psychology emerged and the defining components of multicultural feminist psychology and its major tenets and then illuminate its application in therapy with girls of color. In the application section, we describe the preparation of the therapist, assessment, diagnosis and presenting problem, rapport building, intervention strategies, trauma-informed multicultural feminist therapy, and therapist self-care.

http://dx.doi.org/10.1037/0000140-002
Multicultural Feminist Therapy: Helping Adolescent Girls of Color to Thrive,
T. Bryant-Davis (Editor)

CONTEXT OF THE EMERGENCE OF MULTICULTURAL FEMINIST PSYCHOLOGY

Feminist therapy and multicultural therapy emerged in response to the ways in which the experiences of entire groups of people (e.g., women, people of color) were being neglected in the psychological development of theory, research, practice, and policy. Enns, Williams, and Fassinger (2013) noted that in the aftermath of the civil rights movement of the 1960s and the second wave of feminism during the same time, feminist psychologists began to voice their critiques of psychology, including alignment with one of Weisstein's (1968/1993) primary critiques of psychology's tendency to erase the social context in which behaviors manifest and to overemphasize and pathologize individual traits. The similarities between the psychology of feminist therapy and multicultural therapy became evident at that time. Both psychologies centralize the need for consciousness-raising regarding oppression, agency in the fight for social justice, and empowerment of clients and the larger communities they represent (e.g., women and communities of color; Enns et al., 2013). Both psychologies also noted that clients hold expertise and wisdom about their lives, which should be centralized and celebrated. Interestingly, members of both groups had psychologists who worked to highlight their theories within and outside the American Psychological Association, creating feminist and culturally specific psychological organizations, conferences, and scholarship. From the 1970s to today, these organizations have made advances in institutionalizing attention to and representation of intersectional identities in structure, leadership, membership, mentorship, initiatives, and resources (Enns et al., 2013), which gave way to further the combined efforts as multicultural feminist therapy.

Multicultural feminist therapy emerged in the aftermath of the neglectful treatment of women and girls of color in the feminist and multicultural therapy models. Indeed, feminist psychology theory emerged in the 1960s and 1970s, but it was mostly connected to White feminist psychologists who largely overlooked the needs, ideas, identities, and cultural resources of women and girls of color (Malikiosi-Loizos, 2012). Historically, feminist psychology's views and theories were shaped by gender, whereas other forms of oppression were often marginalized, if not completely ignored (Reid, 2002). Of note are the culturally diverse early feminist psychologists who consistently advocated for the inclusion and redress of the issues facing women of color. Feminist psychology began to grow, and there was a movement focused on multicultural, liberation, and culture-specific psychologies, which centered on race and ethnicity. These theories brought attention to the oppression of communities of color in the larger society and the field of psychology as a whole. The theorists challenged notions of pathology and well-being for racial and marginalized communities. Over many years, multicultural psychology theory has encompassed cultural competence, diversity training, cultural humility, multicultural orientation, and liberation, as well as race-specific psychologies such as Black psychology and Latino psychology. However, these empowerment models often routinely erased the impact of gender identity and gender oppression.

As one can see, there were continued gaps in theorists acknowledging multiple and simultaneous oppressions related to gender, race, and ethnicity. As with feminist psychology, liberation and multicultural psychologies had early women contributors who sought to awaken their subfields to the intersectional challenges facing women and girls of color. The work of women of color in feminist psychology and multicultural psychology was present but was not systemically embraced and integrated into the core of the theories until much later. In the meantime, women of color psychologists working as scholars, practitioners, and researchers began naming and centering on the strengths and needs of their cultured and gendered communities; these theories and efforts gave birth to multicultural feminist therapy.

DEFINING MULTICULTURAL FEMINIST PSYCHOLOGY

Multicultural feminist psychology, also referenced in the literature as feminist multicultural psychology, centralizes the intersections of oppression, power, and privilege in the lives of self-identified women with an understanding of the quest for social justice as an integral component of wellness (Enns et al., 2013). Multicultural feminist psychology aims to center on the experiences and voices of women of color, highlight intersectionality, and emphasize self-definition and empowerment to combat oppression and manifest holistic wellness (Enns, Sinacore, Ancis, & Phillips, 2004; Hill-Collins, 2000; hooks, 1989). Importantly, multicultural feminist psychologists identify as agents of social change (Palmer, 2004). Although race and socioeconomic status have consistently been explored in multicultural feminist psychology, there has been less attention given overall to sexual orientation, disability, migration status, and age. This book seeks to integrate these neglected areas, with a special focus on age—namely, the experience and identities of adolescent girls of color.

Comas-Díaz (2006) described multicultural feminist therapy (with Latinas) as an integrative approach that seeks to cultivate revolutionary acts of healing, transcendence, and rebirth. Multicultural feminist theory argues that to achieve these aims, therapy must empower and raise awareness within clients about the ways their social context has affected their perceptions, behaviors, and affective experience. The context may include such factors as migration status, values, family, culture, and so forth. Multicultural feminist theory builds on a foundation of respect for the cultural values of women and girls while prioritizing the presentation of choices of women and girls of color to facilitate growth and agency. Womanist (feminist theology regarding Black women) and *mujerista* (feminist theology regarding Latina women) psychologies are types of multicultural feminist psychology wherein the core of the theories is not just a form of feminism but goes beyond that to attend to culturally emergent, culturally shaped, and culturally immersed ways of being, knowing, relating, and healing.

Ecological systems theory attends to the context of human development (Barrett & Ballou, 2008; Bronfenbrenner, 1979; Gonzales-Backen, 2013) by exploring individuals' growth through layers of contextual influences, starting with the immediate surrounding environment (i.e., the *microsystem*), where children are influenced through personal relationships and interactions within the home, school, and community settings, to the more distal environment (i.e., the *chronosystem*), where children are more abstrusely influenced by culture and changes in society. Barrett and Ballou (2008) considered these levels through a contextual lens that honors the experience of the clients' lives. An overarching premise is that growth and development at the individual level occur within the context of relationships and influences from other people, who are either immediately connected to the individual or distally removed within society. In this way, identity development can be seen through multiple aspects, such as identity as individual and identity as relational (Barrett & Ballou, 2008).

Treatment approaches from this perspective include relational-cultural therapy and feminist therapy. Relational-cultural therapy views individuals' growth (Jordan, 2001) and challenges (Comstock et al., 2008) through relationship and connection to others and within the context of cultural and societal influence. It aligns with the foundational parts of feminist therapy (West, 2005) and focuses on the well-being of women and social change as integral to individual change. For example, the phrase "the personal is political" has been a staple of feminist therapy since Carol Hanisch used it in 1971 as the title of an essay; it continues to signify the need to address personal problems within the context of social and political influences. Both relational-cultural and feminist therapy complement multicultural therapies by encouraging clients to understand the contextual influences of gender-role socializations, marginalization, power, mutuality, and interconnectedness.

Multicultural feminist models of treatment address the cultural context of clients' lives, with the intention of moving beyond symptom cessation and toward holistic wellness and empowerment (Brown, 2008b; Enns, 2004). Within the framework of multicultural feminist therapy, scholarship has developed on specific approaches, such as womanist psychotherapy and *mujerista* psychotherapy (for a review, see Bryant-Davis & Comas-Díaz, 2016). These treatment approaches address a number of overarching themes, including but not limited to intersectional identity, family, agency, spirituality, community, coping, resistance, healing, and thriving. These themes are applied to contemporary challenges facing multicultural feminist psychologists, such as covert oppression, unconscious bias, denial of inequity, microaggressions, and the complexity of people simultaneously holding roles of privilege and marginalization (Enns et al., 2013).

TENETS OF MULTICULTURAL FEMINIST THERAPY

Key aspects of multicultural feminist psychology are the affirmation of culture, womanhood and girlhood, sociopolitical consciousness, and intersectional awareness. In addition, multicultural feminist therapy centers on an understanding of trauma, oppression, empowerment, healing, and thriving, while attending to connection, spirituality, sexuality, and creativity. Going beyond many feminist theorists who promote acknowledging and resisting multiple forms of oppression, multicultural feminist psychology also centralizes the use of cultural resources and values to shape the therapeutic experience. Healing comes not just from consciousness-raising and empowerment to combat oppression but also in coming home to one's self as a gendered cultural being, both individually and collectively. Foundationally, multicultural feminist theory asserts that along with addressing the multiple forms of oppression, therapists must attend to holistic identity and functioning. The major tenets of multicultural feminist psychology, which will be summarized next, are egalitarian therapeutic relationship, cultural congruence, intersectional lens, empowerment to combat social justice, community engagement, and growth and resilience (Bryant-Davis & Comas-Díaz, 2016; Carr, Green, & Ponce, 2015; Enns et al., 2013).

The first tenet of multicultural feminist therapy is *egalitarian relationships*. The therapist builds the therapeutic relationship on a foundation of respect, honoring the wisdom that girls carry. *Mujerista* psychology, a daughter of multicultural feminist therapy, refers to it as reviving the inner knowing, or intuition, of the client (Comas-Díaz, 2016). Womanist psychology, another daughter of multicultural feminist therapy, would refer to it as *Kujua*, or remembering that which you already know (Bryant, 1993).

Multicultural feminist therapy rejects notions of colonialism, pity, or rescue and instead embraces notions of cocreating and holding space for the inner and outer healing of girls and women. An egalitarian multicultural feminist therapist offers options; asks questions; self-discloses with appropriate awareness; creates space for the client's voice, needs, and priorities; and is comfortable with being flexible and attentive to the wisdom of the client.

The second tenet of multicultural feminist therapy is *self-definition*. Girls are encouraged to define themselves for themselves, as they journey through their cultural identity, racial identity, gender identity, sexual identity, and spiritual or religious identity. Girls are encouraged to explore the meanings, values, and roles they have been directly and indirectly taught and engage in meaning making for themselves. Although the client is encouraged in self-definition, the aim is self-acceptance, affirmation, and celebration of who they are. From this vantage point, girls define what is praiseworthy about the various aspects of themselves as girls of color. Valuing self-definition also means that only persons who self-identify as girls should be addressed as adolescent girls or young women. Adolescents who reject the gender binary or identify as genderqueer or adolescent boys should not have therapists who insist that they embrace girlhood or womanhood. (Clients with fluid or male gender identity may flourish more in a gender queer or adolescent boys group. The therapist does not need to guess. They should honor the wisdom of the client and ask clients how they wish to be identified.) Multicultural feminist therapy creates a path to the client's affirmation of the various aspects of their identity, resisting the societal messages that negate girlhood, diverse racial and ethnic identities, religious and spiritual traditions, and same gender–loving people. Addressing and celebrating aspects of the self that are often marginalized in treatment, multicultural feminist theory maintains an affirming perspective regarding the sexuality and spirituality of women and girls (Hagen, Arczynski, Morrow, & Hawxhurst, 2011). The final aspect of self-definition addressed in multicultural feminist therapy is that adolescent girls of color recognize that although oppression and trauma have affected them, they are more than what others have done to them. Their identities as adolescent girls of color are much more than a series of violations. Multicultural feminist therapists journey with them as they write the script of who they want to be and how they want to cultivate a life of meaning and purpose.

Adolescent girls of color are tasked with determining pathways to address the potential dichotomy between their ideal selves (the image of who they ought to be) and their actual selves (the authentic and integrated truth of who they are). These identity markers are influenced by socializing agents in their lives, which carry both positive and negative messages about the adolescent and society as a whole. For example, they may contend with stereotyped images of themselves as hypersexual, exotic, and animalistic, which carry negative messages in society. They may also find strength in messages that affirm more positive, truthful, and nonstereotyped messages about them and the cultural groups to which they belong. These adolescent girls of color knowingly and unknowingly internalize these messages and experience subsequent influences on their identity, development, and social interactions with others, which may be a central part of their therapy process. Multicultural feminist therapists attend to intersectional identity in a proactive way that addresses the full spectrum of adolescents' identity, including but not limited to gender, age, race, ethnicity, migration status, ability status, socioeconomic status, sexuality, and religion. There is a notion within psychotherapy that clients bring their whole selves into the therapy room and that it is imperative to understand and work with the person as a whole rather than separating them into isolated parts. The underlying tone of this notion is Gestalt, but it is also aligned with multicultural feminist principles focused on the intersection of clients' identities. By naming, incorporating, and affirming the multiple aspects of the self, multicultural feminist therapists empower adolescent girls of color to accept and affirm themselves.

The third tenet of multicultural feminist therapy is *cultural congruence*. The task of the therapist is not to force clients to conform to a psychological model that was not created with them in mind but instead to build on the cultural resources that already exist and use them to shape experiences of healing and empowerment. Traditional psychotherapy uses theories and interventions that were primarily developed on the basis of the experience of middle and upper income, educated, White clients. From this vantage point came the notion that if one wanted to create a therapeutic experience one needed a neutral-colored room, without food, 50 minutes, rates over $100 so the client would value the process, and no one present but the individual client and the therapist. Multicultural feminist therapy decolonizes traditional psychotherapy, which also assumes that if people have not gone to therapy in the way just described, they have not worked on themselves. However, people faced difficulty and discovered ways to heal and grow long before psychotherapy was created. In this regard, multicultural feminist therapy recognizes that generations of cultural healing inform us that vibrant colors, scents, food, family, community, expressive arts, spirituality, and retraditionalization (or embracing of one's legacy of survival) can be therapeutic. Multicultural feminist therapy also recognizes that need for physically and emotionally accessible spaces. Whether the aim in a given moment is insight, psycho-education, or skills building, the approach embraces the cultural traditions of the clients.

The fourth tenet is *sociopolitical consciousness in the form of intersectional awareness*. Adolescent girls experience consciousness-raising in multicultural feminist therapy. They develop critical thinking to identify and analyze the various systems of oppression they encounter. This awareness assists them in resisting internalized oppression, shame, and self-blame for the discrimination, stigma, and bias they experience. It also fosters their ability to relate to other marginalized girls about whom they have adopted negative views as a result of intersectional oppression. This awareness allows girls to look critically at beauty myths in the media, the reporting of history and current events at school, and their feeling about themselves and members of their cultural group.

Identity development is a key component of healthy development for adolescents and includes a number of subthemes, such as racial identity development, gender identity development, sexual identity development, and religious identity development. Adolescence is a time for discovering one's self and of beginning to debate the existential question "Who am I?" In his seminal book on adolescent development, Erikson (1994) identified the stage of *identity versus role confusion*, wherein finding a sense of one's uniqueness and resolving the two polar ends of the stage are essential tasks for adolescent development. This theory places adolescents' identity development in the context of their egos and epigenetic need to move through psychosocial tasks. However, adolescents are faced not only with understanding who they are as unique individuals but also who they are in the context of their surrounding worlds.

To this extent, Marcia (1966, 1980) furthered Erikson's (1994) model and posited that adolescents are tasked with engaging in a thoughtful process of reflective commitment that involves understanding their inner needs, abilities, values, beliefs, history, and self-perceptions. Four proposed identity statuses or resolutions resulted: *identity diffusion* (noncommitment to identity roles and values and without active exploration of related constructs), *moratorium* (noncommitment to identity roles and values but actively exploring identity constructs), *foreclosure* (commitment to identity roles and values but without deep exploration of related constructs), and *identity achievement* (commitment to identity roles and values based on thoughtful exploration of identity constructs). Marcia understood identity in adolescents to be a dynamic process in which elements that constitute identity shift and change over time. Phinney (1989, 1990) understood the same and continued the work of Erikson (1994) and Marcia by conceptualizing a three-stage process of ethnic identity development. This process included the *unexamined stage*, in which adolescents show a lack of exploration of their identity outside the dominant culture's characterizations of it; the *moratorium stage*, in which adolescents begin exploration of their identity; and the *achievement stage*, in which adolescents internalize an understanding of their ethnic identity based on meaningful exploration of it.

Importantly, in both Marcia (1966, 1980) and Phinney's (1989, 1990) theories, adolescence is not seen as the beginning of identity development but rather the first time young people can deconstruct their childhood notions of identity and experiences to resolve a pathway into adulthood. This notion is aligned with Barrett and Ballou (2008), who noted that individual identity changes over time in response to learned experiences within various relationships and environments. Barrett and Ballou discussed the development of a contextual identity through four aspects: identity is that of the individual, identity is relational, identity is based on social units (e.g., race, class, gender), and identity is universal as human. In this model, individuals' lived experiences shape their internalized sense of self and understanding of who they are in ways about which they are consciously and unconsciously aware.

Adolescent girls of color have quite a task in developing their identity because they have multiple selves to consider, and understanding the intersecting nature of those selves must be attended to. They have to consider who they are as themselves, in connection to others, through the multifaceted and intersecting aspects of their identities and subsequent perceived social roles, and with the spoken and unspoken expectations for those roles. In this way, their lived experiences as ethnic and gender minorities play a critical and early role in their identity development. The development of their identity includes *cultural identity*, which is a complex construct whereby an individual's self-concept, thoughts, emotions, behaviors, and overall understanding of him- or herself is connected to multiple cultural group identities, such as racial, gender, sexual, and religious identity, to name a few. Cultural identity can be influenced by experiences with members in- and outside the various cultural groups to which one belongs. For adolescent girls of color, their lived experiences as ethnic and gender minorities play a critical and early role in their identity development process. This concept has been explored through research about ethnic (Kiang, Yip, Gonzales-Backen, Witkow, & Fuligni, 2006; Phinney, 1990; Phinney & Ong, 2007; Umaña-Taylor, Yazedjian, & Bamaca-Gomez, 2004) and gender identity (Kroger, 1997; Steensma, Kreukels, de Vries, & Cohen-Kettenis, 2013; Tobin et al., 2010). Importantly, strong ethnic and gender role attitudes have been found to be protective against negative stereotypes messages that adolescents may encounter on a daily basis (Carlson, Uppal, & Prosser, 2000; Martinez & Dukes, 1997).

Through an ecological, phenomenological, and critical race feminist perspective, Clonan-Roy, Jacobs, and Nakkula (2016) developed a model of positive youth development that is specific to adolescents of color. Their model places critical consciousness at the center of developing a reflective awareness of the self, in relation to the social world, that fosters a deeper understanding of the self and leads to great competences in the domains of connection and caring, competence, character, contribution, confidence, resilience, and resistance. They posited that "developing the skills to critically question and analyze power relationships in the social world, and more subtle and interactional forms of gendered and racial/ethnic marginalization, will empower adolescent girls of color to navigate these multiple marginalities" (p. 104).

The fifth tenet of multicultural feminist therapy is *empowerment*. Some may be concerned that raising the intersectional consciousness of girls could result in them feeling powerless and hopeless. On the contrary, the awareness raising is directly connected to the empowerment. Girls are provided with tools of agency and the freedom to explore the various contexts in which these tools may be used. Honest discussion about potential outcomes of them claiming their voice, as well as attention to the dynamics of when, how, and with whom one chooses to engage, are necessary. Themes such as activism, agency, goal setting, mentorship, and personal and collective response to the problems of injustice also need attention to practical and often urgent responses. Empowerment can take the form of volunteerism, petition creation and signing, letter writing, attending a protest, speaking up about harm that is being done, raising awareness, choosing a career that addresses the issues they are drawn to, using spiritual practices to counter oppression, and showing the radical act of love and celebrating themselves despite the oppression they have experienced.

The sixth tenet of multicultural feminist therapy is *community support* or *interpersonal connection*. Appreciating collective notions of identity underscores how we are all related. Often, those facing distress retreat into isolation, when connection could assist in alleviating the pain. Each of the communities of color has held a long tradition of community support. Multicultural feminist therapy encourages clients to build positive relationships, which can include healing and addressing ruptures in the family regarding intergenerational conflict or conflict between siblings. Building positive relationships and addressing ruptures can also extend to other friends and community members. Positive emotional, informational, and instrumental social support has been identified in the literature as a buffer from the consequences of interpersonal trauma and oppression. Connection can provide a sense of value, support, strength, and guidance. Connection can also take the form of family therapy and group therapy, important modalities for achieving the aims of multicultural feminist therapy, wellness, and empowerment.

The seventh and final tenet of multicultural feminist therapy is *growth and thriving*. Some scholarship refers to this tenet as recovery oriented or resilient. Multicultural feminist therapy aims to do more than provide distress relief or symptom cessation. The cultivation of healing, wellness, wholeness, and thriving echo many of the principles of community psychology and positive psychology. Multicultural feminist therapists facilitate growth, flourishing, and fulfillment. The presence of joy, purpose, connection, inspiration, and motivation are available and accessible for clients. The cultivation of joy, faith, and hope does not remain dormant while waiting for the elimination of all oppression; instead, it provides fuel for the journey and the fullness of life. Adolescent girls of color learn to nourish themselves; develop and maintain reciprocal, healthy relationships; and create lives of meaning and fulfillment.

APPLICATION OF MULTICULTURAL FEMINIST THERAPY WITH ADOLESCENT GIRLS OF COLOR

Preparation of the Therapist

The provision of multicultural feminist therapy requires attention to (a) ongoing self-examination, (b) sharing power, (c) giving voice, (d) facilitating consciousness-raising, (e) building on strengths, and (f) leaving clients the tools to work toward social change (Goodman et al., 2004). Ethically, mental health care necessitates cultural humility, cultural competence, and an intentional moving away from White ethnocentrism. Cultural humility is a self-reflective, other-oriented, and power-attenuating openness to clients as multicultural beings (Hook, Davis, Owen, Worthington, & Utsey, 2013). The therapist places a high value on clients as the experts on their lives and on therapists as active collaborators. In addition, there are centralized values of respect, openness, egolessness, and consideration of the client's cultural background. In addition, across studies, cultural humility involves developing mutual partnerships that address power imbalances and openness to new cultural information (Mosher, Hook, Farrell, Watkins, & Davis, 2016).

Cultural humility is a disposition that values the central role of culture and a commitment to lifelong learning that recognizes the expertise of the client on their cultural experience and identity process (Mosher et al., 2016). Cultural competence encompasses self-awareness, including recognition of one's multiple identities as a clinician and the related points of privilege, power, and oppression, as well as knowledge about the client's culture from sources besides the client (Sue, 2001). The therapist takes on the responsibility and benefit of learning about the historical and contemporary challenges and strengths of the client's cultural group, including the realities of intersectionality. Instead of falling into stereotypes that leave large segments of a community invisible, the therapist attends to the multiple intersecting points of oppression and strength related to gender, race, ethnicity, sexual orientation, age, religion, ability status, and migration status. The reality of living in the United States as an ethnically and/or racially marginalized person is uniquely shaped by additional identity markers of adolescent girls of color. In addition, therapists' skills are related to cultural competence, including the cultural modification of traditional psychotherapeutic interventions and culturally emergent practice strategies that reflect the client's cultural heritage. Therapists have to understand and appreciate that the racial identity of the client can vary and will influence their awareness and appreciation of various cultural values and traditions. While assessing the centrality of racial and ethnic identity of clients, therapists must remain conscious of their racial and ethnic identity and the ways their assumptions, identity, and experiences may shape the progression of treatment. Lack of consciousness and humility can result in tendencies toward stereotyping, pitying, idealizing, pathologizing, or dehumanizing. Clinical ruptures will emerge from these tendencies, and therapists have to address and correct these incidents for the healthy development of the relationship and treatment.

There are also practical and systematic steps that mental health professionals should take to prepare the physical space for adolescent girls of color (see Chapter 2, this volume). Practical steps include having art, magazines, and books that represent the cultures of diverse clients. Systematic steps include having a diverse staff (from the leadership to the clinicians to the administrators) at the counseling agency. In addition, community partnerships and outreach reflect a value of community gatekeepers who are more likely to endorse psychotherapy and refer families of color to the agency. These partnerships can include faith leaders or ministers, local public school administrators, and community centers that serve the holistic and/or cultural needs of potential clients. Finally, a center with flexible hours (weekend and/or evening) as well as a sliding scale is more likely to attract and retain families of color.

Building and maintaining rapport with adolescent girls of color and their families is critical for retention and effectiveness (see Chapter 2, this volume). The intake process has to be flexible to accommodate time for establishing relationships. Beginning the therapeutic relationship with a series of personal questions can result in the erection of emotional and physical walls. Thoughtful use of self-disclosure on the part of the therapist, as well as the integration of culture and arts, can assist in building trust, which is foundational for transformational intervention (see Chapter 5). Along with rapport building, the initial stages of treatment should include an orientation to psychotherapy to address expectations, roles, and stigma related to treatment (see Chapter 4). Attention to issues of confidentiality is highly significant, including disclosure of the conditions under which the therapist will make disclosures of material shared in treatment and to whom—parents, police, and/or child protective services. Although covering confidentiality is a component of all ethical treatment, it is especially relevant for adolescent girls of color who have experienced, witnessed, or been made aware of persons in authority causing harm to families of color, whether intentionally or unintentionally.

Treatment Focus Areas

Therapists have to assess and address a number of major mental health themes in multicultural feminist therapy with adolescent girls of color (see Chapter 3). Positive themes to integrate throughout treatment include identity, empowerment, positive gendered racial socialization, strengths, values, sociocultural networks, academic and vocational goals, and spirituality (see Chapter 5). There are also challenges that therapists should not minimize or overlook in psychotherapy; silence on the part of the therapist can keep adolescent girls of color also struggling in silence. The critical themes that have been established in the literature include trauma; depression; suicidality; substance use and dependence; oppression, discrimination, and microaggressions; body image and phenotype (colorism and biases around non-European features); and sexuality (see Chapter 4). Clinicians have to explore the extent to which each of these issues has emerged in the life of the client, their effect, the client's thoughts and related emotions and behaviors, and the client's coping and resistance strategies. The client's strengths, insights, and sociocultural networks can be helpful in the navigation of these difficult waters (see Chapter 3). To address the critical areas, the therapist has to adopt behaviorally specific questions without shaming attitudes or assumptions.

Assessment

Multicultural feminist therapists must consider youth through the lens of a social-ecological framework, recognizing systems of bidirectional influence (see Chapter 3). *Ecomaps* are an assessment tool used to provide greater clarity of the adolescent's current stressors and strengths; they are a visual representation of relationships, social support, cultural context, and connections between family and the larger community (Crawford, Grant, & Crews, 2016). *Culturagrams* are an additional tool to assess and empower ethnically diverse clients by recording immigration, language, health beliefs; celebrated holidays and special events; the impact of crisis events; values regarding family, education, and work; and contact with cultural institutions (Congress, 2004).

Along with these tools, intake interviews, from a multicultural feminist perspective, have to attend to three primary areas. Therapists have to assess cultural values by engaging in exploratory discourse with the adolescent girl and her family members (see Chapter 2). In a cultural values discussion, the multicultural feminist therapist attends to gendered cultural values, such as ideals regarding gender roles and the impact of discrepancies within the client and between the client and her family's values. In addition, multicultural feminist therapists conduct a full assessment of spirituality and religiosity. This intake includes gathering information about the adolescent's beliefs, engagement in individual and collective religious and spiritual practices, her introduction to her spiritual and religious orientation, and her conceptualization and encounters with a higher power, ancestors, and other spiritual entities.

The therapist should also explore the adolescent's positive and negative feelings and experiences as related to her spiritual and/or religious journey. Finally, it is critical to assess the adolescent's full trauma history, meaning not only assault, abuse, and trafficking but also acts of discrimination, hate crimes, and gendered racism. Asking the question helps to create a safe environment for disclosure and healing.

Diagnosis and Presenting Problems

Many families and communities of color socialize girls of color to adopt roles of caretaker, cultural transmitter, and selfless giver. Beauboeuf-Lafontant (2007) described the *silencing paradigm* that emphasizes feminine goodness, in which girls are socialized to be more attuned and attentive to the needs of others, even to the absence of focus on their own needs and desires. Although these nurturing roles can be assets for girls of color, they can also present in challenging ways that unintentionally lead them to lack self-nurturing and self-care and experience additional stressors. The literature on girls and women of color conceptualizes these roles in various ways, including the stoic sufferer, superwoman syndrome (Woods-Giscombé, 2010), and *marianismo* (Castillo & Cano, 2007). The *stoic sufferer* is related to girls of color being taught to silence their needs and pain, which is reflective of a historical need to be strong in the face of danger, control their emotions in the face of fear, and withstand extreme suffering. The *superwoman syndrome* (historically, the strong Black woman) can be seen in the latter notions of controlled emotions and unmeasurable strength, where girls of color are taught to deal with adversity by moving forward with their heads held high. *Marianismo* (historically, the strong but submissive Latina woman) can also be seen in this way, in which girls of color are taught that they should be pure and moral, humble to others' needs, subordinate and submissive to men, and strong despite pain. In all three cases, girls of color are taught to endure suffering for the sake of others, such as the family, and that there is little place for "weakness" or vulnerability. Because of both the girls' survival strategy of masking pain, as well as the gendered racial biases of the clinician, mental health professionals may misdiagnose girls of color. Studies have shown the potential for clinician bias toward adolescents of color, who are diagnosed with externalizing disorders (such as disruptive behavior disorders) at rates higher than their White counterparts, even when clinical assessment measures do not indicate a diagnosis based on minimal functional impairment (Nguyen, Huang, Arganza, & Liao, 2007). Adolescent girls of color may be more likely to be seen as resistant to care, devaluing of treatment, angry, irritable, paranoid, prone to violence, delusional, hyperreligious, avoidant, and incapable of insight. Under oppressive conditions, some of these survival responses can be mistaken for pathology. Conversely, responses that highlight mental health concerns can be missed. In fact, many adolescent girls carry untreated trauma and undiagnosed depression, eating disorders, and anxiety (Asnaani, Richey, Dimaite, Hinton, & Hofmann, 2010; Sen, 2004; U.S. Department of Health and Human Services, 2001). Some of the presenting problems that adolescent girls of color may face include the school to prison pipeline, with girls of color being disproportionately penalized and criminalized in school and community settings; the trauma of poverty, which opens the door to numerous violations; unexpressed grief from multiple losses; unhealthy relationships; unhealthy coping strategies; complex trauma, including intergenerational trauma; and challenges with language, acculturation, and pressure to shift selves in various cultural contexts. Wun (2016) conducted qualitative interviews with six high school girls of color who had school discipline records. She noted the girls' intersecting experiences of gendered violence and poverty, as well as their feelings of helplessness, pain, and anger. Wun suggested that school faculty establish new ways of understanding and responding to adolescent girls of color and that instead of defining and responding to them as problems, faculty should consider their experiences within their communities and society as a whole, including but not limited to violence, the expression of anger, and the show of resistance. We suggest that multicultural feminist therapists take a similar understanding in working with these adolescent girls of color in therapy.

Rapport Building

Research with clients in multicultural feminist therapy discovered that safety and trust are sacred themes in their evaluation of the therapeutic experience (Abousleman, 2010). Multicultural feminist therapists view adolescent girls of color as experts on their lives with knowledge, creativity, strength, and voice to contribute to the therapeutic process (Brown, 2008b; Enns, 2004; Worell & Johnson, 1997). In fact, multicultural feminist therapists recognize the critical nature of adolescent girls of color having space to share their voice and speak their truth from their unique perspectives. As opposed to viewing adolescent girls of color as merely "vulnerable populations" or "at-risk populations," they are conceptualized as carriers of psychological, vocational, spiritual, and cultural resources and are deserving of care, access, attention, and empowerment. Brown (2008b) further noted that specific symptoms or behaviors that would traditionally lead therapists toward diagnostic labels are reconceptualized in multicultural feminist therapy and understood as evidence of resistance toward experiences of oppression, as well as means to resolve experiences of powerlessness. Understanding a client's distress should then occur in the context of an egalitarian relationship where the power that is inherent in the therapeutic setting is shared with the client, and the course of treatment is approached with a collaborative effort. In this light, multicultural feminist therapy recognizes that "tolerance" is insufficient and respect is necessary for communication, consideration, planning, and implementation of treatment. Further, multicultural feminist therapists use the therapy setting to be social justice agents of change working with and in support of clients to manifest change in their daily lives and the social-political environment as a whole (Goodman et al., 2004).

Therapists working with adolescent girls of color recognize the appropriate use of self-disclosure as well as the need for cultural humility and self-awareness, which are both required to heal any therapeutic ruptures that may occur. Self-disclosure has long been a part of multicultural feminist therapy because it not only helps with rapport building when done appropriately but it also further shares the power of the relationship and allows for mutuality in the therapy process. However, therapists must engage in humility and self-awareness when disclosing so as not to shift the focus of therapy to themselves or to overidentify with the survivors' experience.

In this regard, therapists have a fine line to walk. Goodman and her colleagues (2004) stated that

> even well-intentioned psychologists need to guard against simply imposing their own group's values on another group in the name of consciousness raising. Moreover, we must be careful that in our attempts to use conscientization, we do not end up denigrating or silencing individuals within a group who may think differently. We must engage people with humility and pluralism, acknowledging that our views arise from our own sociocultural experiences and may not be true for the people with whom we are working. (p. 804)

In addition, rapport building with adolescent girls of color requires appreciating and respecting diverse family structures, which may include extended family members and fictive kin, as well as appreciating and respecting diverse communication styles which may use humor, proverbs, high emphasis on nonverbal messaging, references to cultural associations and constructs, and for some girls, dramatic or expressive communication. Therapists recognize the potential for many different cultural definitions of family, expressions of family roles and expectations, as well as a multitude of cultural dimensions that influence communication, expression, and general styles of families (for a review, see McGoldrick, Giordano, & Garcia-Preto, 2005). Multicultural feminist therapists do not create an environment of interrogation or disconnection but of collaboration and engagement across cultures.

Interventions

Adolescent girls of color come from cultures with active oral traditions. Empowering narrative therapy can be helpful and includes the use of storytelling, spoken word, proverbs, and hip-hop (see Chapter 5). Within these traditions, the girls can name, define, and shape themselves in the present and future. These traditions can create a safe place to shatter the silence around trauma and oppression and hold the duality of the ways they have been mistreated and the ways they still hold agency and power.

Working with adolescent girls of color requires attention to body image, beauty myths, and the traumas that many of them have physically endured (see Chapter 3). Talk therapy may be insufficient for them to reclaim their bodies. Embodied treatment that engages holistic awareness and holistic health may include movement, traditional dance, yoga and/or stretching, postures, gestures, walking, and sports. These activities may be directed or nondirected, central to the intervention of the day or used at the beginning or end of session.

Expressive arts are tools for multicultural feminist therapy that can be used for self-exploration, self-expression, healing, and protest (see Chapter 5).

These therapeutic art forms include drumming, beading, dancing, acting, singing, storytelling, and drawing. The visual expressive arts have also been components of multicultural feminist therapy with adolescents of color. Jewelry making, painting, collage making, pottery, photography, multimedia activities, and filmmaking are interests therapists can use to cultivate healing, protest and resistance, and emotional soothing to give adolescent girls psychological space to process difficult material. Therapists have to be mindful not to overinterpret the artwork, give messages that create a sense of perfectionism and performance, or use materials that are not reflective of the girls' culture (e.g., magazines for collage making that do not include models of color).

Spiritual practices are also important components of spiritually integrated psychotherapy with adolescent girls of color (see Chapter 3). These practices can include prayer, meditation, smudging (burning leaves or smelling oils associated culturally with cleansing and healing), connecting with ancestors by speaking about them or pouring libations to honor them, and rebuilding trust of their inner wisdom, intuition, or the higher power alive in them (see Chapter 5).

Retraditionalization, decolonization, cultural education, and tapping into cultural resources are all significant aims for holistic health and development for adolescent girls of color (see Chapter 2). Positive racial socialization and knowledge of cultural resources can serve as protective factors for adolescents' healthy development, academically and socially. Integrating interventions in session and homework assignments that connect girls with their rich heritage can be one pathway to fostering resilience and recovery from stressors and life challenges (see Chapter 2). Adolescent girls of color can receive cultural psychoeducation about the contributions and creativity of their ancestors and elders, as well as contemporary role models. Multicultural feminist therapy aims to reconnect adolescent girls of color with their culture, decolonize their thinking and behavior, and connect them with the cultural wealth of their ancestry.

Critical consciousness-raising is an essential component of empowerment and multicultural feminist therapy (see Chapter 5). Therapists should provide adolescent girls of color with awareness-raising psychoeducation about the realities of intersectionality and oppression in its multiple forms, as well as its effects, healthy coping strategies, and diverse ways to resist (see Chapter 3). Resistance strategies, such as artivism (i.e., the use of art as a medium for activism), can provide girls with lifelong tools to combat oppression and resist internalizing messages that are demeaning, dehumanizing, and marginalizing (see Chapter 5). The intervention does not end with consciousness-raising but empowers girls with knowledge and skills to pursue justice in their lives. At their core, multicultural feminist therapy, womanist therapy, and *mujerista* therapy are pathways to liberation wherein adolescent girls of color can reclaim their identities and authentically thrive through actualization and activism (see Chapter 5).

Another important aspect of multicultural feminist therapy is spirituality (see Chapter 2). Psychotherapy requires *hope*—the belief that things can get better than they are now and that people can grow beyond what they currently see in themselves. Spiritually integrated psychotherapy engages in reflection and holistic practices, attending to the spiritual, emotional, cognitive, and physical aspects of our identity. In the Latina tradition, adolescent girls are encouraged to reconnect with and honor their intuition, or inner wisdom (see Chapter 5). In the Latina, African American, American Indian, and Asian tradition, spiritual practices may include prayer, meditation, yoga, praise dance, reading inspiring texts, or attending collective services or rituals that reconnect the girls to their spiritual source and community (see Chapter 2). Solution-focused therapy involves exploring with the girls whether there are any spiritual practices they have found nourishing and whether they are considering reactivating those practices. One specific example is the use of cultural proverbs and/or spiritual verses to soothe, encourage, motivate, and inspire adolescent girls of color (see Chapter 5).

Building, enhancing, and maintaining healthy social support are all important for adolescent girls of color (see Chapter 3). The manifestation of this value can take the form of family therapy or group therapy. Discussions about sisterhood or friendship and healthy peer relationships are necessary areas of focus for intervention. Regarding family therapy, it is important to build rapport with the family, whether the entire intervention is family based or the therapist involves the family for the initial sessions and/or the culminating sessions. In meeting with the family, multicultural feminist therapists recognize the importance of acknowledging and demonstrating respect for the family elders and obtaining information from the elders on the family history; assessment of family strengths and struggles is critical, including history of intergenerational trauma and family triumphs (see Chapter 2). In addition, multicultural feminist therapists explore family perceptions regarding gender roles and the transition from girlhood to womanhood. Multicultural feminist, womanist, and *mujerista* therapists recognize the need to empower families to see the strengths and gifts of girls and women, along with the challenges they may face (see Chapter 5). When the family can celebrate their daughter's present and future, the daughter can more readily celebrate herself. Group interventions should be culturally emergent, such as emancipation circles or cultural modifications of traditional psychotherapy interventions, such as culturally modified trauma-focused cognitive behavior therapy. In family, group, and individual interventions, adolescent girls of color should find the safety and support to explore their cultural values, including those they may fully adopt, those they may reject, and those they may choose to modify.

Multicultural feminist therapy uses both prevention and intervention models across modalities of individual, family, and group practice. An ecological systems approach is the frame of this intervention, recognizing the multiple layers of interaction that have a bidirectional influence on the lives of adolescent girls of color. There is an appreciation for the culturally modified evidence-based treatments that have been developed and evaluated as well as the interventions that are derived from the cultural heritage of girls of color. Culturally modified evidence-based treatments have been shown to result in significant improvements across a variety of mental health concerns (Griner & Smith, 2006). These treatments should be grounded in a framework that provides an understanding of the unique and complex challenges that survivors face. They should be flexibly geared toward the client's needs. They should also consider the cultural appropriateness of involving family members and extended networks in the healing process, of course with clear informed consent and a review of confidentiality at the beginning of therapy sessions (Brown, 2008a). These interventions aim to assist in the healthy development of adolescent girls of color through the healing of emotional wounds and empowerment for the transition from surviving to thriving. Empowerment treatment models, such as multicultural feminist therapy, value attainment of joy, purpose, and wholeness as experienced by the client and as observed by the therapists and community members.

Trauma-Informed Multicultural Feminist Therapy

Multicultural feminist therapy also acknowledges and addresses the existence and impact of oppression as a potential form of societal and/or intergenerational trauma (Brown, 2008a; Bryant-Davis, 2007; Kirmayer, Gone, & Moses, 2014). The denial or minimization of trauma in the forms of discrimination, stigma, and microaggressions (i.e., intentional or unintentional communications of racial slights or insults; Sue et al., 2007) is a violation of the therapist's commitment to client-centered, compassionate care. Treating these experiences as unreal or unimportant does not show respect for clients or acknowledge their narratives as influenced by the social context in which their experiences have occurred. Instead, therapists should take an ethnopolitical approach that recognizes and bears witness to (vs. suppressing) the trauma and oppression of clients' experiences and that uses language to speak to clients' experiences in ways that promote individual, community, and political change (Comas-Díaz, 2000). In fact, the feminist view that the "personal is political" acknowledges external conditions, such as oppression, as contributors to internalized trauma. Multicultural feminist therapists screen for these and other experiences of oppression, as well as their impact on the lives of adolescent girls of color.

Treatment goals and interventions are selected collaboratively to address these experiences. Interventions aimed at addressing oppression incorporate positive racial and ethnic identity, affirming humanity, enhancing community support, attending to gendered racism (i.e., interconnected sexism and racism), and developing resistance strategies such as artivism and activism (Bryant-Davis & Comas-Díaz, 2016; Bryant-Davis & Tummala-Narra, 2017). These interventions have long existed in communities of color as a means of surviving the many levels of degradation they have experienced. Working with adolescents of color through interventions that highlight these and other cultural strengths supports them in practices that are normative within their communities and that have historically facilitated healing. For example, the integration of artivism into treatment aligns with cultural traditions of using music, poetry, dance, and other forms of artistry to express pain and anger and transform them into resistance and action.

Other Forms of Interpersonal Trauma

Adolescent girls of color, particularly American Indian and African American girls, are at increased risk of a number of forms of interpersonal trauma. For example, there is an increased risk of intimate partner abuse and sexual assault (Morgan & Kena, 2017; Smith et al., 2017), police brutality (Bryant-Davis, Adams, Alejandre, & Gray, 2017; Hansen, 2017), and sex trafficking (Banks & Kyckelhahn, 2011; Farley, 2003; Pierce, 2012). These assaults, which are all rooted in issues of power and control, leave adolescent girls of color and their families further marginalized, silenced, and traumatized by the inequitable injustices they face in society. It is imperative to approach treatment with an understanding of the sociocultural context that impacts the experience of trauma of survivors of color as well as the mental health effects and aftermath (Bryant-Davis, Chung, & Tillman, 2009). Whittier (2016) used a feminist framework to understand the intersectional dimensions that impact sexual abuse in communities of color and specifically against children; she noted that "theorizing sexual violence intersectionally allows us to consider how gender, race, class, and age interact to shape experiences, interpretations, and responses, and points to the need for research guided by this approach" (p. 99). We add that it also points to the need for therapy guided by that approach, such as multicultural feminist therapy.

Multicultural feminist therapy incorporates a full trauma history assessment and relevant trauma-focused interventions to address these violations with added attention to cultural barriers, disclosure, and cultural strengths, as well as resources for coping and healing, such as spiritual practices and the use of the expressive arts (BigFoot & Dunlap, 2006; Bryant-Davis & Tummala-Narra, 2017; Drake-Burnette, Garrett-Akinsanya, & Bryant-Davis, 2016; Singh, 2009). Multicultural feminist therapists should work with clients to interrupt the powerlessness that comes with enduring abuses, assaults, and exploitations while encouraging clients' exploration and promotion of self-power and cultural healing. Attention to cultural strengths, resources, and coping can aid in healing and resilience for these youth.

Therapists' Self-Care

Multicultural feminist therapy recognizes the humanity of the therapist. Therapists are not blank slates without needs of their own. Instead, therapists bring their whole selves into the room with intersecting identities, related experiences in the world, potential trauma of their own, and/or potential vicarious trauma from engagement as a trauma therapist. As Brown (2008a) eloquently put it,

> Because [vicarious trauma] is a profound and sometimes hidden experience for trauma psychotherapists, it touches on all aspects of the psychotherapist's multiple identities and social locations and may aggravate a therapist's hidden wounds of insidious trauma, betrayal, or cultural experiences of danger. Thus, just as cultural competence is of importance in working with clients so that psychotherapists can hear and know the multiple meanings of their trauma experience in light of their various identities, so such competence is a necessary component of responding to [vicarious trauma] in themselves. (p. 253)

Multicultural feminist therapists provide the best care by actively creating ways to refill their therapeutic well. They engage in self-care through cultural practices; spiritual practices; mutual and reciprocal, healthy relationships; supervision and consultation; appropriate limit and boundary setting; lifelong learning; and engagement in activity, advocacy, or activism for community-level empowerment. They may even do so through self-exploration and seeking therapy from a multicultural feminist therapist who is relationally unknown to them.

CONCLUSION

Multicultural psychology and feminist psychology call for attention to and respect for persons who have been systemically underserved, marginalized, and oppressed. The psychological literature has routinely neglected adolescent girls of color, both their needs and their strengths. Adolescent girls of color deserve to be more than an afterthought to developers of practice models. As an act of justice and care, this approach centers on adolescent girls of color, recognizing their gifts, cultural heritage, and praiseworthy girlhood.

Multicultural feminist psychology is holistic, extending beyond mind–body approaches to integrate mind, body, and spirit. From this viewpoint of healing work being sacred, this approach is open to and drawn to the use of expressive arts as well as awareness that manifests in the form of activism. The therapist and the client are not only change agents of the interior self but also potential change agents of family, community, and society. Adolescent girls treated with multicultural feminist therapy are empowered to combat oppression in ways that resonate with them. With the support of internal and cultural resources, they shed the layers of internalized oppression and awaken to their full possibility, which allows them to not only heal but also to thrive. Adolescent girls of color transform when both their wounds and wings are recognized. Multicultural feminist therapists declare to them with spirit, word, and action, "I see you, and I stand with you."

REFERENCES

Abousleman, T. M. (2010). *Safety and trust are so sacred: A qualitative study of women clients in feminist multicultural therapy* (Doctoral dissertation). Available on Pro-Quest Information & Learning.

Asnaani, A., Richey, J. A., Dimaite, R., Hinton, D. E., & Hofmann, S. G. (2010). A cross-ethnic comparison of lifetime prevalence rates of anxiety disorders. *Journal of Nervous and Mental Disease, 198*, 551–555. http://dx.doi.org/10.1097/NMD.0b013e3181ea169f

Banks, D., & Kyckelhahn, T. (2011). *Characteristics of suspected human trafficking incidents, 2008–2010*. Washington, DC: U.S. Department of Justice: Office of Justice Programs, Bureau of Justice Statistics. http://dx.doi.org/10.1037/e725812011-001

Barrett, S., & Ballou, M. (2008). The person of the client: Theory. In M. Ballou, M. Hill, & C. West (Eds.), *Feminist therapy theory and practice: A contemporary perspective* (pp. 39–53). New York, NY: Springer.

Beauboeuf-Lafontant, T. (2007). You have to show strength: An exploration of gender, race, and depression. *Gender & Society, 21*, 28–51. http://dx.doi.org/10.1177/0891243206294108

BigFoot, D. S., & Dunlap, M. (2006). Storytelling as a healing tool for American Indians. In T. M. Witko (Ed.), *Mental health care for urban Indians: Clinical insights from Native practitioners* (pp. 133–153). Washington, DC: American Psychological Association. http://dx.doi.org/10.1037/11422-007

Bronfenbrenner, U. (1979). *The ecology of human development*. Cambridge, MA: Harvard University Press.

Brown, L. S. (2008a). *Cultural competence in trauma therapy: Beyond the flashback*. Washington, DC: American Psychological Association.

Brown, L. S. (2008b). Feminist therapy. In J. L. Lebow (Ed.), *Twenty-first century psychotherapies: Contemporary approaches to theory and practice* (pp. 277–306). Hoboken, NJ: Wiley.

Bryant, C. (1993). *Kujua: A spirituality of the Hidden Way* (pp. 35–39). Baltimore, MD: Akosua Visions.

Bryant-Davis, T. (2007). Healing requires recognition: The case for race-based traumatic stress. *The Counseling Psychologist, 35*, 135–143. http://dx.doi.org/10.1177/0011000006295152

Bryant-Davis, T., Adams, T., Alejandre, A., & Gray, A. A. (2017). The trauma lens of police violence against racial and ethnic minorities. *Journal of Social Issues, 73*, 852–871. http://dx.doi.org/10.1111/josi.12251

Bryant-Davis, T., Chung, H., & Tillman, S. (2009). From the margins to the center: Ethnic minority women and the mental health effects of sexual assault. *Trauma, Violence, & Abuse, 10*, 330–357. http://dx.doi.org/10.1177/1524838009339755

Bryant-Davis, T., & Comas-Díaz, L. (Eds.). (2016). *Womanist and* mujerista *psychologies: Voices of fire, acts of courage*. Washington, DC: American Psychological Association. http://dx.doi.org/10.1037/14937-000

Bryant-Davis, T., & Tummala-Narra, P. (2017). Cultural oppression and human trafficking: Exploring the role of racism and ethnic bias. *Women & Therapy, 40*, 152–169. http://dx.doi.org/10.1080/02703149.2016.1210964

Carlson, C., Uppal, S., & Prosser, E. C. (2000). Ethnic differences in processes contributing to the self-esteem of early adolescent girls. *The Journal of Early Adolescence, 20*, 44–67. http://dx.doi.org/10.1177/0272431600020001003

Carr, E. R., Green, B., & Ponce, A. N. (2015). Women and the experience of serious mental illness and sexual objectification: Multicultural feminist theoretical frameworks and therapy recommendations. *Women & Therapy, 38*, 53–76. http://dx.doi.org/10.1080/02703149.2014.978216

Castillo, L. G., & Cano, M. A. (2007). Mexican American psychology: Theory and clinical application. In C. Negy (Ed.), *Cross-cultural psychotherapy: Toward a critical understanding of diverse client populations* (2nd ed., pp. 85–102). Reno, NV: Bent Tree Press.

Clonan-Roy, K., Jacobs, C. E., & Nakkula, M. J. (2016). Towards a model of positive youth development specific to girls of color: Perspectives on development, resilience, and empowerment. *Gender Issues, 33*, 96–121. http://dx.doi.org/10.1007/s12147-016-9156-7

Comas-Díaz, L. (2000). An ethnopolitical approach to working with people of color. *American Psychologist, 55*, 1319–1325. http://dx.doi.org/10.1037/0003-066X.55.11.1319

Comas-Díaz, L. (2006). Latino healing: The integration of ethnic psychology into psychotherapy. *Psychotherapy: Theory, Research, Practice, Training, 43*, 436–453. http://dx.doi.org/10.1037/0033-3204.43.4.436

Comas-Díaz, L. (2016). *Mujerista* psychospirituality. In T. Bryant-Davis & L. Comas-Díaz (Eds.), *Womanist and* mujerista *psychologies: Voices of fire, acts of courage* (pp. 149–169). Washington, DC: American Psychological Association.

Comstock, D. L., Hammer, T. R., Strentzsch, J., Cannon, K., Parsons, J., & Salazar, G., II. (2008). Relational-cultural theory: A framework for bridging relational, multicultural, and social justice competencies. *Journal of Counseling & Development, 86*, 279–287. http://dx.doi.org/10.1002/j.1556-6678.2008.tb00510.x

Congress, E. P. (2004). Book review [Review of the book *Evidence-based practice manual: Research and outcome measures in health and human services*, by Albert R. Roberts & Kenneth R. Yeager (Eds.)]. *Brief Treatment and Crisis Intervention, 4*, 195–196. http://dx.doi.org/10.1093/brief-treatment/mhh016

Crawford, M. R., Grant, N. S., & Crews, D. A. (2016). Relationships and rap: Using ecomaps to explore the stories of youth who rap. *British Journal of Social Work, 46*, 239–256. http://dx.doi.org/10.1093/bjsw/bcu096

Drake-Burnette, D., Garrett-Akinsanya, B., & Bryant-Davis, T. (2016). Womanism, creativity, and resistance: Making a way out of "no way." In T. Bryant-Davis & L. Comas-Díaz (Eds.), *Womanist and* mujerista *psychologies: Voices of fire, acts of courage* (pp. 173–193). Washington, DC: American Psychological Association. http://dx.doi.org/10.1037/14937-008

Enns, C. Z. (2004). *Feminist theories and feminist psychotherapies: Origins, themes, and diversity* (2nd ed.). New York, NY: Haworth Press.

Enns, C. Z., Sinacore, A. L., Ancis, J. R., & Phillips, J. (2004). Toward integrating feminist and multicultural pedagogies. *Journal of Multicultural Counseling and Development, 32*, 414–427.

Enns, C. Z., Williams, E. N., & Fassinger, R. E. (2013). Feminist multicultural psychology: Evolution, change, and challenge. In C. Z. Enns & E. N. Williams (Eds.), *The Oxford handbook of feminist multicultural counseling psychology* (pp. 3–26). New York, NY: Oxford University Press.

Erikson, E. H. (1994). *Identity: Youth and crisis*. New York, NY: Norton.

Farley, M. (2003). Prostitution and the invisibility of harm. *Women & Therapy, 26*, 247–280. http://dx.doi.org/10.1300/J015v26n03_06

Gonzales-Backen, M. A. (2013). An application of ecological theory to ethnic identity formation among biethnic adolescents. *Family Relations, 62*, 92–108. http://dx.doi.org/10.1111/j.1741-3729.2012.00749.x

Goodman, L. A., Liang, B., Helms, J. E., Latta, R. E., Sparks, E., & Weintraub, S. R. (2004). Training counseling psychologists as social justice agents: Feminist and multicultural principles in action. *The Counseling Psychologist, 32*, 793–836. http://dx.doi.org/10.1177/0011000004268802

Griner, D., & Smith, T. B. (2006). Culturally adapted mental health intervention: A meta-analytic review. *Psychotherapy: Theory, Research, Practice, Training, 43*, 531–548. http://dx.doi.org/10.1037/0033-3204.43.4.531

Hagen, W. B., Arczynski, A. V., Morrow, S. L., & Hawxhurst, D. M. (2011). Lesbian, bisexual, and queer women's spirituality in feminist multicultural counseling. *Journal of LGBT Issues in Counseling, 5*, 220–236. http://dx.doi.org/10.1080/15538605.2011.633070

Hanisch, C. (1971). The personal is political. In J. Agel (Ed.), *The radical therapist* (pp. 152–157). New York, NY: Ballantine Books.

Hansen, E. (2017, November 13). *The forgotten minority in police shootings.* CNN. Retrieved from https://www.cnn.com/2017/11/10/us/native-lives-matter/index.html

Hill-Collins, P. (2000). *Black feminist thought: Knowledge, consciousness, and the politics of empowerment.* Boston, MA: Unwin Hyman.

Hook, J. N., Davis, D. E., Owen, J., Worthington, E. L., Jr., & Utsey, S. O. (2013). Cultural humility: Measuring openness to culturally diverse clients. *Journal of Counseling Psychology, 60*, 353–366. http://dx.doi.org/10.1037/a0032595

hooks, b. (1989). *Talking back: Thinking feminist, thinking Black*. Boston, MA: Between the Lines.

Jordan, J. V. (2001). A relational-cultural model: Healing through mutual empathy [Special issue]. *Bulletin of the Menninger Clinic, 65*, 92–103.

Kiang, L., Yip, T., Gonzales-Backen, M., Witkow, M., & Fuligni, A. J. (2006). Ethnic identity and the daily psychological well-being of adolescents from Mexican and Chinese backgrounds. *Child Development, 77*, 1338–1350. http://dx.doi.org/10.1111/j.1467-8624.2006.00938.x

Kirmayer, L. J., Gone, J. P., & Moses, J. (2014). Rethinking historical trauma. *Transcultural Psychiatry, 51*, 299–319. http://dx.doi.org/10.1177/1363461514536358

Kroger, J. (1997). Gender and identity: The intersection of structure, content, and context. *Sex Roles, 36*, 747–770. http://dx.doi.org/10.1023/A:1025627206676

Malikiosi-Loizos, M. (2012). A feminist multicultural approach to counselling psychology. *Psychology, 19*, 215–229.

Marcia, J. E. (1966). Development and validation of ego-identity status. *Journal of Personality and Social Psychology, 3*, 551–558. http://dx.doi.org/10.1037/h0023281

Marcia, J. E. (1980). Identity in adolescence. In J. Adelson (Ed.), *Handbook of adolescent psychology* (pp. 109–137). New York, NY: Wiley.

Martinez, R. O., & Dukes, R. L. (1997). The effects of ethnic identity, ethnicity, and gender on adolescent well-being. *Journal of youth and adolescence, 26*, 503–516. http://dx.doi.org/10.1023/A:1024525821078

McGoldrick, M., Giordano, J., & Garcia-Preto, N. (Eds.). (2005). *Ethnicity and family therapy* (3rd ed.). New York, NY: Guilford Press.

Morgan, R. E., & Kena, G. (2017). *Criminal victimization 2016*. Washington, DC: U.S. Department of Justice: Office of Justice Programs, Bureau of Justice Statistics.

Mosher, D. K., Hook, J. N., Farrell, J. E., Watkins, C. E., Jr., & Davis, D. E. (2016). Cultural humility. In E. Worthington, D. Davis, & J. Hook (Eds.), *Handbook of humility* (pp. 107–120). New York, NY: Routledge.

Nguyen, L., Huang, L. N., Arganza, G. F., & Liao, Q. (2007). The influence of race and ethnicity on psychiatric diagnoses and clinical characteristics of children and adolescents in children's services. *Cultural Diversity and Ethnic Minority Psychology, 13*, 18–25. http://dx.doi.org/10.1037/1099-9809.13.1.18

Palmer, L. K. (2004). The call to social justice: A multidiscipline agenda. *The Counseling Psychologist, 32*, 879–885. http://dx.doi.org/10.1177/0011000004269278

Phinney, J. S. (1989). Stages of ethnic identity development in minority group adolescents. *The Journal of Early Adolescence, 9*, 34–49. http://dx.doi.org/10.1177/0272431689091004

Phinney, J. S. (1990). Ethnic identity in adolescents and adults: Review of research. *Psychological Bulletin, 108*, 499–514. http://dx.doi.org/10.1037/0033-2909.108.3.499

Phinney, J. S., & Ong, A. D. (2007). Conceptualization and measurement of ethnic identity: Current status and future directions. *Journal of Counseling Psychology, 54*, 271–281. http://dx.doi.org/10.1037/0022-0167.54.3.271

Pierce, A. S. (2012). American Indian adolescent girls: Vulnerability to sex trafficking, intervention strategies. *American Indian and Alaska Native Mental Health Research, 19*(1), 37–56. http://dx.doi.org/10.5820/aian.1901.2012.37

Reid, P. T. (2002). Multicultural psychology: Bringing together gender and ethnicity. *Cultural Diversity and Ethnic Minority Psychology, 8*, 103–114. http://dx.doi.org/10.1037/1099-9809.8.2.103

Sen, B. (2004). Adolescent propensity for depressed mood and help seeking: Race and gender differences. *Journal of Mental Health Policy and Economics, 7*, 133–145.

Singh, A. A. (2009). Helping South Asian immigrant women use resilience strategies in healing from sexual abuse: A call for a culturally relevant model. *Women & Therapy, 32*, 361–376. http://dx.doi.org/10.1080/02703140903153229

Smith, S. G., Chen, J., Basile, K. C., Gilbert, L. K., Merrick, M. T., Patel, N., . . . Jain, A. (2017). *The national intimate partner and sexual violence survey (NISVS): 2010–2012 State report*. Atlanta, GA: National Center for Injury Prevention and Control, Centers for Disease Control and Prevention.

Steensma, T. D., Kreukels, B. P., de Vries, A. L., & Cohen-Kettenis, P. T. (2013). Gender identity development in adolescence. *Hormones and Behavior, 64*, 288–297. http://dx.doi.org/10.1016/j.yhbeh.2013.02.020

Sue, D. W. (2001). Multidimensional facets of cultural competence. *The Counseling Psychologist, 29*, 790–821. http://dx.doi.org/10.1177/0011000001296002

Sue, D. W., Capodilupo, C. M., Torino, G. C., Bucceri, J. M., Holder, A. M., Nadal, K. L., & Esquilin, M. (2007). Racial microaggressions in everyday life: Implications for clinical practice. *American Psychologist, 62*, 271–286. http://dx.doi.org/10.1037/0003-066X.62.4.271

Tobin, D. D., Menon, M., Menon, M., Spatta, B. C., Hodges, E. V., & Perry, D. G. (2010). The intrapsychics of gender: A model of self-socialization. *Psychological Review, 117*, 601–622. http://dx.doi.org/10.1037/a0018936

Umaña-Taylor, A., Yazedjian, A., & Bamaca-Gomez, M. (2004). Developing the Ethnic Identity Scale using Eriksonian and social identity perspectives. *Identity: An International Journal of Theory and Research, 4*, 9–38. http://dx.doi.org/10.1207/S1532706XID0401_2

U.S. Department of Health and Human Services. (2001). *Mental health: Culture, race and ethnicity*. Rockville, MD: U.S. Department of Health and Human Services, Substance Abuse and Mental Health Services Administration, Center for Mental Health Services.

Weisstein, N. (1993). Psychology constructs the female; or the fantasy life of the male psychologist. *Feminism and Psychology, 3*, 195–210. (Original work published 1968)

West, C. K. (2005). The map of relational-cultural theory. *Women & Therapy, 28*, 93–110. http://dx.doi.org/10.1300/J015v28n03_05

Whittier, N. (2016). Where are the children? Theorizing the missing piece in gendered sexual violence. *Gender & Society, 30*, 95–108. http://dx.doi.org/10.1177/0891243215612412

Woods-Giscombé, C. L. (2010). Superwoman schema: African American women's views on stress, strength, and health. *Qualitative Health Research, 20*, 668–683. http://dx.doi.org/10.1177/1049732310361892

Worell, J., & Johnson, N. G. (1997). Creating the future: Process and promise in feminist practice. In J. Worell & N. G. Johnson (Eds.), *Shaping the future of feminist psychology: Education, research, and practice* (pp. 1–14). Washington, DC: American Psychological Association. http://dx.doi.org/10.1037/10245-011

Wun, C. (2016). Angered: Black and non-Black girls of color at the intersections of violence and school discipline in the United States. *Race, Ethnicity and Education, 21*, 1–15. http://dx.doi.org/10.1080/13613324.2016.1248829

2

CULTURE, RESILIENCE, AND INDIGENIST FEMINISM TO HELP NATIVE AMERICAN GIRLS THRIVE

JACQUELINE S. GRAY, DEVON S. ISAACS, AND MELISSA J. WHEELER

Native American (NA)[1] adolescent girls are a group as diverse as the myriad indigenous cultural and ethnic backgrounds from which they descend. They represent a demographic that endured numerous systematic hardships from both a historical standpoint and contemporary experience. From historical trauma and loss due to the colonization of Native American lands to modern-day instances of extreme poverty, discrimination, objectification, and trauma, there is little doubt that NA adolescent girls are at high risk. Yet there is also an incredible amount of resiliency to be found in this group. This resiliency is deeply rooted in the very cultures from which NA adolescent girls have been disenfranchised.

In this chapter, we give both historical and modern context to the experience of NA adolescent girls by highlighting some of the areas of risk these girls face today. These include issues of identity development, disintegration of traditional family structures, educational and employment barriers,

---

[1]*Native American* as used in this chapter denotes the indigenous people of the United States, including American Indians, Alaskan Natives, Native Hawaiians, and American Pacific Islanders.

http://dx.doi.org/10.1037/0000140-003
Multicultural Feminist Therapy: Helping Adolescent Girls of Color to Thrive,
T. Bryant-Davis (Editor)

misrepresentation and objectification of NA and female identity, interpersonal violence, and the cumulative effects of trauma and discrimination.
In each of these contexts of risk lie great reserves of personal and cultural
resilience, with important implications for good mental health and increased
well-being. Individuals in helping professions can draw from these deep
wells of strength to create healing in a therapeutic context, given that both
intervention and practice are culturally adaptable (or culturally derived) and
relevant to the intersectionality of identities that exist among these young
women. This chapter explores indigenist feminist therapeutic interventions
and how they can effectively address healing for NA adolescent girls.

DEMOGRAPHICS

In 1977, the Office of Management and Budget defined the Native American
as any person having "origins in any of the original peoples of North America
[including South and Central America], and who maintains cultural identification through tribal affiliation or community recognition" (Centers for
Disease Control and Prevention [CDC], 2016, para. 2). In 2017, roughly
6.8 million individuals identified as American Indian or Alaskan Native (AIAN)[2]
alone or in combination with other races, accounting for 2% of the total U.S.
population. Of the total AIAN, 2.7 million are AIAN alone (40.1%), leaving
4.1 million who are more than one ethnicity (U.S. Census Bureau, 2018a).
There are currently 573 federally recognized tribes situated in 35 states across
the country, along with more than 60 state-recognized tribal entities and over
550 tribal groups that have not yet gained state or federal recognition (Bureau
of Indian Affairs [BIA], 2018; National Conference of State Legislatures, 2016;
U.S. Department of the Interior–Indian Affairs, 2017). There are also 1.5 million Native Hawaiian or Pacific Islanders (NHPI) alone or in combination with
other ethnicities (U.S. Census Bureau, 2018b). According to these statistics,
there are over 1.25 million AIAN/NHPI females under the age of 19, each
representing tribal groups with unique cultures, value systems, spiritual
beliefs, and traditional practices (U.S. Census Bureau, 2018b). It is difficult

---

[2]*American Indian–Alaska Native (AIAN)* denotes the indigenous people of the
48 contiguous United States and Alaska. This is a political designation that the
United States uses to denote eligibility for those things granted for the lands
the United States gained through treaties with indigenous nations. This is the
designation the U.S. government uses in collecting data on ethnicity. AIAN is
the term preferred by the National Congress of American Indians.

to differentiate indigenous Pacific Islanders from NA groups because data collected by U.S. government programs include them with Asian groups. However, many of the issues detailed in this chapter also impact indigenous Pacific Islanders through similar mechanisms of colonization by Western patriarchal societies.

Understanding the identity of the NA girl means taking into consideration the numerous ways in which that identity is formed as it pertains to local, national, and global spheres of influence (Markstrom, 2011). In a broad sense, NA personhood is defined by U.S. government recognition of tribal sovereignty and influenced by historical frames of reference, sense of belonging, inter-relatedness, perceptions of NAs by nonindigenous groups, and sociocultural factors such as education, politics, and legal determinants of membership. Most commonly, shared cultural practices and language, tribal affiliation, recognition by tribal community members, the Certificate Degree of Indian Blood (CDIB),[3] and self-identification as tribal members are all ways NAs identify today (Thornton, 1997). Interestingly, AIANs are the only ethnic group in the United States required to prove their membership in the group. During the 19th century, the Bureau of Indian Affairs began keeping records of blood quantum (defined as the percentage of blood as recorded by documented lineage) as a means of determining tribal membership. Some would argue that the original intent of the use of blood quantum in classification "was to determine the point at which the various responsibilities of [the] dominant society to (American) Indian peoples ended" (Garroutte, 2001, p. 225). Thus, the CDIB and blood quantum have a large capacity to determine the treaty rights and benefits of the NA However, NA identity is also tied to connection with land, ancestors, clan membership, language, shared beliefs, traditional practices, and spirituality. HeavyRunner and Morris (1997) emphasized that "[Native Americans] experience the world through a cultural framework that help [them] understand where they originated from, where they are presently, and where they are headed, which further makes cultural identity a predominant foundation and source of strength" (as cited in Stumblingbear-Riddle, 2010, p. 23).

Thus, identity is also strongly tied to geographic location. Throughout the process of ethnic and cultural diaspora, NAs who once occupied vast tracts of land across the United States are now clustered in communities located

---

[3] The Certified Degree of Indian Blood (CDIB) and Certified Degree of Alaska Native Blood (CDANB) are official tribal identification cards required for an American Indian or Alaska Native to be eligible for certain benefits such as housing, food, education, and health care. At times, these cards have been acceptable as identification to move between the United States and Canada or Mexico.

in urban, rural, and geographically defined reservation areas. A 2014 American Community Survey reported that the largest populations of NAs in the United States (those populations greater than 100,000) now reside primarily in 15 states: California, Oklahoma, Arizona, Texas, New York, New Mexico, Washington, North Carolina, Florida, Michigan, Alaska, Oregon, Colorado, Pennsylvania, and Minnesota (U.S. Census Bureau, 2018a). Policies such as the Voluntary Relocation Program and Indian Relocation Act of 1956 have shifted the population of NAs to more urban areas (Brave Heart & DeBruyn, 1998; Wilkins, 2016). As a result, AIANs are gradually becoming more urban, more educated, and more "economically advantaged," although pockets of extremely disadvantaged groups still exist (Sarche, Spicer, Farrell, & Fitzgerald, 2011). Hence, the NA adolescent girl's experience is informed in many ways by the location in which she lives. For example, urban areas may represent greater access to education and employment opportunities but may also mean less cultural connectivity and increased acculturative stress. Rural and reservation areas, which provide greater connection to indigenous culture and ancestral lands, are often much more indicative of lower socioeconomic status and isolation.

HISTORICAL AND INTERGENERATIONAL TRAUMA AND THE IMPORTANCE OF FAMILY AND KINSHIP

When considering therapeutic approaches for NA adolescent girls, it is extremely important to understand identity and experiences in terms of historical and modern context and to do so using a holistic and community-focused approach (Guttmannova et al., 2017). Unlike their European counterparts, NA women in many tribal groups held positions of power, authority, and decision making within tribal kinship and family systems before colonization (Green, 1992). NA women were skillful leaders and decision makers with power, strength, and respect in their communities. This is evidenced in creation stories, women's roles in leadership, and in having a voice during important meetings and discussions (Green, 1992, pp. 31–42). It was only with the European, patriarchal influence of the settlers that women were not consulted and were often left out of important decisions (Mankiller, 2011, pp. 97–98). It could be said that feminism was the norm in American indigenous communities before 1492, with some cultures being matriarchal and taking an egalitarian approach to leadership (Maltz & Archambault, 1995). For example, some tribes required the agreement of the women before they would go to war. However, the identity of the NA woman changed greatly as NA women and girls were forced, through colonization, into sexual submission and required to take on domestic roles modeled after the roles of their European American counterparts. An added layer of identity loss occurred as part of the forced assimilation of NAs during the boarding school era. During the boarding school era from the 1880s to the 1970s, NA children as young as 5 years of age were forcibly removed from their homes and kinship groups. Children were placed in industrial and mission schools where they were stripped of their cultural identities and spirituality using assimilative practices such as the cutting of hair and taking away of traditional clothing, by feeding them strange foods, and forbidding them to speak their language or practice their spiritual beliefs (Brave Heart & DeBruyn, 1998; Duran & Duran, 1995, pp. 27–28; LaPointe, 2008). Children who attempted to engage in their traditional spiritual and cultural practices were often subjected to severe violence and brutality as punishment. Those who survived this horrific experience were often left with multiple traumas, including rape and assault by workers at the schools (Brave Heart & DeBruyn, 1998).

Historical trauma refers to a series of complex traumas that are "inflicted on a group of people that share a specific group identity or affiliation" (Sarche et al., 2011, p. 8) through means of war, genocide, forced assimilation, violence, poverty, and illness (Brave Heart & DeBruyn, 1998; Sarche et al., 2011; Walters et al., 2011). It is hypothesized that the effect of these types of traumas persists today and may be transmitted intergenerationally through parenting behaviors that were damaged by the NA boarding school era. These traumas were further exacerbated by the inability to practice culturally grounded methods of grieving and compounded by restricted access to healing ceremonies and practices. Deprived of cultural guidance and stripped of traditional ways of knowing and being, many of these individuals transmitted their trauma and loss through their families, establishing a cycle of deeply ingrained loss and grief (Brave Heart & DeBruyn, 1998). The stripping away of parenting skills also resulted in a loss of protective factors for future generations, resulting in the perpetuation of physical and sexual abuse and neglect of successive generations of NA children (D. S. BigFoot, personal communication, June 6, 2007).

Many protective factors have survived in NA families and communities. However, mental health interventions for NA youth often fail to implement the increasingly well-recognized number of protective factors that still exist in tribal families and communities in favor of a more deficit-based, individualized approach. Focusing on individual symptoms and cures occurs at the risk of neglecting interrelatedness and social connectivity as key descriptors of well-being across many indigenous worldviews (Rountree & Smith, 2016). Research has found social support, protective family and peer influence, cultural identity, parental support, and parental nurturing are important factors for good mental health among NA youth (Allen, Mohatt, Fok, Henry, & Burkett, 2014; Baldwin, Brown, Wayment, Nez, & Brelsford, 2011; Goodkind, LaNoue, Lee, Freeland, & Freund, 2012; Griese, Kenyon, & McMahon, 2016; Hawkins et al., 2000; Johnson et al., 1998; Kenyon & Carter, 2011; Masten & Coatsworth, 1998; Mmari, Blum, & Teufel-Shone, 2010). In addition, family and kinship networks often extend beyond parents and siblings to include grandparents and elders within the community at great benefit to NA youth (Fuller-Thomson & Minkler, 2005). For example, elders have a great deal to contribute in terms of resilience. Oral transmission of stories relating to the Wounded Knee Massacre, the Navajo Long Walk, and the Trail of Tears (to name just a few) are important reminders of historical loss and trauma but are also important reminders of survival and remembrance. It is important to note here, in terms of contemporary adversities, that many elders view issues of substance abuse and suicide in terms of a continuation of those events (Reinschmidt, Attakai, Kahn, Whitewater, & Teufel-Shone, 2016). NA families and kinship networks have been described as consisting of a "larger social unit" (p. 2) where membership is defined by the way in which children are cared for and provided for (Goodluck & Willeto, 2009). On the basis of an indigenous framework of "interrelatedness" and a shared sense of self-efficacy, the concept of the family directly contributes to themes of self-esteem, cultural connectedness, and the development of value systems derived from relational worldviews. It is possible that NA communities already have much of the knowledge needed for healing embedded within their cultures, and helping professions should draw on this knowledge to inform practice.

THE IMPACT OF VIOLENCE, DISCRIMINATION, AND STEREOTYPING ON INDIGENOUS WOMEN AND GIRLS

Amnesty International (2007) reported that "data gathered by the U.S. Department of Justice indicates that American Indian and Alaska Native women are more than 2.5 times more likely to be raped or sexually assaulted than women in the U.S., in general" (p. 2). This has tremendous implications for the types of traumas seen in clinical and counseling settings. In at least 86% of these "reported cases of rape or sexual assault against women, survivors report that the perpetrators are non-Native men" (Amnesty International, 2007, p. 4). This presents an added complication because 46% of people living on reservations in 2010 were not Native American. Jurisdictional issues where tribal police cannot arrest non-NA offenders means federal authorities may only bring charges in major felony cases (Futures Without Violence, 2012; Gray & Anderson, 2013). Due to the frequency of occurrences, NA adolescent girls might feel the push to accept this type of trauma as a "way of life" or "just something that happens." In addition, these issues of jurisdiction in reservation communities may allow interpersonal violence and sexual victimization to go underreported for fear that perpetrators will not be punished and victims or their families will experience retribution. The report of the National Congress of the American Indian (NCAI; 2013) on violence against NA women stated that "U.S. attorneys declined to prosecute nearly 52% of violent crimes that occur in Indian country, and 67% of cases declined were sexual abuse related cases" (p. 8). Outcomes of interpersonal violence for NA women living on reservations are often fatal. It has been estimated that murder rates for indigenous women in some reservation areas are more than 10 times the national average (NCAI, 2013).

Many NA girls and women go missing every year, but police reports are not taken, and families are often left on their own to determine what has happened to their loved one (Young, Dejarlais, & Smith, 2017). This culture of disempowerment and NA female victimhood may also contribute to a disproportionate amount of sex trafficking of NA adolescent girls. A 2015 *Marie Claire* article documented the effects of the Bakken Shale oil boom near Fort Berthold, North Dakota, which resulted in thousands of single male oil workers settling in the area (Webley Adler & Hillstrom, 2015). The increase in sex trafficking of NA adolescent girls and women that occurred after the boom was so great that it sparked a piece of tribal legislation called Loren's Law. This law defines human trafficking as a breach of tribal law and increases penalties for human sex traffickers under tribal jurisdiction. Savannah's Act has also been introduced into Congress to address the issue of missing and murdered NA women and girls. This act will aid in the collection of data, the reporting of those that are missing, and the coordination of crime information systems and will also create and expand AMBER Alert child abduction warnings to and beyond Indian Country[4] (Heitkamp, 2017).

---

[4]As used in this chapter, *Indian country* means (a) all land within the limits of any Indian reservation under the jurisdiction of the U.S. government, notwithstanding the issuance of any patent, and including rights-of-way running through the reservation, (b) all dependent Indian communities within the borders of the United States whether within the original or subsequently acquired territory thereof, and whether within or without the limits of a state, and (c) all Indian allotments, the Indian titles to which have not been extinguished, including rights-of-way running through the same (June 25, 1948, ch. 645, 62 Stat. 757; May 24, 1949, ch. 139, §25, 63 Stat. 94).

Lesbian, gay, bisexual, and transgender (LGBT) NA adolescent girls also face increased psychosocial risks for poor mental health and poor health outcomes. Individuals with these sexual identities are often referred to in NA communities as *Two-spirit*. Historically, most NA cultures honored and respected alternative sexual lifestyles and gender roles (L. B. Brown, 1997). Just as NAs are carriers of sacred gifts of the Great Spirits, so too are the Two-spirits. Some NA cultures emphasize the sacredness of the alternative gender status and lifestyles that provide Two-spirits with a sacred purpose and plan that is to be shared with others (L. B. Brown, 1997). For instance, the Navajos called Two-spirits *nádlaeehí*, whereas European colonists referred to both female and male as *berdaches*.[5] Nádlaeehí were often responsible for managing the family property, supervising the household, and handling agricultural as well as domestic responsibilities. Nádlaeehí combined both female and male activities, including hunting, warfare, herding sheep, weaving, and basketry, which contributed to their unique status (Roscoe, 1998). In prereservation times, nádlaeehí often held religious specialist roles because their unique identity was as much a sacred occupational status as a secular social role (Roscoe, 1998). Children with nádlaeehí tendencies were given special care and encouragement. In contemporary times, however, issues of housing and job discrimination lessen the chance for economic opportunity, and stigma and discrimination in schools abound for LGBT youth. These adversities may be compounded by intersectionality of ethnic and sexual identities. When counseling LGBT or Two-spirit young women, it is important to include information about the cultural value of Two-spirit individuals to the tribe and their honored position, in addition to addressing the struggles of the contemporary experiences.

Studies have shown that positive self-esteem and positive self-regard among NA adolescents are linked to unconditional acceptance by others, positive perceptions of self by others, cultural identification, preservation of cultural identity, and experiences of success (Dvorakova, 2003; Whitesell, Mitchell, & Spicer, 2009). Building a positive concept of self can be greatly undermined by discrimination and stereotyping. Media plays a large role in this discrimination by perpetuating misrepresentations of the NA (e.g., the noble savage, warrior chief, Indian princess, squaw, lazy drunkard). These stereotypes occur via popular culture in a variety of forms, including television, movies, printed media such as magazines, fashion, Halloween costumes, and sports team mascots (Fryberg, Markus, Oyserman, & Stone, 2008). To illustrate, Fryberg and Morse (2003) found that NAs who had been primed with negative social representations reported lower self-esteem, "lower collec-

---

[5] *Berdache* is an early European, often offensive, term to describe a Native American who assumes the dress, social status, and role of the opposite sex.

tive self-efficacy and fewer future achievement selves" (p. 62). Most recently, sports team mascots have been recognized as especially problematic for positive identity formation among NA youth. Further, Fryberg and Morse (2003) found NAs experienced lower collective self-efficacy and fewer future achievement-related selves regardless of whether they agreed with using NAs as mascots or not. Research such as this has created a call for an increasing number of psychological organizations to take a position on the need for eliminating derogatory representations of NAs as mascots (e.g., Society of Indian Psychologists, American Psychological Association). The pervasive influence of media and team mascot stereotyping is a continuation of historical trauma in a modernized sense. Rather than understanding the diversity and heterogeneity of the NA population, media portray indigenous individuals as derogatory archetypes of themselves, often with serious psychological consequences (Leavitt, Covarrubias, Perez, & Fryberg, 2015).

BARRIERS TO EDUCATION AND EMPLOYMENT

The academic success of NA students hinges largely on retention in academic settings. Currently, NA students are faced with a dropout crisis in the educational system, with overall graduation rates that fall well below the national average. When compared with other racial and ethnic groups (Asians, 77.9%; Whites, 69.8%; Blacks, 54.7%; Hispanics, 50.8%), graduation rates for NA youth are only 46.6% (Faircloth & Tippeconnic, 2010). This has tremendous implications for NA youth joining the workforce, earning a livable wage, and pursuing higher education. NA adolescents who go on to pursue higher education as first-generation students may also experience a sense of survivor guilt, known as *family achievement guilt*, that may go unrecognized by helping professionals (Covarrubias & Fryberg, 2015a, 2015b). As caregivers, NA girls may be especially vulnerable to experiencing guilt about leaving families and kinship networks to pursue higher education. NA adolescent girls often play an integral role in the well-being of the family and the community by caring for siblings, parents, and elders. Students who perceive that they have left especially difficult home lives (e.g., family trauma, substance use, extreme poverty) may experience higher levels of this guilt.

Positive representations of NA identity can greatly alleviate how NA students view the difficulties of pursuing both secondary and higher education. NA students overall experience less exposure to self-relevant positive role models in academic settings than their White counterparts (Covarrubias & Fryberg, 2015a; Fryberg, 2003). Self-relevant role model exposures can occur through consumption of literature, art, and music created by NA individuals; through opportunities to read and learn about positive NA role models; and by attending events and learning opportunities connected to NA educators and professionals. Contrary to historical views, the NA student does not experience cultural deprivation. Rather, the emphasis on learning in education systems has to be shifted toward a theme of self-determination rooted in the awareness of cultural differences and similarities. Differences in the NA student compared with other ethnic or cultural groups are often misunderstood as a lack of intelligence and even as learning disabilities. Perceived problematic behavioral differences for these students may actually center on feelings of isolation, anxiety, or rejection; perceptions of forced acculturation; contradictions with values systems that prize noncompetition and sharing; preference for private (vs. public) recognition; conflict of spatial and temporal concepts; complex nonverbal communication centered on showing respect; value of noninterference; and connection to nature (Parrish, Klem, & Brown, 2012).

IMPLICATIONS FOR MENTAL HEALTH

NA adolescent girls' risk of developing poor mental health outcomes can be influenced by complications to cultural identity development, historical and intergenerational trauma, the disintegration of family and kinship structures, interpersonal violence and discrimination, and barriers to education and employment. Walters, Simoni, and Evans-Campbell (2002) related that "by the 12th grade, the lifetime prevalence of alcohol use is almost universal, with 96% of Native American boys and 92% of Native American girls having used alcohol" (p. S107). NA youth currently face disparate proportions of substance use and alarmingly high rates of suicide in tribal communities. According to a 2015 National Youth Risk Survey (CDC, 2017), AIAN youth engaged in risky behaviors (e.g., drug use, risky sexual behavior, suicide attempts, criminal activity, violence and gang activity, truancy, behaviors related to unintentional injuries) at a much higher rate overall when compared with either White or Black youth (Baldwin et al., 2011; CDC, 2016; Frank & Lester, 2002). In a comprehensive assessment of prevalence rates, the CDC (2008b) reported that "alcohol-attributable deaths accounted for 4 times as many deaths among American Indian/Alaskan Natives as in the U.S. general population (11.7 vs. 3.3 %, respectively)" (para. 7). In addition, AIAN youth in the United States report higher suicidality, including suicidal ideation and suicidal behavior, compared with other racial and ethnic groups (see Figure 2.1; Gray & McCullagh, 2014; Manzo, Tiesman, Stewart, Hobbs, &

FIGURE 2.1. Suicide Rates Between 1999 and 2016 by Race for Females 10 to 24 Years of Age

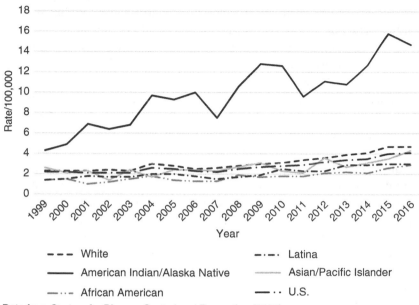

Data from Centers for Disease Control and Prevention (2018).

Knox, 2015). It is estimated that violence, homicide, suicide, and unintentional injuries account for 75% of annual deaths in AIAN youth ages 12 to 20 (Aspen Institute, 2016). When paired with psychosocial risk factors (e.g., low socioeconomic status, low educational attainment, adverse childhood experiences, domestic violence and lifetime prevalence of abuse or assault, perceived lack of purpose and low self-worth, historical trauma or loss), risky behaviors may be especially salient precursors for the development of chronic mental disorders and high mortality rates among AIAN youth (Substance Abuse and Mental Health Services Administration [SAMHSA], 2013).

NA adolescents use substances to cope with stressors earlier in childhood than their counterparts and are also far more likely to deal with severe consequences of drug and alcohol use, such as mental illness, high mortality rates, and incarceration. In addition, NA women with histories of alcohol dependence reported higher rates of depression, anxiety, hostility, phobic anxiety, paranoid ideation, psychoses, and obsessive–compulsive behaviors than NA women with no alcohol dependence (Walker et al., 1996). Use of alcohol and illicit drugs also greatly increases the likelihood of engaging in risky behaviors (including risky sexual behaviors). The indigenist stress-coping paradigm is a useful tool for understanding these trends because it incorporates a sociohistorical view that considers the impact of colonization on NA peoples (Walters et al., 2002). This paradigm suggests that maladaptive coping schemes often relate to proximal and distal traumas, childhood abuse and neglect, unresolved grief and mourning, and discrimination stemming from historically driven situations that continue to influence the modern context of NA individuals (Walters et al., 2002). In the indigenist stress-coping model, the association between stressors and adverse consequences is moderated by culturally situated factors, and consistent themes emerge to highlight the importance of family and community, traditional and spiritual healing practices, and NA identity as a means of overcoming substance use (Walters et al., 2002). Using this model during therapeutic work may help elicit pertinent information for understanding both interpersonal difficulties and institutional barriers such as lack of access to mental health care. Walters et al. (2002) referred to the model as a "decolonized conceptual framework" (p. 10) that is preferable to the Eurocentric models of stress coping that are currently the status quo. Consistent with the indigenist feminist view, this model promotes the autonomy and empowerment of NA peoples.

According to Langhinrichsen-Rohling, Friend, and Powell (2009), NA females are more likely than African American, Asian American, and Latina American females to report suicidal ideation and suicide attempts, with females reporting more ideation and fewer attempts than males. Adolescent girls living on or near reservation areas have an increased risk due to high levels of poverty and isolation and higher rates of alcohol and drug use. There is little doubt that suicide in Indian country has reached epidemic status. Clusters of suicides occurring in reservation areas have received national attention and have prompted health initiatives aimed at addressing the issue. Gray and McCullagh (2014) stated that "disparities in health, education, and employment opportunities, coupled with the high prevalence of violence and substance abuse, serve to both exacerbate mental health problems and disconnect Native American youth from their community and culture" (p. 1). The cumulative risk and protective model for suicide attempts indicates that each risk factor an NA adolescent is exposed to makes them 1.4 times as likely to attempt suicide, whereas each additional protective factor decreases that likelihood by 50% (Mackin, Perkins, & Furrer, 2012). In addition, a study by Cummins, Ireland, Resnick, and Blum (1999) indicated that a lack of family caring, poor body image and low self-esteem, negative feelings about going to school, and increased worries and concerns (mostly related to themes of interpersonal violence) were strong correlates for poor emotional health in NA girls.

A culturally relevant, strengths-based approach geared toward increasing resilience across the life span may be one of the most effective ways to address mental health disparities among NA adolescent girls (Clauss-Ehlers,

2008; Fergus & Zimmerman, 2005; Oré, Teufel-Shone, & Chico-Jarillo, 2016; Stumblingbear-Riddle, 2010). As helping professionals, we must look at the experience of the NA adolescent girl holistically while examining social and contextual factors for mental health. Weaving culturally relevant practices that address interrelatedness as a key factor of the NA experience into mental health treatment is of the utmost importance (Mohatt, Fok, Burket, Henry, & Allen, 2011). This includes recognizing the importance of traditional knowledge and ceremony, the role of spirituality, and awareness of historical context and social support (Kulis, Hodge, Ayers, Brown, & Marsiglia, 2012; Nebelkopf & Phillips, 2004; Wexler & Gone, 2012).

PSYCHOLOGICAL TREATMENT OF NATIVE AMERICAN ADOLESCENT GIRLS

Evidence-based practice is a difficult process for therapists working with NAs. Substance abuse is one of the few areas that have evidence-based, culturally relevant treatment processes for NAs. Many other NA treatments are evidence-based for the dominant culture and some of the racial and ethnic groups with larger populations but not for NAs (Gray, 2012). Many add a feather or some NA symbol or term and consider it to be "culturally adapted." Unfortunately, that is not a relevant adaptation to the culture. Some of the examples provided next are ways to integrate the culture and teachings into the therapy to address the needs of NA adolescent girls. Over centuries of challenges, the indigenous peoples of the United States have shown exceptional strength and healthy ways of coping with the genocide, loss of land and culture, forced acculturation, loss of tribal languages, and tragic deaths of ancestors and loved ones (Barcus, 2003). Among the greatest coping mechanisms for NAs are their culture, identity, family connections, and spirituality. These mechanisms have sustained NA resiliency through the impact of sociopolitical, cultural, and physical environments and stressors from oppression and hostility (LaFromboise, Hoyt, Oliver, & Whitbeck, 2006). Many youths living in urban and nonreservation areas do not have access to the support networks and cultural values that provide needed resiliency (LaFromboise, Trimble, & Mohatt, 1990). This makes it important that the therapeutic environment provide opportunities for these protective factors. There are less than 300 indigenous psychologists in North America (J. P. Gone, personal communication, November 21, 2016). The severe shortage of NA mental health providers and lack of culturally competent providers make gaining cultural competence important for NAs seeking services initially and for continuing treatment after the initial visit (Barcus, 2003). Fear and mistrust of non-Indigenous providers may be compounded by the cultural insensitivity of these providers, resulting in those seeking help not returning after the first appointment (Barcus, 2003; Gray, 2012). Differences between NA culture and the dominant culture must be examined when approaching therapy with NAs.

Welcoming Therapy Environment

It is important to prepare a safe and welcoming environment for NA adolescent girls in therapy. This often includes traditional art and medicine (e.g., sage, sweetgrass, tobacco, cedar, water). Seeing objects that are familiar to the adolescent girl's culture as she enters the therapy center or office can create a sense of acceptance of who she is and the culture with which she identifies. The display of artwork, pottery, NA dolls, or NA designs in cloth or beadwork can create this connection to culture (Gray, 2012). You may ask the client whether particular things would make her more comfortable in the space. If your facility does not allow for smudging (burning of sage, sweetgrass, tobacco, cedar, or other medicines to cleanse and purify the area)—most facilities do not allow burning of anything inside the building—it would be good to consider smudging outside (weather permitting) or providing an alternative. This can include the use of medicinal oils or leaves to breathe in the fragrance before and after the session and to cleanse the area of the disturbing information (or spirits) shared from the session (Gray, 2012). A non-NA therapist might offer the client a braid of sweetgrass (sweetgrass is a woman's medicine) or some sage leaves to hold and smell during the session. This can lead to a discussion of smudging. It is important here to clarify what is comfortable for the NA girl based on cultural knowledge and level of acculturation.

In addition to the welcoming environment, it is important to address a few myths, stereotypes, and misinformation about NAs to make the environment more welcoming. Much of what the majority culture knows about NAs comes from the film industry and the Hollywood western. This creates biases through false information and misunderstanding of NA culture. The relationship between NAs and alcohol and being lazy, shifty, and stoic are common descriptors of NAs. Common assumptions include NAs receiving money or being supported by the federal government, receiving a free education, and receiving free housing. When first meeting the NA client and her family, rapport building may begin by the therapist introducing her- or himself and by including more of who they are than just credentials. This can be seen in Case Example 1 in Appendix 2.1. It is important to include some background regarding where you come from and what brought you to this place. Then, the therapist should provide the family or girl the opportunity to introduce themselves, remembering that many traditional introductions include who their parents and grandparents are and identification of tribal membership or descendancy. Also, the helping professional should recognize that in some cases the introduction will defer to the oldest relative in attendance, depending on how traditional the family may be. The introduction is a time to establish our interrelatedness or connection as people or relatives. This reinforces the NA premise of *mitákuye oyás'in* (in Lakota, "we are all related"). Service providers should understand that some NA clients go to family or traditional healers before going to a therapist, especially a nonindigenous therapist. The establishment of the relationship or relatedness at the beginning of treatment is important (see Case Example 2 in Appendix 2.1).

Cultural History and Connection

During the intake process, it is important to gather a cultural history in addition to the family, social, health, and counseling information from the client and family. The cultural history will contain not only tribal membership but also involvement in traditional tribal activities, participation in ceremonies, and family history of any cultural involvement. This history includes family relationships, who the client has lived with, where she has lived, types of cultural activities and participation, types of ceremonies and participation, whether she or any family members speak the tribal language, who makes decisions in their family, whether the decision making changes when they are with other family, what they call sickness in their family, and how it is treated. Family relationships in NA communities differ from Western definitions of *family*, where direct blood relatives are identified (note the interrelatedness that was described earlier). Within NA communities someone who is close, although not a blood relative, may be called *Mom* or *Auntie* because that describes the closeness of the relationship irrespective of the blood relationship. It is also common to refer to cousins or close peers as *sisters* or *brothers* because they may be raised in a close emotional relationship like siblings rather than cousins or friends. It can be complicated if a therapist is trying to create a genogram, a diagram of family relationships and generations, when the client is referring to multiple people as *mom* or referring to *sisters* and *brothers* if there are no biological siblings in the family. Elders or esteemed members of the community may be referred to as *grandmother* or *grandfather* as well.

Participation or lack of participation in cultural activities and ceremonies can provide important information about how closely the client and her family are connected to the culture and history of their family and tribe. If they live in an urban setting, it is important to ask about how the family came to live in that city and whether they return to their tribal community for visits or special events. This is common, especially when the family lives within a few hours of the tribal community. It can also explain absences from school for days or weeks at a time while the family travels "home." There may be particular feasts, celebrations, ceremonies, or other events that occur at specific times. The client and her family need to know you do not have to know all the specifics of the ceremony but that you want to understand how things you talk about may relate to her cultural involvement.

Sometimes, young people go to live with other relatives for periods. It is important to know about these changes in living situation, who was included in the household, how long the client lived with that particular relative, how it was different from where she lives now, and who she lives with currently. This can help determine important relationships, preferences for living environment, what activities are looked forward to or missed when in a particular residence, and stability in her living situation. Knowing who she talks to within the family for support and problem solving and whether the family makes use of traditional medicines or healers are integral parts of treatment (Barcus, 2003; see Case Example 2 in Appendix 2.1).

In the initial session, time should be allowed to explain how psychotherapy treatment differs from traditional healing methods, including the length of each session, the number of sessions, and scheduling of and arriving for appointments (Barcus, 2003). Because of the differences between the Western concept of time used by most service providers and an NA concept of time, this may have to be negotiated as to what will and will not be accepted. It may also help to brainstorm possible barriers to timely attendance of sessions and how to handle them. When discussing how decisions are made in the family, who is in charge, and how "sickness" is described, it is important to know who the key decision makers are. Some tribes are matriarchal, and others are patriarchal (Green, 1992, pp. 21–29). The decision maker may not be the mother or father, but the oldest male or female relative. Trust in the Western mental health system is low due to a lack of indigenous providers and culturally competent non-NA providers. The provider must earn the trust and respect of the adolescent client and her family by being transparent about expectations of what is going to happen and by providing culturally sensitive and relevant services (Barcus, 2003).

Know the Tribal History

The history of each tribe and their experience with colonization is different, so it is important to understand the history of a person's tribe in order to provide culturally competent treatment. Tribes and individuals within the tribes differ greatly, and cultural knowledge has to be tribally specific (Barcus, 2003). As has been described, historical trauma or intergenerational trauma is based on shared traumas of a specific tribe or group, so references made to specific events are more important to some tribes and not relevant to others. Some tribes have history or cultural centers that may have a brief tribal history available. The client knowing or not knowing the history may not be as important as the events imprinted on their DNA. Knowing what events are important and how ancestors were able to survive those traumas can provide important skills and success stories for the client.

Values of Native American Women

In its commentary on the American Psychological Association's (2017) *Ethical Principles of Psychologists and Code of Conduct*, the Society of Indian Psychologists (SIP) put together a list of common values shared by tribes, although tribal values may vary, and it is important to work within the tribal values in the psychological treatment of NA adolescent girls (Garcia & Tehee, 2014). This document was created with over 100 tribes participating. The 12 common values identified by SIP include (a) all things are sacred; (b) life and development are understood in cycles; (c) everything is connected; (d) events in life can be understood as lessons; (e) respect and honoring are essential to true and long-lasting relationships; (f) relevant healing emphasizes the social, historical, and political contexts that shape indigenous experience; (g) relevant healing encourages balance and harmony, positive growth, and resilience; (h) individuality is valued by how it improves the community with collaboration, more highly valued than autonomy; (i) sustainability is essential to survive and thrive; (j) mystery, awe, wonder, intuition, and miracles occur naturally in everyday life; (k) the best way to understand one's place and identity is in the context of the past, present, and future of one's community; and (l) compartmentalism misses the beauty of the whole (Garcia & Tehee, 2014). In some indigenous cultures, they are spoken of as teachings instead of values. The Anishinaabe speak of wisdom, love, respect, bravery, honesty, humility, and truth as the Seven Grandfathers (Fiola, 2014). The Lakota have the Seven Great Lakota Sioux Laws that include prayer, respect, compassion, honesty, generosity, humility, and wisdom (J. E. Brown, 1971). When NA women gather and talk, the subjects of family and community are usually at the center, with topics of tradition, values, and culture mixed within that context (Mankiller, 2011, p. xxviii). Spirituality is a common core of everything. Rocks, trees, animals, and water all have spirits and are part of the whole. The ceremony is part of spirituality, but many people look at the ceremony as the spirituality, not as a piece of the whole concept of how we (including rocks, animals, plants, etc.) are all related (Mankiller, 2011).

Ceremonies

Each tribe has its own rites and ceremonies. Two common ceremonies for many tribes that can be important in adolescent development are coming of age ceremonies and naming ceremonies. Although they may be conducted differently from tribe to tribe, the concepts are the same. In *The Sacred Pipe*, the seven rites of the Lakota are explained: (a) keeping of the soul; (b) *Inipi*, the rite of purification; (c) *Hanblecheyapi*, the crying for a vision; (d) *Wiwanyag Wachipi*, the Sun Dance; (e) *Hunkapi*, the making of relatives; (f) *Ishna Ta Awi Cha Lowan*, preparing a girl for womanhood; and (g) *Tapa Wanka Yap*, the throwing of the ball (J. E. Brown, 1971; Powers, 1986, pp. 66–73). The sixth rite, *Ishna Ta Awi Cha Lowan*, is the most important for this book because it deals with the transition of a girl to woman and traditionally takes place following her first menstrual period to explain the expectations and duties that come with the role of being a woman. The coming of age ceremony symbolizes the transition from childhood to womanhood and is conducted by the women of the family or community. This is a rite of passage and usually is built on stories and activities that are important to being a woman with power and strength. Bringing in the true roles of women in NA culture helps the adolescent girl to value her role, power, and strength as a woman (see implementation in Case Example 1 in Appendix 2.1).

Similarly, the naming ceremony is common in most tribes. NAs may receive four or five names in their lifetime. One may be given in their youth, but others are earned throughout their lifetime (Powers, 1986, pp. 60–61). Usually, an elder in the family or community is asked to name someone. This takes hours of prayer and meditation for the spirits to provide the name the person will carry, maybe for an ancestor, an event that occurred, or some other occurrence that is seen as represented in the child (Powers, 1986, p. 61). When these ceremonial rites of passage are not observed, many times the adolescent is left adrift and feels disconnected. Developing a process for an NA girl to receive a name to describe her or to live up to can be powerful. In many tribes, a person may be considered to have multiple spirits—for example, a spirit that remains on the earth after they pass to watch over family and loved ones and a spirit that passes to the Spirit World; some may have other spirits for other parts of who they are. If someone is disoriented, is not sure where they fit in, is traveling a lot between locations, or has wandered off, the individual may have left a spirit behind somewhere, and it is necessary to call the spirit home, so it knows where to go to find the person to whom it belongs. This is why mothers and grandmothers in NA communities may be found calling for their children at times to bring the child and their spirit back home.

Busy Hands

"We learn better when our hands are busy" (D. S. BigFoot, personal communication, June 6, 2007). When working with NA women and girls, it is important they have something to do while they are talking: Beading, making quilts, coloring, painting, and other cultural activities can make it easier to discuss difficult issues without worrying about looking at someone or talking (Atkins & Snyder, 2017). These activities can help the client relax and lessen the focus of attention on the individual. Either encouraging the adolescent to bring something she likes to work on with her hands or providing options such as clay, play dough, drawing or painting materials, beads, or other materials to be creative with her hands while she is talking can open up quiet and reserved adolescent girls (Levine & Levine, 2004; Malchiodi, 2005; McNiff, 2004). Finding other than verbal ways of expression is important to help NA girls find their voices.

Diagnosis and Presenting Problems

Any diagnosis of NA adolescent girls should be made with caution and consideration of cultural aspects that may influence that diagnosis. Because identity and mental health are mutually co-informed and cultural contexts in identifying the criteria of the *Diagnostic and Statistical Manual of Mental Disorders* (fifth ed. [*DSM–5*]; American Psychiatric Association, 2013), SIP addressed many concerns about how the manual could cause harm to clients and the public. In a letter providing feedback to the *DSM–5* task force (Garcia & Gray, 2011), SIP recommended the manual be used with extreme caution. NA girls are often overrepresented as crime victims requiring forensic evaluation. Many of the diagnoses that do not consider the cultural context and spiritual orientation should be used with caution in diagnosing NA girls in this setting because the potential for harm in legal settings and misuse by attorneys may have a lasting impact. *DSM–5* does not consider cultural fit, context, and spiritual orientation when applying diagnoses, including the transgenerational transmission of trauma (Garcia & Gray, 2011).

Caution is also urged when using standardized assessments with NA adolescent girls. When conducting an assessment, it is important to consider culture, tribal history, spirituality, traditional belief systems, collectivistic orientation, and acculturation, particularly when interpreting assessments that have not been validated with any NA population (Gray, Peters, & McCullagh, 2016). It is also important for the clinician to take into consideration her or his biases, attitudes, and assumptions to understand how the assessment process may be impacted. Some NA adolescents may be bilingual or not have English as their first language. Because many NA people are faced with socioeconomic barriers and disparities in health, education, and career opportunities, clinicians must understand how these factors impact assessment with NA adolescent girls (Gray et al., 2016).

Substance Use and Abuse

NA health disparities include a range of behavioral health problems, the most prevalent of which appear to be substance use disorders (SUDs; Gone & Calf Looking, 2015). These disproportionate rates impact nearly all members of an NA community, including vulnerable NA girls. Many girls grow up in homes with parents and family members dealing with SUDs or other mental health illnesses; some have family members who have been in prison, some grow up in abusive homes, and some have experienced bullying and trauma (Coyhis Publishing, 2010). These negative cycles of violence and self-destructive behaviors in the NA culture point to the introduction of alcohol and other drugs. Although there are disproportionate rates of SUDs in conjunction with sexual and physical assaults, there are low levels of reporting made by NA girls. These low reporting rates may contribute to feelings of isolation and hopelessness among victims because most often perpetrators are not caught, arrested, and prosecuted due to gaps caused by mistrust of the legal system (Wahab & Olson, 2004). Numerous barriers contribute to the challenges NA women and girls face when seeking help, including racism, fear of familial alienation, language barriers, lack of trust, fear of being fostered to outsiders, fear of White-dominated agencies, and cultural and value differences (Wahab & Olson, 2004). It is for these reasons and more that community-oriented programs and providers are necessary to help NA girls learn new ways of thinking and feeling about themselves. Many NA counselors believe that the integration of cultural and spiritual values in substance treatment programs is the only effective solution to the rates of substance abuse problems of NAs (Beauchamp, 1997).

Community culturally oriented approaches to prevention have great potential to address the needs of communities that are in line with NA values and principles (Guttmannova et al., 2017). Retraditionalization, or the return to traditional cultural forms, promotes cultural, individual self-esteem. The retraditionalization process teaches about NA values and traditions that can be incorporated into treatment modalities, including individual and group counseling, psychoeducation groups, and the Red Road to Recovery based on the work of Eugene Thin Elk (1993), focusing on traditional cultural values and spirituality (Nebelkopf & Phillips, 2004). One such cultural approach to the prevention and treatment of SUDs, dysfunctional families and relationships, and suicide rates is the White Bison Wellbriety Movement, which uses the Medicine Wheel and 12 Step program (Coyhis Publishing, 2010). The White Bison Wellbriety Movement, established in 1988, provides culturally based tools to heal from intergenerational trauma. The Medicine Wheel and 12 Step program is an inclusive culturally and spiritually relevant approach to substance abuse for NA people. The model is based on the Teachings of the Medicine Wheel, the Cycle of Life, and the Four Laws of Change presented in a series of modules that enable NA individuals to meet their needs by sharing insights and experiences through activities such as mind mapping. This activity empowers the individual to focus on their innate knowledge of the cultural teachings and then to apply that knowledge to their daily lives and decision-making process. This holistic model accounts for the mental, physical, spiritual, and emotional aspects of an individual. The approach emphasizes teachings about truth and life, as well as the power to influence significant change in attitudes, behaviors, values, and intent. The Medicine Wheel and the 12 Step program connects principles of living with each step combined with a cultural approach allowing each person's tribal traditions to be used as she works the steps (Coyhis Publishing, 2010). There is a specific White Bison curriculum for women and girls that focuses on their cultural and personal traumas and losses. Using this model may improve social and emotional bonds that help individuals develop trust, autonomy, and other positive emotions and thought patterns that will help emotional, mental, physical, and spiritual growth in NA girls. This model is important to NA adolescent girls because it provides culturally based healing for the next seven generations of indigenous people (Coyhis Publishing, 2010).

An inclusive program should have a strength-based curriculum tailored to the needs of the individual dealing with issues of SUDs and trauma and applied as a prevention curriculum for NA youth. Participating in a culturally relevant program that recognizes the importance of culture and spirituality may support the adolescent girl to cultivate a set of values and philosophies about what it means to be an NA female.

It is important for mental health providers to appreciate the importance and meaning of cultural practices in terms of healing and holistic balance because it demonstrates key cultural perspectives and influences the identity development of the individual. Such cultural healing practices are based on traditions and perspectives that are outside the realm of Western psychological tenets (Rybak & Decker-Fitts, 2009). Healing and wellness from an NA perspective include "recovering one's wholeness," or reestablishing harmony and balance within the four areas of mental, physical, emotional, and spiritual aspects of life. Although this may sound like a Gestalt therapy approach, it comes from the NA perspective of thousands of years of all things being related and necessary to be a whole person (Blanchard, 2011). Typically, mental health providers use a Western approach in which the provider is trained to isolate problem areas in human functioning for which interventions are then developed (Hodge, Limb, & Cross, 2009). However, in NA culture, the healer treats the balance, adjusting the four areas to wellness (Cross, 1997). Connecting spiritual elements to all living elements is an important dimension of living in wellbriety. It is recommended that mental health providers pinpoint effective programs in the general population and culturally adapt them for NA adolescents (Guttmannova et al., 2017; see Case Example 3 in Appendix 2.1).

As stated in the previous section, spirit, body, mind, and context are all interconnected with the ability to change and influence one another. Changes in one variable result in changes throughout the larger system (Hodge et al., 2009). Cultural perspective should include balance and harmony as the pathway to wellness. Implications for mental health professionals are not limited to the following areas and should consider the holistic picture of the NA adolescent girl when initiating healing practices. These practices may include drumming, beading, pipe ceremonies, dancing, or coming of age ceremonies, but we highlight two commonly used practices that can support NA adolescent girls. Talking circles in conjunction with talking sticks provide healing and have been used as a learning format for the decision-making process, conflict management, and general healing process (Coyhis Publishing, 2010). Talking circles can help individuals explore concepts, teachings, and issues and validate feelings and experiences. Talking circles can provide space for NA girls to establish a support network, make autonomous decisions, manage conflict, develop healthy ways of coping, and discover important values (Coyhis Publishing, 2010). The few rules for the talking circle and talking stick require those participating to be seated or standing, one person to speak at a time who cannot be interrupted, and the bearer of the talking stick to be mindful and speak the truth but not engage in negative talk (J. E. Trimble, personal communication, August 3, 2000). Following this advice provides validation, acknowledgment, and healing that otherwise may not be provided outside of sessions. This activity requires the girl to engage in deep thought processes about pressing issues in her life and, when prompted, to find the answers within herself. Circles also create a sense of being cared for by others that can be a powerful transformational experience because it reinforces self-love and allows individuals to risk experiencing difficult feelings that were previously masked by substance use (Nebelkopf & Phillips, 2004).

Most NA tribes have used storytelling as a way to convey teachings and lessons from generation to generation. Storytelling can provide individuals with a better sense of self, understanding of the environment, and the path toward healing and can influence a person's perception of reality (Bigfoot & Dunlap, 2006). Sharing of such stories can provide healing in unresolved trauma, grief, shame, and guilt and provide hope to those suffering (Mehl-Madrona, 2007), especially those vulnerable, at-risk NA girls. The power of storytelling with positive role models in the community can often act as good medicine for the girl. In sharing stories and experiences, the girl can create a network of role models who can provide wisdom and insight, which often is a powerful medium for healing (Coyhis Publishing, 2010). Learning and sharing with her circle can accelerate healing and connectedness that helps her overcome barriers, brings about personal growth, and builds character (Coyhis Publishing, 2010). The underlying principle is again related to the interconnectedness of all things while empowering the NA girl to tell her story. It is clear that holistic prevention and intervention programs should use an integrated, culturally adapted treatment model for those dealing with SUDs and other behavioral health issues. As the mental health provider for NA adolescents, it is important to acknowledge the indigenous psychology underlying NA healing practices. Knowledge of cultural practices and ceremonies can deepen the non-NA provider's understating of NA adolescent youth. The integration and use of the previously mentioned retraditionalization treatment modalities can provide NA girls with an experiential healing process in substance abuse treatment, thus reducing the disproportionate rates of SUDs among NA girls.

Victimization: Violence, Sexual Assault, and Trafficking

As was previously mentioned, NA adolescent girls are at high risk of victimization through violence, sexual assault, and trafficking. This high risk makes it imperative that the issues be addressed and discussed with NA adolescents. These behaviors may be viewed as the norm unless confronted from a cultural, feminist, and social perspective. NA girls must know that an attack on her being is not part of every girl's life and should not be accepted as if it were. NA women are seen in increasing numbers in the corrections system. It is common for intimate partners of these women to intimidate them to admit to the criminal behavior because the women do not have a criminal record, unlike the intimate partner who may have an extensive criminal record and may thus be more likely to experience the consequences of their criminal behavior. The women are told they will not "do time" or will serve only a light sentence and do not realize that they may lose custody of their children and may be incarcerated for years, while their intimate partner goes free (C. I. LaCounte, personal communication, July 12, 2012). NA adolescents are extremely overrepresented in state and federal corrections systems (Rountree, 2015). Although AIAN youth represent about 1% of the population, they represent 2 to 3 times that number in the juvenile justice system (Rountree, 2015). According to the Office of Juvenile Justice and Delinquency Prevention (2017), AIAN adolescent girls are incarcerated at five times the rate of White girls, at the highest rate of any ethnic group. NA girls provide an easy target for traffickers and murderers because law enforcement officers do not have a centralized database to identify and track information on NA girls and young women who disappear. Canada is now addressing this issue (Royal Canadian Mounted Police, 2014). In the United States, there is no official database, and little is known of these missing, murdered, assaulted, and trafficked NA girls and women except in their own families and communities (Young et al., 2017). Jurisdictional issues and dismissal by legal authorities put these young NA women at more risk than other adolescent girls in this country.

Another form of violence in NA communities is suicide. NA adolescent girls' complete suicides at the highest rate of any racial or ethnic group in the United States (CDC, 2018). Rates began increasing from about four per 100,000 in 1999 to over 15 per 100,000 in 2015 (see Figure 2.1; CDC, 2018). These rates are nearly 400% the national rate for females from 10 to 24 years of age (CDC, 2018). These higher rates have included suicide clusters (three or more connected suicides in a short period), some involving relationships established on social media (National Suicide Prevention Taskforce, personal communication, December 15, 2013). It is important to note that these numbers may vary greatly by the tribe. Although some tribes may have extremely high rates, some over 100 per 100,000, other tribes have a suicide rate that is near zero over a number of years.

It is important to gather information about whether the adolescent has ever considered suicide; when, where, why, and what stopped her; or if she attempted suicide, what happened. Other important information is her social and family exposure to suicides. Does she know anyone who attempted or completed a suicide? Again, who, where, when, and why, the relationship to her, and how she felt about it. The more common a suicide is in her social and family circles, the higher the risk of her seeing that as an option to dealing with her problems. This has to be addressed openly and honestly with the adolescent. It is important to identify multiple reliable sources of people available to her when she is having suicidal thoughts or tendencies because it develops a wall of resilience. Resources may come from many places, including medical support, spirituality, generosity, healthy activities, mentors, positive friends, family support, and mental health support (http://sourcesofstrength.org). When working with adolescents in tribal communities, it is quite common to ask whether anyone has been affected by suicide and have every hand in the room be raised. These communities are small, and one death can impact everyone in the community. In urban areas, it is more difficult to identify the connections except within urban NA centers or programs. Knowing the social circles of NA adolescent girls in urban settings can help locate those relationships. At times, myths have been perpetuated among the youth of a particular tribe that glamorizes suicide as part of their culture. If this is the case, elders or cultural leaders have to state the truth that committing suicide is not a part of traditional culture. Some good resources for this include two culturally relevant resources: *Native American Life Skills Development Curriculum* (LaFromboise, 1995) and *Live to See the Great Day That Dawns: Preventing Suicide by American Indian and Alaska Native Youth and Young Adults* (SAMHSA, 2010). In addition, many tribes are implementing the Zero Suicide curriculum, also available through SAMHSA (http://zerosuicide.sprc.org/toolkit).

CONCLUSION

It is important that those providing therapeutic services to NA adolescent girls understand the complexities of their lives, the barriers to resources, the disruptions to identity development, and the healing steps toward becoming the best person they can be. Providing a cultural context to their issues helps to add to the wholeness of who they are to be as they grow into women. Understanding and acceptance of the cultural and spiritual part of the NA adolescent girl help her to value herself and all that she is.

Wilma Mankiller's (2011) book, *Every Day Is a Good Day: Reflections by Contemporary Indigenous Women*, provides a look into modern-day NA women leaders who discuss NA values and perspectives. NA adolescent females, especially those who do not have access to NA female elders to teach them and provide wisdom, could be helped by providing a context for their journey and grounding their identity. *Women and Power in Native North America* (Klein & Ackerman, 1995) is another book that helps to identify and provide context of who NA women are in NA society and traditional cultures.

The use of culturally based treatment is important in addressing that "missing piece" in NA adolescent girls' development, but it is also important for the service provider to view NA healing through the lens of feminism and resilience. When addressing the trauma experienced by NA adolescent girls, it is as important to provide a supportive, familiar, and accepting environment as it is to point out the ways that NA women and girls have been resilient throughout history, thus giving them a heritage of resilience and strength. NA adolescent girls come from strong, resilient, female leaders who were the very definition of feminism in their time. This source of strength, wrapped in the indigenous culture, provides the framework for help, support, social justice, and healing of NA young women.

APPENDIX 2.1: CASE EXAMPLES

CASE EXAMPLE 1: THE IMPORTANCE OF CEREMONY IN DEVELOPMENT OF IDENTITY

Angela[6] is a 14-year-old indigenous female runaway with a family history of alcoholism who ended up in the child welfare system with a White family because Indian child welfare was unable to find a placement with a Native American family. She was referred for therapy in an urban community. Angela felt she was lost and did not belong anywhere. She was taking care of herself. Angela did not feel wanted or a part of her tribal community because she had not been raised in a traditional way and was living in a non-Indian home. When she and the therapist talked about her expectations of life, her goals, what success means, and her needs to be successful, the therapist uncovered a longing to have a home and linkage to her tribal community.

The therapist, with Angela's permission, contacted the local Urban Indian Center to locate a female elder from her tribe who could answer Angela's questions and meet with Angela and the therapist. When they met, the elder, Rose, told Angela, the therapist, and the foster mother about the Womanhood Ceremony, including what it involves and what it means to be a woman in that tribe. After hearing more, Angela expressed interest in having the ceremony. Rose worked with Angela and her foster mother for the preparation and what she needed to do before the ceremony. The therapist also talked about how therapy is a ceremony and has a process for preparation, just as the Womanhood Ceremony does. Rose gathered women from the community center to conduct the ceremony when Angela was prepared.

Throughout the year of preparation, the therapist encouraged Angela to engage in storytelling activities to deepen insight into her feelings. At the end of each session, the therapist provided space for Angela to smudge and purify

---

[6] Client descriptions have been anonymized to protect confidentiality.

herself before she left the session. Angela enjoyed the smell of sage because it reconnected her to other female role models in the community. After the preparation process, Angela went through the Womanhood Ceremony with her foster mother supporting her. Angela is now closer to her foster mother and also has a support network of women to go to with questions and provide guidance in her life. These women are considered "aunties" or "grandmothers." As Angela made this connection, she wanted to receive an Indian name and worked with Rose to prepare for the naming ceremony when she is given a name based on who she became in the past year. This builds the framework for positive progress in therapy, development of supports, and strengthening of identity and self-esteem. The therapist also provided a ceremony for Angela's growth in that process through the past year.

CASE EXAMPLE 2: A PROBLEM WITH FAMILY FOLLOW-THROUGH IN THERAPY

A young adolescent American Indian girl was referred to counseling by the school because of poor attendance and not turning in her homework. The sessions were divided between time with the girl and time with the girl and her mother. At the end of each session, the mother and daughter left in full agreement with the therapist about a plan for the following week. The mother and daughter would return to the next session without having implemented any of the approaches that were agreed on in the previous session. The frustrated therapist sought consultation from a senior therapist who asked who the decision maker was in the family. After exploring this during the next session, the therapist invited the grandmother, who was determined to be the person blocking any change, to come to the next session. When the grandmother was involved in accomplishing the goal of the granddaughter being successful in school and being included in making a plan for success, changes began happening quickly. The grandmother was key to supporting the granddaughter making it to school and getting her homework done and making sure the rest of the family did the same.

CASE EXAMPLE 3: FROM SUBSTANCE ABUSE TO RECONNECTING WITH CULTURAL PRACTICES

Nina, a 17-year-old Native American, was admitted into an all-woman counseling group. Nina described initially living with her grandmother, who passed away when Nina was 12. She moved back into an unstable home with her verbally abusive parents. She described growing up learning about her Native American background from her grandmother but had not been to any ceremonies since her grandmother's passing. She admitted to coping by drinking and getting high to numb her feelings. Nina initially resisted individual and group sessions until she was challenged to do a mind-mapping activity that involved feelings of pain, anger, and hurt. She was gently challenged to deepen her insight into her feelings. Although she sobbed throughout the exercise, she was provided support from her peers and counselors. At the end of the activity, she asked to be smudged because she wanted to "get rid of bad vibes." She told the counselor the smell of sage reconnected her to her grandmother. She later wrote an apology letter to her grandmother asking for forgiveness for straying from her path.

REFERENCES

Allen, J., Mohatt, G. V., Fok, C. C., Henry, D., & Burkett, R. (2014). A protective factors model for alcohol abuse and suicide prevention among Alaska Native youth. *American Journal of Community Psychology, 54*, 125–139. http://dx.doi.org/10.1007/s10464-014-9661-3

American Psychiatric Association. (2013). *Diagnostic and statistical manual of mental disorders* (5th ed.). Arlington, VA: Author.

American Psychological Association. (2017). *Ethical principles of psychologists and code of conduct* (2002, Amended June 1, 2010 and January 1, 2017). Retrieved from http://www.apa.org/ethics/code/index.aspx

Amnesty International. (2007). *Maze of injustice: The failure to protect indigenous women from sexual violence in the USA.* Retrieved from https://www.amnestyusa.org/pdfs/mazeofinjustice.pdf

Aspen Institute. (2016). *State of Native youth: Drawing strength from our cultures.* Retrieved from http://www.cnay.org/docs/state-of-native-youth-report-2016-web-spread.pdf

Atkins, S., & Snyder, M. (2017). *Nature-based expressive arts therapy: Integrating the expressive arts and ecotherapy.* Philadelphia, PA: Jessica Kingsley.

Baldwin, J. A., Brown, B. G., Wayment, H. A., Nez, R. A., & Brelsford, K. M. (2011). Culture and context: Buffering the relationship between stressful life events and risky behaviors in American Indian Youth. *Substance Use and Misuse, 46*, 1380–1394. http://dx.doi.org/10.3109/10826084.2011.592432

Barcus, C. (2003). *Recommendations for the treatment of American Indian populations: Council of National Psychological Associations for the Advancement of Ethnic Minority Interests.* Washington, DC: Association of Black Psychologists.

Beauchamp, D. (1997). Healing alcoholism in indigenous people. *Social Work Perspectives, 8*, 35–40.

Bigfoot, D. S., & Dunlap, M. (2006). Storytelling as a healing tool for American Indians. In T. M. Witko (Ed.), *Mental health care for urban Indians: Clinical insights from Native practitioners* (pp. 133–153). Washington, DC: American Psychological Association.

Blanchard, G. (2011). *Ancient ways: Indigenous healing innovations for the 21st century.* Holyoke, MA: Neari Press.

Brave Heart, M. Y. H., & DeBruyn, L. M. (1998). The American Indian Holocaust: Healing historical unresolved grief. *American Indian and Alaska Native Mental Health Research, 8*(2), 56–78.

Brown, J. E. (1971). *The sacred pipe: Black Elk's account of the seven rites of the Oglala Sioux.* Norman: University of Oklahoma Press.

Brown, L. B. (1997). *Two spirit people: Native American, lesbian women and gay men.* New York, NY: Haworth Press.

Bureau of Indian Affairs. (2018, July 23). Indian entities recognized and eligible to receive services from the United States Bureau of Indian Affairs. *Federal Register.* Retrieved from https://www.federalregister.gov/documents/2018/07/23/2018-15679/indian-entities-recognized-and-eligible-to-receive-services-from-the-united-states-bureau-of-indian

Centers for Disease Control and Prevention. (2008a). Adverse health conditions and health risk behaviors associated with intimate partner violence—United States, 2005. *Morbidity and Mortality Weekly Report, 57,* 113–117.

Centers for Disease Control and Prevention. (2008b). Alcohol-attributable deaths and years of potential life lost among American Indians and Alaska Natives—United States, 2001–2005. *Morbidity and Mortality Weekly Report, 57,* 938–941.

Centers for Disease Control and Prevention. (2016). *Office of Management and Budget (OMB), Directive No. 15: Race and ethnic standards for federal statistics and administrative reporting.* Retrieved from https://wonder.cdc.gov/wonder/help/populations/bridged-race/directive15.html

Centers for Disease Control and Prevention. (2017). *YRBS data and documentation.* Retrieved from https://www.cdc.gov/healthyyouth/data/yrbs/data.htm

Centers for Disease Control and Prevention. (2018). *WISQARS fatal injury data visualization tool.* Retrieved from https://wisqars-viz.cdc.gov:8006/

Clauss-Ehlers, C. S. (2008). Sociocultural factors, resilience, and coping: Support for a culturally sensitive measure of resilience. *Journal of Applied Developmental Psychology, 29,* 197–212. http://dx.doi.org/10.1016/j.appdev.2008.02.004

Covarrubias, R., & Fryberg, S. A. (2015a). The impact of self-relevant representations on school belonging for Native American students. *Cultural Diversity and Ethnic Minority Psychology, 21,* 10–18. http://dx.doi.org/10.1037/a0037819

Covarrubias, R., & Fryberg, S. A. (2015b). Movin' on up (to college): First-generation college students' experiences with family achievement guilt. *Cultural Diversity and Ethnic Minority Psychology, 21,* 420–429. http://dx.doi.org/10.1037/a0037844

Coyhis Publishing. (2010). *Medicine Wheel and 12 Steps for Women: Facilitator manual.* Colorado Springs, CO: Author.

Cross, T. (1997). *Understanding the relational worldview in Indian families.* Retrieved from http://oregon.4h.oregonstate.edu/sites/default/files/information/staff/inclusive/RelationalWorldView.pdf

Cummins, J. R., Ireland, M., Resnick, M. D., & Blum, R. W. (1999). Correlates of physical and emotional health among Native American adolescents. *Journal of Adolescent Health, 24,* 38–44. http://dx.doi.org/10.1016/S1054-139X(98)00063-9

Duran, E., & Duran, B. (1995). *Native American postcolonial psychology.* Albany: SUNY Press.

Dvorakova, A. (2003). The low self-esteem Indian stereotype: Positive self-regard among Indigenous peoples of the United States. *Indigenous Nations Studies Journal, 4*(2), 1–23.

Faircloth, S. C., & Tippeconnic, J. W. (2010). *The dropout/graduation crisis among American and Alaska Native students: Failure to respond places the future of Native peoples at risk.* Retrieved from https://www.civilrightsproject.ucla.edu/research/k-12-education/school-dropouts/the-dropout-graduation-crisis-among-american-indian-and-alaska-native-students-failure-to-respond-places-the-future-of-native-peoples-at-risk

Fergus, S., & Zimmerman, M. A. (2005). Adolescent resilience: A framework for understanding healthy development in the face of risk. *Annual Review of Public Health, 26,* 399–419. http://dx.doi.org/10.1146/annurev.publhealth.26.021304.144357

Fiola, C. (2014). *Rekindling the sacred fire: Métis ancestry and Anishinabe spirituality.* Winnipeg, Canada: University of Manitoba Press.

Frank, M. L., & Lester, D. (2002). Self-destructive behaviors in American Indian and Alaska Native high school youth. *American Indian and Alaska Native Mental Health Research, 10*(3), 24–32. http://dx.doi.org/10.5820/aian.1003.2002.24

Fryberg, S. A. (2003). Really? You don't look like an American Indian: Social representations and social group identities. *Dissertation Abstracts International: Section B. The Sciences and Engineering, 64*(3-B), 1549.

Fryberg, S. A., Markus, H. R., Oyserman, D., & Stone, J. M. (2008). Of warrior chiefs and Indian princesses: The psychological consequences of American Indian mascots. *Basic and Applied Social Psychology, 30,* 208–218. http://dx.doi.org/10.1080/01973530802375003

Fryberg, S. A., & Morse, G. L. (2003). *Really? You don't look like an American Indian: Social representations and social group identities the relationships among cultural affiliation, perceived quality of life and mental health in a Native American population.* Retrieved from http://www.indianmascots.com/ex-17---fryberg-final_disse.pdf

Fuller-Thomson, E., & Minkler, M. (2005). American Indian/Alaskan Native grandparents raising grandchildren: Findings from the Census 2000 Supplementary Survey. *Social Work, 50,* 131–139. http://dx.doi.org/10.1093/sw/50.2.131

Futures Without Violence. (2012). *The facts on violence against American Indian/Alaskan Native women.* Retrieved from https://www.futureswithoutviolence.org/userfiles/file/Violence%20Against%20AI%20AN%20Women%20Fact%20Sheet.pdf

Garcia, M. A., & Gray, J. S. (2011). *Letter from the Society of Indian Psychologists to the Chair of the DSM-5 Task Force of the American Psychiatric Association.* Albuquerque, NM: Society of Indian Psychologists.

Garcia, M. A., & Tehee, M. (Eds.). (2014). *Society of Indian Psychologists commentary on the American Psychological Association's (APA)* Ethical Principles of Psychologists and Code of Conduct. Albuquerque, NM: Society of Indian Psychologists.

Garroutte, E. M. (2001). The racial formation of American Indians: Negotiating legitimate identities within tribal and federal law. *American Indian Quarterly, 25,* 224–239. http://dx.doi.org/10.1353/aiq.2001.0020

Gone, J. P., & Calf Looking, P. E. (2015). The Blackfeet Indian culture camp: Auditioning an alternative indigenous treatment for substance use disorders. *Psychological Services, 12,* 83–91. http://dx.doi.org/10.1037/ser0000013

Goodkind, J. R., LaNoue, M. D., Lee, C., Freeland, L. R., & Freund, R. (2012). Involving parents in a community-based, culturally grounded mental health intervention for American Indian youth: Parent perspectives, challenges, and results. *Journal of Community Psychology, 40,* 468–478. http://dx.doi.org/10.1002/jcop.21480

Goodluck, C. W., & Willeto, A. A. (2009). *Seeing the protective rainbow: How families survive and thrive in the American Indian and Alaska Native community*. Retrieved from https://www.aecf.org/m/resourcedoc/aecf-howfamilies surviveindianandalaskan-2009.pdf

Gray, J. S. (2012). Cultural adaptations for American Indian clients. In G. Bernal & M. M. Domenech-Rodriguez (Eds.), *Cultural adaptations: Tools for evidence-based practice with diverse populations* (pp. 201–221). Washington, DC: American Psychological Association. http://dx.doi.org/10.1037/13752-010

Gray, J. S., & Anderson, N. (2013). *Violence in Native American communities.* Paper presented at the Confronting Family and Community Violence: The Intersection of Law and Psychology Conference, Washington, DC.

Gray, J. S., & McCullagh, J. A. (2014). Suicide in Indian country: The continuing epidemic in rural Native American communities. *Journal of Rural Mental Health, 38,* 79–86. http://dx.doi.org/10.1037/rmh0000017

Gray, J. S., Peters, W. M. K., & McCullagh, J. A. (2016). Psychological assessment considerations for American Indian, Alaska Natives, and Native Hawaiians. In F. T. L. Leong & Y. S. Park (Eds.), *Testing and assessment with persons and communities of color* (pp. 12–17). Washington, DC: American Psychological Association.

Green, R. (1992). *Women in American Indian society.* New York, NY: Chelsea House.

Griese, E. R., Kenyon, D. B., & McMahon, T. R. (2016). Identifying sexual health protective factors among Northern Plains American Indian youth: An ecological approach utilizing multiple perspectives. *American Indian and Alaska Native Mental Health Research, 23*(4), 16–43. http://dx.doi.org/10.5820/aian.2304.2016.16

Guttmannova, K., Wheeler, M. J., Hill, K. G., Evans-Campbell, T. A., Hartigan, L. A., Jones, T. M., . . . Catalano, R. F. (2017). Assessment of risk and protection in Native American youth: Steps toward conducting culturally relevant, sustainable prevention in Indian country. *Journal of Community Psychology, 45,* 346–362. http://dx.doi.org/10.1002/jcop.21852

Hawkins, J. D., Herrenkohl, T., Farrington, D. P., Brewer, D., Catalano, R. F., Harachi, T. W., & Cothern, L. (2000). *Predictors of youth violence.* Retrieved from https://files.eric.ed.gov/fulltext/ED440196.pdf

HeavyRunner, I., & Morris, J. S. (1997). *Traditional native culture and resilience.* Retrieved from https://conservancy.umn.edu/bitstream/handle/11299/145989/TraditionalNativeCulture-and-Resilience.pdf?sequence=1&isAllowed=y

Heitkamp, H. (2017). *Heitkamp introduces "Savannah's Act" to help address the crisis of missing and murdered Native American women.* Retrieved from https://www.congress.gov/bill/115th-congress/senate-bill/1942/text?q=%7B%22search%22%3A%5B%22Heitkamp%22%2C%22Missing+Murdered+Native+Women%22%5D%7D&r=3&s=8

Hodge, D. R., Limb, G. E., & Cross, T. L. (2009). Moving from colonization toward balance and harmony: A Native American perspective on wellness. *Social Work, 54,* 211–219. http://dx.doi.org/10.1093/sw/54.3.211

Johnson, K., Bryant, D. D., Collins, D. A., Noe, T. D., Strader, T. N., & Berbaum, M. (1998). Preventing and reducing alcohol and other drug use among high-risk youths by increasing family resilience. *Social Work, 43,* 297–308. http://dx.doi.org/10.1093/sw/43.4.297

Kenyon, D. B., & Carter, J. S. (2011). Ethnic identity, sense of community, and psychological well-being among Northern Plains American Indian youth. *Journal of Community Psychology, 39,* 1–9. http://dx.doi.org/10.1002/jcop.20412

Klein, L. F., & Ackerman, L. A. (1995). *Women and power in native North America.* Norman: University of Oklahoma Press.

Kulis, S., Hodge, D. R., Ayers, S. L., Brown, E. F., & Marsiglia, F. F. (2012). Spirituality and religion: Intertwined protective factors for substance use among urban American Indian youth. *The American Journal of Drug and Alcohol Abuse, 38,* 444–449. http://dx.doi.org/10.3109/00952990.2012.670338

LaFromboise, T. D. (1995). *American Indian life skills development curriculum.* Madison: University of Wisconsin Press.

LaFromboise, T. D., Hoyt, D. R., Oliver, L., & Whitbeck, L. B. (2006). Family, community, and school influences on resilience among American Indian adolescents in the upper Midwest. *Journal of Community Psychology, 34,* 193–209. http://dx.doi.org/10.1002/jcop.20090

LaFromboise, T. D., Trimble, J. E., & Mohatt, G. V. (1990). Counseling intervention and American Indian tradition: An integrative approach. *The Counseling Psychologist, 18,* 628–654. http://dx.doi.org/10.1177/0011000090184006

Langhinrichsen-Rohling, J., Friend, J., & Powell, A. (2009). Adolescent suicide, gender, and culture: A rate and risk factor analysis. *Aggression and Violent Behavior, 14,* 402–414. http://dx.doi.org/10.1016/j.avb.2009.06.010

LaPointe, C. A. (2008). Sexual violence: An introduction to the social and legal issues for Native women. In S. Deer, B. Clairmont, C. A. Martell, & M. L. White Eagle (Eds.), *Sharing our stories of survival: Native women surviving violence* (pp. 31–48). New York, NY: Altamira Press.

Leavitt, P., Covarrubias, R., Perez, Y., & Fryberg, S. (2015). "Frozen in time": The impact of Native American media representations on identity and self-understanding. *Journal of Social Issues, 71,* 39–53. http://dx.doi.org/10.1111/josi.12095

Levine, S. K., & Levine, E. G. (2004). *Foundations of expressive arts therapy: Theoretical and clinical perspectives.* Philadelphia, PA: Jessica Kingsley.

Mackin, J., Perkins, T., & Furrer, C. (2012). The power of protection: A population-based comparison of Native and non-Native youth suicide attempters. *American Indian and Alaska Native Mental Health Research, 19*(2), 20–54. http://dx.doi.org/10.5820/aian.1902.2012.20

Malchiodi, C. A. (2005). *Expressive therapies.* New York, NY: Guilford Press.

Maltz, D., & Archambault, J. (1995). Gender and power in Native North America. In L. F. Klein & L. A. Ackerman (Eds.), *Women and power in Native North America* (pp. 230–249). Norman: University of Oklahoma Press.

Mankiller, W. (2011). *Every day is a good day: Reflections by contemporary indigenous women* (2nd ed.). Golden, CO: Fulcrum.

Manzo, K., Tiesman, H., Stewart, J., Hobbs, G. R., & Knox, S. S. (2015). A comparison of risk factors associated with suicide ideation/attempts in American Indian and White youth in Montana. *Archives of Suicide Research, 19,* 89–102. http://dx.doi.org/10.1080/13811118.2013.840254

Markstrom, C. A. (2011). Identity formation of American Indian adolescents: Local, national, and global considerations. *Journal of Research on Adolescence, 21,* 519–535. http://dx.doi.org/10.1111/j.1532-7795.2010.00690.x

Masten, A. S., & Coatsworth, J. D. (1998). The development of competence in favorable and unfavorable environments. Lessons from research on successful children. *American Psychologist, 53,* 205–220. http://dx.doi.org/10.1037/0003-066X.53.2.205

McNiff, S. (2004). *Art Heals: How creativity cures the soul.* Boston, MA: Shambhala.

Mehl-Madrona, L. (2007). *Narrative medicine: The use of history and story in the healing process*. New York, NY: Simon & Schuster.

Mmari, K. N., Blum, R. W., & Teufel-Shone, N. (2010). What increases risk and protection for delinquent behaviors among American Indian youth? Findings from three tribal communities. *Youth & Society, 41*, 382–413. http://dx.doi.org/10.1177/0044118X09333645

Mohatt, N. V., Fok, C. C. T., Burket, R., Henry, D., & Allen, J. (2011). Assessment of awareness of connectedness as a culturally-based protective factor for Alaska native youth. *Cultural Diversity and Ethnic Minority Psychology, 17*, 444–455. http://dx.doi.org/10.1037/a0025456

National Conference of State Legislatures. (2016). *Federal and state recognized tribes*. Retrieved from http://www.ncsl.org/research/state-tribal-institute/list-of-federal-and-state-recognized-tribes.aspx#State

National Congress of American Indians. (2013). *Policy insights brief—statistics on violence against Native Women*. Retrieved from http://www.ncai.org/attachments/PolicyPaper_tWAjznFslemhAffZgNGzHUqIWMRPkCDjpFtxeKEUVKjubxfpGYK_Policy%20Insights%20Brief_VAWA_020613.pdf

Nebelkopf, E., & Phillips, M. (2004). *Healing and mental health for Native Americans: Speaking in red*. Lanham, MD: AltaMira Press.

Office of Juvenile Justice and Delinquency Prevention. (2017). *Juvenile incarceration*. Retrieved from https://www.childtrends.org/indicators/juvenile-detention

Oré, C. E., Teufel-Shone, N. I., & Chico-Jarillo, T. M. (2016). American Indian and Alaska Native resilience along the life course and across generations: A literature review. *American Indian and Alaska Native Mental Health Research, 23*(3), 134–157. http://dx.doi.org/10.5820/aian.2303.2016.134

Parrish, M. S., Klem, J. L., & Brown, D. R. (2012). *Diversity in learning: A comparison of traditional learning theories with learning styles and cultural values of Native American students*. Retrieved from https://www.counseling.org/docs/default source/vistas/vistas_2012_article_45.pdf?sfvrsn=4f6df61c_11

Powers, M. N. (1986). *Oglala women: Myth, ritual, and reality*. Chicago, IL: University of Chicago Press. http://dx.doi.org/10.7208/chicago/9780226677507.001.0001

Reinschmidt, K. M., Attakai, A., Kahn, C. B., Whitewater, S., & Teufel-Shone, N. (2016). Shaping a Stories of Resilience Model from urban American Indian elders' narratives of historical trauma and resilience. *American Indian and Alaska Native Mental Health Research, 23*(4), 63–85. http://dx.doi.org/10.5820/aian.2304.2016.63

Roscoe, W. (1998). *Changing ones: Third and fourth genders in Native North America*. New York, NY: Saint Martin's Press.

Rountree, J. (2015). *American Indian and Alaska Native youth in the juvenile justice system*. Retrieved from https://www.ncmhjj.com/wp-content/uploads/2015/07/American-Indian-and-Alaska-Native-Youth.pdf

Rountree, J., & Smith, A. (2016). Strength-based well-being indicators for Indigenous children and families: A literature review of Indigenous communities' identified well-being indicators. *American Indian and Alaska Native Mental Health Research, 23*(3), 206–220. http://dx.doi.org/10.5820/aian.2303.2016.206

Royal Canadian Mounted Police. (2014). *Missing and murdered Aboriginal women: A national operational overview*. Retrieved from http://www.rcmp-grc.gc.ca/wam/media/460/original/0cbd8968a049aa0b44d343e76b4a9478.pdf

Rybak, C., & Decker-Fitts, A. (2009). Understanding Native American healing practices. *Counselling Psychology Quarterly, 22*, 333–342. http://dx.doi.org/10.1080/09515070903270900

Sarche, M. C., Spicer, P., Farrell, P., & Fitzgerald, H. E. (2011). *American Indian and Alaska Native children and mental health.* Santa Barbara, CA: ABC-CLIO.

Stumblingbear-Riddle, G. (2010). *Resilience among American Indian adolescents: Investigation into the role of culture.* Available from ProQuest Dissertations and Theses database. (AAT 3422296)

Substance Abuse and Mental Health Services Administration. (2010). *The NSDUH Report: Substance use among American Indian or Alaska Native adults.* Rockville, MD: Author.

Substance Abuse and Mental Health Services Administration. (2013). *Risk and protective factors for substance abuse and/or mental health problems among Alaska Native and American Indian populations.* Retrieved from https://www.samhsa.gov/capt/sites/default/files/resources/factors-substance-abuse-mental-health.pdf

ThinElk. (1993). Walking in balance on the red road. *Journal of Emotional and Behavioral Problems, 2*, 54–57.

Thornton, R. (1997). Tribal membership requirements and the demography of 'old' and 'new' Native Americans. *Population Research and Policy Review, 16*, 33–42.

U.S. Census Bureau. (2018a). *American Indian and Alaska Native Heritage Month: November 2018.* Retrieved from https://www.census.gov/newsroom/facts-for-features/2018/aian.html

U.S. Census Bureau. (2018b). *Annual estimates of the resident population by sex, single year of age, race alone or in combination, and Hispanic origin for the United States: April 1, 2010 to July 1, 2017.* Retrieved from https://factfinder.census.gov/faces/tableservices/jsf/pages/productview.xhtml?src=bkmk

U.S. Department of the Interior–Indian Affairs. (2017). *American Indian population and labor force reports.* Retrieved from https://www.bia.gov/knowledge-base/american-indian-population-labor-force-reports

Wahab, S., & Olson, L. (2004). Intimate partner violence and sexual assault in Native American communities. *Trauma, Violence, & Abuse, 5*, 353–366. http://dx.doi.org/10.1177/1524838004269489

Walker, R. D., Lambert, M. D., Walker, P. S., Kivlahan, D. R., Donovan, D. M., & Howard, M. O. (1996). Alcohol abuse in urban Indian adolescents and women: A longitudinal study for assessment and risk evaluation. *American Indian and Alaska Native Mental Health Research, 7*(1), 1–47. http://dx.doi.org/10.5820/aian.0701.1996.1

Walters, K. L., Mohammed, S. A., Evans-Campbell, T., Beltrán, R. E., Chae, D. H., & Duran, B. (2011). Bodies don't just tell stories, they tell histories: Embodiment of Historical Trauma among American Indian and Alaska Natives. *DuBois Review, 8*, 179–189. http://dx.doi.org/10.1017/S1742058X1100018X

Walters, K. L., Simoni, J. M., & Evans-Campbell, T. (2002). Substance use among American Indians and Alaska natives: Incorporating culture in an "indigenist" stress-coping paradigm. *Public Health Reports, 117*, S104–S117.

Webley Adler, K., & Hillstrom, C. (2015, September 22). Sex trafficking on the reservation: One Native American Nation's struggle against the trade. *Marie Claire Magazine.* Retrieved from http://www.marieclaire.com/culture/news/a16028/native-american-sex-trafficking/

Wexler, L. M., & Gone, J. P. (2012). Culturally responsive suicide prevention in indigenous communities: Unexamined assumptions and new possibilities. *American Journal of Public Health, 102*, 800–806. http://dx.doi.org/10.2105/AJPH.2011.300432

Whitesell, N. R., Mitchell, C. M., & Spicer, P. (2009). A longitudinal study of self-esteem, cultural identity, and academic success among American Indian adolescents. *Cultural Diversity and Ethnic Minority Psychology, 15*, 38–50. http://dx.doi.org/10.1037/a0013456

Wilkins, D. E. (2016). The history of federal Indian policy and changes to tribal governments. In S. Lobo, S. Talbot, & T. L. Morris (Eds.), *Native American voices* (pp. 82–101). London, England: Routledge.

Young, A., Dejarlais, C., & Smith, M. (2017, October). Solidarity with our indigenous sisters. Paper presented at the American Indian Health Research Conference, Grand Forks, ND.

3

AFRICAN AMERICAN ADOLESCENT GIRLS

Embracing the Strength in Intersectionality

MONIQUE CLINTON-SHERROD, STEPHANIE HAWKINS, AND TIFFANY G. TOWNSEND

African American girls are a diverse, resilient group whose members experience a range of strengths and challenges. The varied lived experiences of African American girls highlight the importance of an intersectional lens when considering therapeutic approaches and ways in which practitioners can work to empower them. However, as with other ethnic minorities, there is often underutilization of mental health treatment by African American girls (Garland et al., 2005; L. M. Miller, Southam-Gerow, & Allin, 2008). This chapter examines such approaches from the perspective of individual, family, and group therapy, with a focus on assessment, barriers to treatment, strategies for treatment retention, and effectiveness of treatment.

Although African American girls have myriad presenting problems, trauma is, unfortunately, a common underlying issue for many (Voisin, 2007; Wilson, Woods, Emerson, & Donenberg, 2012). We examine the impact of varied traumatic experiences, such as violence, racism, and other forms of oppression (e.g., sexism, classism, homophobia), and identify how these experiences may manifest as presenting problems in the therapeutic setting.

The contents of this chapter represent the first author's views and not those of the U.S. Department of Defense or the United States Navy.

http://dx.doi.org/10.1037/0000140-004
Multicultural Feminist Therapy: Helping Adolescent Girls of Color to Thrive,
T. Bryant-Davis (Editor)

We also discuss special considerations according to treatment modality that may require attention when working with African American girls. Much of the focus here is guided by Black feminist theory perspectives, which maintain that therapeutic approaches with African American girls have to attend to race, class, gender, and sexuality as critical factors (Collins, 2000; Crenshaw, 1991).

The chapter provides an overview of the developmental context for African American adolescent girls and a variety of factors that have a potential impact on seeking and engaging in therapy. This is followed by some key considerations for the use of individual, family, and group therapy approaches with African American girls. For individual therapy, we explore the importance of cultural congruence and therapeutic alliances between African American girls and mental health practitioners and the need for holistic, trauma-informed, empowering approaches. For family therapy, we discuss the intergenerational transmission of trauma and how it affects parenting, educational and career aspirations, and romantic relationships. Finally, for group-level therapy, the discussion is focused on the integral cultural role of female group support for African American girls and young women, which may facilitate this therapeutic approach.

Following the presentation of each modality, we discuss the treatment of Tasha, a 14-year-old African American girl. We use Tasha's case to help illustrate the use of our recommended approach in the therapeutic setting. Our discussion of culturally congruent treatment for African American girls is framed in the shared experiences of trauma at community and broader societal levels, which may further impact individual, family, and group dynamics. Each of these therapeutic modalities is discussed in relation to how they facilitate resiliency in African American girls for addressing not only presenting problems but also broader intersecting issues that impact long-term mental and physical health.

BACKGROUND

The U.S. Census identifies an African American or Black individual as "a person having origins in any of the Black racial groups of Africa" (U.S. Census Bureau, 2018, para. 3). The 2016 U.S. Census found that African American girls and young women make up about 14% of the youth population. These numbers include girls from a range of backgrounds, including African American, Haitian, Nigerian, Jamaican, Kenyan, and other representation across the African and Black diaspora. Although not specific to just girls, a sense of the extent of immigrant adolescents can be gleaned from data indicating that 25% of all children (ages 0–17 years) are first- or second-generation immigrants (Federal Interagency Forum on Child and Family Statistics, 2018). This diverse representation brings a culturally rich, resilient array of girls throughout the United States; however, the magnificence of these girls is often minimized, suppressed, and continuously challenged through injustices and disparities to social, judicial, educational, and other socioecological domains in their lived experiences.

Developmentally, adolescents experience a multitude of changes and adaptations that seem to play a key role in their daily functioning and decision-making processes regarding both risk and protective behaviors. It is not surprising that in the context of these intense cognitive and rapid physical changes, impairments in psychological adjustment begin to emerge and problem behaviors become more prevalent. Although their numbers are a fraction of the general population, African American girls are found to have increased risk compared with other adolescents for exposure to traumatizing events and the various maladaptive behaviors that often stem from this exposure (K. M. Harris, Gordon-Larsen, Chantala, & Udry, 2006). This risk is quite evident with behaviors that can heighten harm exposure, such as risky sexual behavior and substance use. African American adolescent girls are more likely to engage in sexual activity and at an earlier age compared with other ethnicities, which in turn increases the risk of teen pregnancy, sexually transmitted infections, and HIV (Centers for Disease Control and Prevention [CDC], 2016; Faryna & Morales, 2000). Although African American girls report lower drug use, findings regarding substance use by African American adolescents from the 2016 Monitoring the Future Survey speak to changing risk among the group for drugs such as marijuana (Miech et al., 2017). In addition, even with lower substance use rates overall for African American youth, the negative impacts stemming from substance use are disproportionately higher for African Americans.

As previously mentioned, impairments in psychological functioning are also noted during this period. According to epidemiological studies, depression and depressive symptoms increase in early adolescence, and this increase is overwhelmingly seen among adolescent girls (Keenan & Hipwell, 2005). For girls, research has suggested that the physical changes that occur during puberty have a psychological impact and have been linked to changes in mood, cognition, and behavior (Keenan, Culbert, Grimm, Hipwell, & Stepp, 2014). Pubertal changes such as menarche and breast growth are milestones in the development of adolescent girls, and many girls see these changes as the onset of their transition to womanhood. Accordingly, these more salient physical changes may prompt members of the girls' social networks to expect more mature behavior, such as early involvement in romantic relationships and sexual behavior, stimulating transitions in social relationships that these girls may or may not be ready to manage.

Early Pubertal Development

With so many physical, cognitive, and psychological changes, the transition to womanhood may be stressful for many girls, and this is particularly problematic if pubertal development is perceived to occur too early. In fact, early pubertal timing has been linked to negative outcomes, such as early sexual activity (Townsend, 2002) and an increased risk of depression (Joinson, Heron, Lewis, Croudace, & Araya, 2011). Given that African American girls tend to experience pubertal changes at a younger age than their European American counterparts (Biro et al., 2006), the link between early pubertal development and depression may place African American girls at an increased risk of the manifestation of depressive symptoms and other mental health vulnerabilities. As indicated in the report *Girlhood Interrupted: The Erasure of Black Girls' Childhood*, this may also contribute to the "adultification" of African American girls, in which adults have been found to view African American girls between the ages of 5 and 14 as more sexually mature and less "innocent" than their White counterparts (Epstein, Blake, & González, 2017).

Impacts of Racism and Sexism

Development for African American girls is further complicated by their experience of racism and sexism. In fact, some scholars have suggested that trauma and mental illness among African Americans must be viewed within the larger historical and sociopolitical context of racism, discrimination, political oppression, and often poverty (Shorter-Gooden, 2009; Whaley, 2003). The task for African American girls is to develop a healthy sense of themselves as African Americans and as future women in a society that devalues both identities, and for many, this process occurs in low-resource communities, which can further limit opportunities for healthy self-exploration (Sanders & Bradley, 2005). Restricted, often negative views of African American women in the media and mainstream culture can help to shape the way African American girls come to view themselves, and these images can influence the way in which others value and interact with them (Gordon, 2008; Stephens & Phillips, 2005).

Lewis and Neville (2015) expanded the often-siloed examination of overt racism and sexism independently or attempts at extrapolating quantitative interactions between the two to focus on gendered racism within an intersectional framework, with a particular focus on pervasive, subtle microaggressions. Their taxonomy of gendered racial microaggressions highlights three higher level themes with gendered racism experienced by African American girls and women: (a) projected stereotypes that revolve around Jezebel and angry black woman projections, (b) silenced and marginalized themes stemming from struggles for respect and invisibility within professional contexts, and (c) assumptions about style and beauty that minimize African American girls and women to assumed stereotypes for communication styles and physical appearance (Lewis, Mendenhall, Harwood, & Huntt, 2016). For instance, the highly sexualized Jezebel image of Black women as indicated by the first theme has colored society's view of African American women's sexuality (T. M. Harris & Hill, 1998). Accordingly, Donovan (2007) found that White men perceived African American women to be sexually promiscuous. This perception led White men to judge African American women to be responsible for their sexual assault when the perpetrator was said to be a White male. Similarly, Gillum (2002) found that 48% of African American men in her study viewed African American women as sexual temptresses, which was significantly related to these men's justification of violence against them. As previously mentioned, African American girls are viewed as more sexually mature (Epstein et al., 2017), which increases the likelihood that they too are perceived in the context of the sexually promiscuous Jezebel stereotype. Not surprisingly, African American women and girls are at an increased risk of sexual victimization and abuse (Bent-Goodley, 2004; Kilpatrick, Resnick, Ruggiero, Conoscenti, & McCauley, 2007; Paulozzi, Saltzman, Thompson, & Holmgreen, 2001).

The objectification of African American girls also contributes to the increased risk of other types of violations such as sex trafficking. The Victims of Trafficking and Violence Protection Act of 2000 defines *sex trafficking* as occurring when "a commercial sex act is induced by force, fraud, or coercion, or in which the person induced to perform such act has not attained 18 years of age" (§7102. Definitions, Section 9). Media images of human trafficking victims are often focused on high-profile cases that perpetuate society's image of a typical victim as a White, middle class, and ultimately rescued survivor. However, statistics indicate that African Americans, especially those in marginalized communities, are the most vulnerable groups for sex trafficking, with over 40% of victims of human trafficking being African American adult and youth (Banks & Kyckelhahn, 2011; Task Force on Trafficking of Women and Girls, 2014). African American girls are also at greater risk of trafficking at younger ages compared with girls of other races (Sherman & Grace, 2011). The grim reality for African American girls and levels of sexual exploitation is further explained through the Department of Justice's findings that 52% of juvenile prostitution arrests are of African American girls (Banks & Kyckelhahn, 2011). The lens for viewing African American girls who are held hostage in the sex trade is that of prostitutes or sex workers rather than the more appropriate lens of sexually exploited children, again a reflection of the adultification that occurs with these girls (Phillips, 2015).

Impacts of Trauma

Although sexual development, sexual decision making, and the formation of satisfying romantic relationships are major developmental tasks for adolescent girls, the experience of interpersonal trauma and exploitation often disrupts this normal developmental trajectory (Loeb et al., 2002), particularly if someone the girl trusts perpetuates the abuse. According to Freyd (1996), abuse (sexual or emotional) by a perpetrator whom the victim trusts and to whom she has an attachment may lead to damaged cognitive mechanisms (e.g., damaged self-esteem and faulty reality-detecting mechanisms). For instance, experiencing sexual abuse as a child may lead girls to believe that interpersonal engagement and relatedness is contingent on sexual behavior. These girls may accept sexual activity as a way of connecting, even when they are not interested in sex (Cloitre, 1998; Underwood, Stewart, & Castellanos, 2007). In addition, feelings of shame and self-blame may make it difficult for those girls who have been abused to form satisfying friendships or romantic relationships (Feiring, Rosenthal, & Taska, 2000). In one instance, a girl who has been abused or exploited may view subsequent relationships as dangerous. Because her model of interpersonal interaction is negative, she may enter relationships with a more defensive stance than is appropriate (McCann & Pearlman, 1990). In contrast, other girls may react to abuse and interpersonal trauma with inadequate self-protection. Given the relationship violations they have experienced, they may have difficulty knowing what appropriate boundaries are or may not feel that they have the right to establish clear limits with others. Feeling hungry for attention or frightened about being alone, they may attach quickly without getting to know a person and may even tolerate maltreatment in an effort to stay connected (McCann & Pearlman, 1990).

This can place many African American girls at an increased risk of teen dating violence victimization (Black et al., 2015). Teen dating violence among African American girls varies in reported prevalence rates, but African American teens are generally found to have higher rates of physical violence compared with other teens (CDC, 2018). African American teens who are survivors of physical dating violence are also at greater risk than those without this violence for a litany of other maladaptive behaviors, including substance use, risky sexual behavior, unhealthy dieting practices, and suicidal ideation (Silverman, Raj, & Clements, 2004; Wiemann, Agurcia, Berenson, Volk, & Rickert, 2000; Wingood, DiClemente, McCree, Harrington, & Davies, 2001).

Girls who have experienced sexual victimization may begin to believe that they must rely on their sexuality as a means to survive (American Psychological Association [APA], Task Force on the Sexualization of Girls, 2007), and frequently the development of healthy body awareness can become stunted (Underwood et al., 2007). This—coupled with the limited, often sexually exploitive images that emphasize the appearance and sexual appeal of African American women—can foster self-objectification among African American adolescent girls, in which girls may begin to internalize the observers' perspective to evaluate their bodies (Fredrickson & Roberts, 1997), reinforcing a belief that their value and self-worth are functions of their appearance and sex appeal (Gordon, 2008).

African American women depicted in current media outlets (e.g., music videos, reality TV) who use sexuality for material gain may glorify the exploitation of a woman's body as a viable means to obtain financial resources. These oversexualized images not only suggest how African American girls should act but also provide implicit messages about how African American girls should look to be considered attractive (Peterson, Wingood, DiClemente, Harrington, & Davies, 2007; Robillard, 2012). African American girls and women with lighter skin and keener, European features are often revered as most desirable in the media, conveying the message that African Americans who are aesthetically closer to White are more appealing (Townsend, Jones Thomas, Neilands, & Jackson, 2010). For African American girls, self-objectification may be manifested in a preference for physical characteristics they believe will be judged more favorably (e.g., lighter skin, longer hair, keen features, fine hair texture). Those who judge themselves to be too far outside of this narrow, Eurocentric standard of beauty may be left with feelings of shame and low self-worth (Shorter-Gooden, 2009).

In addition to sexual victimization and abuse, African American girls who live in low-resource communities are often exposed to multiple forms of interpersonal violence (e.g., robberies, gang activity) and community trauma (Aldwin, 2007; Graves, Kaslow, & Frabutt, 2010; Norris, 1992; Perilla, Norris, & Lavizzo, 2002). For instance, social media has increased the visibility of racial oppression in the United States law enforcement system; however, a limited focus has been given to the intersection of race and gender and aggressive or abusive policing (Brunson & Miller, 2006). Although its occurrence is not new, African American girls are developing against a highly visible backdrop of mass incarceration and are now regularly exposed to horrifying images of unarmed African Americans being killed at the hands of police and others with little justice for the victims. Highly visible cases of injustice, such as those highlighted through the "Say Her Name" social movement and murders of unarmed youth such as Trayvon Martin, highlight the pervasiveness of racialized societal conditions that contribute to community-level stressors experienced by African Americans (Crenshaw, Ritchie, Anspach, Gilmer, & Harris, 2015; Yancy & Jones, 2012). In the Fatal Interactions With Police Study, researchers found that the odds of African Americans being killed while unarmed was 6.6 to 1, with large impacts on the odds from the number of unarmed African American women killed (Johnson, Gilbert, & Ibrahim, 2018). This has heightened their experiences of alienation, stress, and vicarious trauma (Westcott, 2015).

TREATMENT SEEKING AND ATTRITION

The contextual factors just described provide a snapshot of how gender, class, and race intersect to impact African American girls' lived experiences. These experiences provide powerful contextual forces that contribute to the mental health vulnerabilities faced by African American girls. Due to many of the circumstances outlined earlier, African American girls are at an increased risk of depression, posttraumatic stress disorder, anxiety, dissociation, and substance abuse (Kilpatrick et al., 2003), as well as suicidal ideation and low self-esteem (M. P. Thompson et al., 2000).

Despite exposure to factors that increase vulnerabilities to mental illness, African American girls, like their male counterparts, are less likely to use mental health services compared with European American youth (Caldwell, Assari, & Breland-Noble, 2016; Flores, 2016). This has major implications for long-term outcomes because untreated psychological disorders increase the risk that African American girls will experience challenges in social mobility and adaptive functioning as adults (Assari & Caldwell, 2017). Although limited access to resources and low health literacy may contribute to reduced rates of mental health use among African American youth (Assari & Caldwell, 2017), it does not fully explain the disparity.

According to Breland-Noble, Burriss, and Poole (2010), African American youth hold negative views of psychological treatment, citing mistrust of clinicians as a primary concern. Psychotherapy process scholars point to the importance of the therapeutic alliance for helping to improve treatment outcomes; however, there is less agreement concerning the factors that increase client trust and facilitate the formation of a strong therapeutic alliance. Wintersteen, Mensinger, and Diamond (2005) found that for adolescent girls, gender matching helped to facilitate the development of an alliance, and those girls who had a gender-matched therapist were more likely to remain in treatment. Similarly, African American adolescents who had a same-race therapist in this study were also more likely to remain in treatment and less likely to terminate prematurely, suggesting that African American girls may develop an early alliance and remain in therapy longer with a therapist who is an African American woman. However, Wintersteen et al. also found that the quality of the connection and the respect in the therapeutic relationship superseded racial match. In other words, the demographic mismatch between the therapist and the adolescent client can be overcome if the adolescent feels respected and connected to the therapist. How, then, do therapists, regardless of the demographic match, engage and retain African American girls in treatment and help to ensure positive treatment outcomes?

AFRICAN AMERICAN GIRLS AND INDIVIDUAL THERAPY

Clinicians and psychotherapy process scholars agree that efficacious treatment starts with therapeutic techniques that are culturally relevant and tailored to the specific needs of the client (APA, 2017; Breland-Noble et al., 2010; Shorter-Gooden, 2009). An approach grounded in a framework of multicultural feminist therapy (e.g., womanist psychotherapy) helps to ensure that the therapeutic strategies used align with the sociocultural experience of African American girls (Drake-Burnette, Garrett-Akinsanya, & Bryant-Davis, 2016; Harrell & Rowe, 2014). When working with this population, the goal of the treatment is to foster self-knowledge and empower these girls to take control over their health, even in the face of the powerful contextual forces described earlier.

Overcoming Barriers to Individual Therapy

The first step in helping African American girls to assume responsibility for their health and start the healing process is for them to identify and acknowledge when there is a problem. Treatment engagement for African American adolescent girls includes helping them to identify when normal "growing pains" or "issues" have become severe enough to require professional attention. In their study examining the engagement of African American youth in mental health treatment, Breland-Noble and her colleagues (2010) found that African American adolescents were reluctant to acknowledge having depression even if they endorsed several depressive symptoms that would meet the clinical threshold for a diagnosis. Instead of seeing these symptoms as a sign of a medical issue that required treatment, many of the youth in their study described their symptoms in nonclinical terms (e.g., "feeling sleepy a lot" or "angry a lot") that would reduce the likelihood that these young people would see the need for professional intervention. Breland-Noble et al. suggested providing culturally relevant psychoeducational sessions (i.e., public forums, panel discussions in conjunction with community-based organizations) in the community to help educate adolescents and their parents about the signs of clinically significant mental health issues and the potential impact of these issues on youth development.

Reducing the stigma associated with mental health issues is another important strategy to increase engagement of African American adolescent girls in treatment (Murry, Heflinger, Suiter, & Brody, 2011). Discussing well-known African Americans who have experienced and learned to manage mental health challenges can help reduce potential feelings of isolation and shame while educating adolescents and their parents about what happens in therapy can demystify the therapeutic process and help to reduce the anxiety associated with seeking mental health treatment. For example, in a *New York Times* article (Baquet, 2017) and a CNN interview (2018), Jay-Z, a high-profile celebrity, discussed mental health disparities among African Americans and how he has benefited from therapy, including impacts on his perceptions and reactions to racism. It may also be helpful to avoid the overuse of clinical jargon and a focus on risk behaviors in session, focusing instead on functional outcomes that the adolescent finds important, such as positive relationships with family and friends and success with academic and personal goals (Sanders & Bradley, 2005). In this way, adolescent girls are empowered to serve as active participants in their treatment, instead of passive recipients of a "medical procedure" (Breland-Noble et al., 2010).

Factors That Facilitate Individual Therapy

The therapeutic alliance is the active ingredient that supports successful therapy outcomes. As previously mentioned, a demographic match may help facilitate the development of this alliance for African American adolescent girls. However, there are other important considerations. African American girls must establish trust and feel safe in the therapeutic relationship, particularly if an abuse or trauma history is present (Underwood et al., 2007). In addition, many African American girls have been socialized to be independent and self-reliant, which may make them feel uncomfortable in a relationship that requires them to show vulnerability (Shorter-Gooden, 2009). Therapists working with these clients must be aware that they may encounter some initial resistance in therapy. Thus, more sessions may be required to establish rapport (Underwood et al., 2007). Selective and appropriate self-disclosure by the therapist in session can help promote trust in the therapeutic relationship and can establish the authenticity and transparency that is so important when treating African American youth (Harrell & Rowe, 2014; Shorter-Gooden, 2009). Appropriately maintaining confidentiality and immediately disclosing exceptions to confidentiality when they arise are particularly important when working with African American girls because of the overrepresentation of African American children in the child welfare system and the high risk that an African American child could be removed from the home because of a report of suspected abuse or neglect (Child Welfare Information Gateway, 2016). In addition, establishing a more flexible role as the therapist in session, including a more collaborative, interpersonal style and accessible appointment times, has also been identified by African American youth as an effective way that therapists can create a safe, welcoming environment for treatment (Breland-Noble et al., 2010; Shorter-Gooden, 2009).

Using the framework of multicultural feminist therapy, there are additional points that must be considered when working with African American girls. Therapists should not function as if they are working with an individual in a vacuum. Rather, African American girls should be conceptualized in the context of a full ecosystem that includes their immediate family, school, neighborhood and community, and the broader society (APA, 2017). In this way, there is an appreciation for the "person–culture–context transaction" (Harrell & Rowe, 2014, p. 7), in which the client is viewed in relation to her environment and her social networks. The symptoms that are presented in therapy must be understood as part of a system of norms and sociocultural experiences that help give meaning to the presenting problems (Harrell & Rowe, 2014). As described for diverse populations in the APA Multicultural Guidelines (2017), therapists should be knowledgeable about African American history and culture and the sociohistorical background of African Americans' experiences in the United States.

For instance, the division of labor based on gender that was traditionally seen in the majority culture would have been detrimental in the African American community. African American women have always worked, and shared responsibility by the mother and the father for financial support of the children was necessary for the survival of the African American family (Hill, 2000). Consequently, African American girls develop in a family and community context in which gender roles are more flexible. In fact, many African American girls are raised in families in which their mother, grandmother, or female caretaker is the sole provider. Through observation of these role models, African American girls are socialized toward independence, self-sufficiency, and survival (Shorter-Gooden, 2009).

However, this self-confidence and self-assurance may interact with racially charged, gendered images and messages in some settings, causing African American girls to be viewed as loud, overbearing, and overly challenging of authority (Townsend et al., 2010). This may help to explain the harsher punishments that African American girls receive in the educational system and their disproportionate representation in the juvenile justice system (Annamma et al., 2016; Department of Education Office for Civil Rights, 2014). Using this sociohistorical knowledge, therapists can help African American girls understand their experience of oppression and distinguish between those problems that may stem from internal conflicts versus those that may stem from external forces (Shorter-Gooden, 2009).

Armed with a cultural understanding, therapists working with African American girls should focus on the strengths and assets of the client, her environment, and the broader African American community (Sanders & Bradley, 2005). African Americans in general, particularly African American girls and women, often espouse values of collective survival, emotional energy, and a being orientation to time (i.e., a person is viewed as valuable by virtue of their existence; S. P. Brown, Lipford-Sanders, & Shaw, 1995). African American girls are also likely to value spirituality, be collective in orientation, and place high importance on nurturing relationships within extended family and community (Abdullah, 1998; Boyd-Franklin, 1991; Greene, 1994). It is through these nurturing relationships, particularly with their mothers, that African American girls learn to cope with oppression. Therapists working with African American girls can build on these and other cultural strengths to nurture resilience, competence, and self-efficacy (Harrell & Rowe, 2014: Shorter-Gooden, 2009). Again, the goal of treatment using a framework of multicultural feminist therapy is empowerment. This can be accomplished by helping the girls develop critical consciousness and infusing aspects of culture in treatment—such as African American art, literature, poetry, and music—as appropriate (Drake-Burnette et al., 2016). Individual sessions that provide a safe space for African American girls to conduct healthy self-exploration, while receiving validation and affirmation for their strengths, culture, and experiences, can help to fortify a population that has historically been largely marginalized and ignored.

Treating Tasha Individually: A Case Study

Tasha[1] is a 14-year-old African American adolescent. She lives with her mother, Vivian (28 years old), and her grandmother (53 years old). Tasha's father

---

[1] Client descriptions have been anonymized to protect confidentiality.

(27 years old) has never been a consistent presence in her life due to his frequent incarceration. Since Tasha began eighth grade, she has been involved with a group of girls who are known troublemakers in the school. As a result, Tasha has engaged in behaviors that resulted in two in-school suspensions. Because Tasha is 3 months away from her middle school graduation, Tasha's guidance counselor met with Vivian several times regarding Tasha's declining behavior. Tasha's guidance counselor suggested that Tasha receive individual counseling with a therapist. Although Tasha's mother thought counseling would be a good idea, Tasha was not enthusiastic and was initially quite resistant, particularly because she did not see her behavior as a mental health problem.

Tasha was referred to a community mental health clinic where she was assigned to an individual therapist, an African American graduate student in psychology. At the start of treatment, Tasha's resistance was manifested in sporadic attendance, and when she did attend sessions, she often had little to share. Building trust became a major treatment goal for the therapist. As the two continued to learn about each other, the therapist shared aspects of her life that mirrored that of Tasha's experience, while being careful to acknowledge and appreciate those areas that Tasha identified as divergent. Those areas of divergence (e.g., living with a father who was incarcerated) began to represent important aspects of Tasha's identity that needed to be explored. As time progressed, it became clear that Tasha began to relate to her therapist and seemed much more comfortable in session. However, the therapist realized that the discussions remained superficial. Tasha continued to have difficulty discussing sensitive topics, and her acting out behavior in school had not improved.

One day, Tasha brought a notebook full of her drawings into session. Initially, she insisted she did not want to show the therapist her drawings, and out of respect, the therapist honored this decision. In fact, Tasha brought the book to session several times, and although the therapist acknowledged the book, she assured Tasha that she would wait to view the book until Tasha was ready. Eventually, Tasha felt safe enough to show the drawings to the therapist. The drawings revealed themes of loneliness, pain, and issues of body image. The body image theme appeared to be grounded in a colorism ideology (Tasha was darker skinned, but her mother was lighter). Tasha had been teased about her complexion by her peers, and her drawings depicted an idealization of a Eurocentric aesthetic. The therapist used this as an opportunity to have a frank discussion with Tasha about the history and origins of colorism in this country, while also appropriately disclosing her struggle with the issue. This process seemed to solidify Tasha's alliance with the therapist, and more sensitive topics began to emerge.

In addition to Tasha bringing drawings that she created outside of session, the therapist encouraged Tasha to draw in session to help communicate her feelings when words were too difficult. It soon became clear that Tasha's family structure and her father's incarceration were painful for her, and although the therapist began to help Tasha process some her feelings about these issues, working with Tasha's family seemed warranted.

AFRICAN AMERICAN GIRLS AND FAMILY THERAPY

The family therapeutic modality can be particularly impactful for African American girls, given the evolving nature of families. In 2016, 66% of Black or African American children lived in single-parent households compared with 35% of all kids in the United States. Families headed by unmarried parents are diverse (Waller, 2012; Waller & Emory, 2014). In some situations, the mother and father are in a committed relationship and are parenting together; in others, the parenting is negotiated between individuals who ended a committed relationship, and still others may have never had a committed relationship before conception (McHale, 2011). An underlying assumption with the family therapy modality is that individuals of a family system, regardless of how the system is composed, are interrelated, influencing one another in important ways (Becvar & Becvar, 2009). From a historical trauma perspective, families can transmit the damage of slavery and other trauma through several generations and in many ways by the learned behavior of the generation before them. Engaging the family as a therapeutic modality can assist the family unit, rather than individual members, to identify and break generational patterns of behavior.

The challenge of family therapy for some African American families, as described by Boyd-Franklin (1989), is the issue of mistrust and resistance to therapy. There is a lack of consensus on the views held by African Americans related to mental illness. However, actual help seeking is low, regardless of the view African Americans hold about seeking mental health services. Poor access to quality care and stigma are considered some of the key barriers to seeking services (DeFreitas, Crone, DeLeon, & Ajayi, 2018; V. L. S. Thompson, Bazile, & Akbar, 2004; Ward, Wiltshire, Detry, & Brown, 2013). The perceptions about mental health services can be more debilitating in the context of family therapy because it takes more than one person having to overcome their perceptions about treatment to have a positive experience. Next, we highlight the role of historical trauma, parenting, and the inclusion of the arts—specifically music—as important factors to address for African American girls in the family therapy context.

Historical Trauma

Historical trauma (e.g., slavery) and other types of trauma impact the types of presenting problems African American families may bring to therapy. For generations post slavery, African Americans have experienced oppression that has led to racial disparities across a number of indicators of well-being (Wilkins, Whiting, Watson, Russon, & Moncrief, 2013). In similar ways that parents during slavery taught their children how to survive in the midst of dangerous conditions, current African American parents also view teaching their children how to navigate the dangers of oppressive circumstances, including community violence and disparate justice systems, as a crucial parental role (Wilkins et al., 2013). The resilience of the African American community, as evidenced by the ability of the African American family to survive the various permutations of oppression and progress over 4 centuries, should give family therapists insight on the psychological and cultural resources that can be leveraged in the therapeutic setting.

Family Structure

The essence of family structure is greatly influenced by culture; it defines the role of men, women, and children, and it also creates cross-generational influences unique to every family (Connell, 2010). The family role flexibility that exists in many African American households (e.g., matriarchal African American family) are structural configurations that are often a response to systemic economic disadvantage and a demonstration of resilience. The custom of grandparents caring for the grandchildren dates back to slavery, when nonworking feeble and/or elderly grandparents could no longer work and became primary caretakers of children (Billingsley, 1992). The practice of nonkin relatives caring for children is an African tradition that became prominent during slavery and continues today to ensure dignity despite oppression (Boyd-Franklin, 1991; Wilkins et al., 2013).

Failure to consider these experiences in the therapeutic environment may lead to ineffective treatment. In fact, Laszloffy and Hardy (2000) contended that the awareness and consideration of these experiences are not sufficient for effective treatment; rather, family therapists should operate from a place of racial sensitivity, which involves actively challenging racial injustice. The importance of this approach in therapeutic engagement with African American girls and their families is that the therapeutic process is situated in a place of support and valuing of the families' resilience as opposed to a place of judgment and lack of knowledge.

Parenting

Parenting offers the opportunity to transmit values and beliefs based on cultural knowledge and the realities of one's society (Gershoff, 2002; Harrison, Wilson, Pine, Chan, & Buriel, 1990). One of the ways in which this is done with African American families is through racial socialization. Racial socialization includes parenting practices to increase self-esteem and mitigate the potential for negative outcomes associated with racial injustices and/or discrimination (Hughes et al., 2006). Hughes and Chen (1997, 1999) categorized four types of racial socialization typically used by African American parents: (a) cultural socialization, which involves teaching about history and heritage; (b) preparation for bias, which involves preparing for future encounters with racial discrimination and prejudice; (c) promotion of (racial) mistrust; and (d) egalitarianism and silence, which involves increasing understanding of one's sociohistorical background as well as those of other racial groups, whereas silence about race reflects conversations that do not address race at all. The relevance of racial socialization for African American girls and family therapy is that research has shown that maternal caregivers more frequently relay racial socialization messages to their female adolescent children than to their male adolescent children (T. L. Brown, Linver, & Evans, 2010).

Family therapists working with African American girls and their families would benefit from exploring whether racial socialization was developed in a deliberate or unintended manner. This exploration could uncover the reasons for parenting practices. For example, although African American mothers are known for spanking their kids (Gershoff, Lansford, Sexton, Davis-Kean, & Sameroff, 2012), the reasons for the use of this type of discipline often are not discussed. These mothers may feel compelled to use physical punishment to protect their children because of the fears and dangers from life in violent communities, disproportional contact of African American youth with the justice system, or police brutality (Thomas, 2017). Family therapists may also be able to highlight communication patterns among the adults in the family that are rooted in their own racial socialization experiences. Family therapists should consider how culture and social context inform parenting practices and explore how some of these practices may be gendered. An example of gendered racial socialization is African American mothers giving their daughters African American dolls and highlighting their daughter's beauty, whereas boys are told to behave appropriately in public and to respect authority (Edwards & Few-Demo, 2016).

Family Therapy and Music

Although adolescence is a period of intense change and development, it is also a period when the time spent listening to music increases. On average, adolescents listen to music for up to 3 hours daily (Roberts, Henriksen, & Foehr, 2009; Tarrant, North, & Hargreaves, 2000; Zillmann & Gan, 1997). Music is mostly an emotional experience (Miranda, 2013), and given the prominence of music in the lives of adolescents, it can be a useful tool in the context of family therapy for African American girls.

Family music therapy is a small but developing discipline in the family therapy field (Nemesh, 2017). Music reflects an individual's emotions. One benefit of incorporating music in family therapy is that the experience with music can create a relaxed atmosphere and bypass the typical defenses clients bring into the therapeutic space, overcome rigid family structures, and enable family members to gain insight regarding their family relationships (Kerr, Hoshino, Sutherland, Parashak, & McCarley, 2008; Nemesh, 2017). E. B. Miller (1994) incorporated the use of music as a tool in family therapy and found the musical sessions had a positive impact on promoting positive family communication and family cooperation, facilitated the practice of healthy parenting skills, and enhanced productive family dynamics. In the context of family music therapy, family members improvise together using musical instruments without prior training or experience (Nemesh, 2017). It is thought that this nonverbal, playful musical exchange is the basis for facilitating family interactions (Oldfield, Bell, & Pool, 2012). Research conducted by Nemesh (2017) found the initial family clinical assessment for family music therapy can highlight a broad picture of a family's interactions (e.g., communication patterns, roles, dysfunctions). For example, the choice of instruments in a session can reveal family members' underlying beliefs, self-worth, dynamics, and roles. When families begin their musical improvisation, strengths and challenges with family cohesion, support, consideration, control, problem solving, and leadership may be revealed (Nemesh, 2017). As these issues are highlighted, family music therapy can have as its goal to strengthen parent–child family relationships and enhance child development.

Treating Tasha in Context: Family Therapy

Tasha's therapist recommended to Tasha's mother, Vivian, that they explore family therapy. Despite a strong therapeutic alliance, Tasha's behavior had not substantively improved, and pain regarding family dynamics was becoming more apparent. Vivian did not like the idea of talking about her family's business with a stranger. Vivian talked to her mother about the recommendation to see a family therapist and was surprised that her mother was supportive of the idea. Vivian's mother confided that when she found out Vivian was pregnant at 14 years old with Tasha, she talked with a therapist to help her deal with the news. With that information, Vivian felt more comfortable seeking a family therapist (under the condition that her mother join the therapy sessions with them, given the critical role her mother plays in Tasha's life).

When Vivian told Tasha about family therapy, Tasha was extremely uncomfortable. She had finally connected with her therapist, and she worried about sharing some of her feelings with her mother and grandmother. During the first session, Tasha did not speak at all. The therapist used that opportunity to get Vivian and Vivian's mother's perspective on Tasha. Despite having seen Tasha individually for weeks, the therapist was unaware of Tasha's love of singing. The therapist decided to use music to break down resistance to the family process. The therapist engaged the whole family in a task to create a song together describing how they use each other for support. This exercise created a good opportunity for the therapist to see how the family communicates, the lyrics or instruments they selected to create the song, and how they depended on each other to develop the song.

A couple of important findings were revealed during family therapy. During the music improvisation, the leadership and collaboration dynamics within their family played out during the song-writing exercise. Both Tasha and Vivian looked to Vivian's mother to guide them in how they should start the exercise; however, all three of them worked together to develop lyrics that they all agreed described how they support each other. Another important revelation involved Tasha sharing her feelings about her father, who had been incarcerated most of her life. She also shared that during the end of her seventh-grade year some of her friends found out about her father's incarceration and began to bully her. Although Tasha had always had a close relationship with her mother and grandmother, she told them that she did not feel comfortable talking to them about the bullying because of the parental discord already present. The therapist asked Vivian how she felt hearing about Tasha's experience in school. Vivian began to sob and said she was also bullied during middle school, and she talked about how supportive her mother (Tasha's grandmother) was. She also said that she would like to give that same level of support to Tasha. As a family, they agreed to have more honest conversations in their home. The therapist pointed out to Tasha how similar her middle school experience appeared to be to her mother's experience and reminded her that she has two women in her life she can lean on for support.

AFRICAN AMERICAN GIRLS AND GROUP THERAPY

Group therapy can take shape in various contexts, from formal sessions in office settings to facilitated groups in school and community settings, with both structured and unstructured formats (Cramer-Azima, 2002; Haen & Aronson, 2017). When effectively implemented, this therapeutic approach can provide a safe environment for adolescents to experience mental and behavioral health interventions with their peer groups (Shechtman, 2007). Whereas individual and family therapy allow for the direct tailoring of sessions on the specific individual and family needs of adolescents and their immediate support system, group therapy can have the added challenge of addressing the common and unique needs of the various individuals in the group (Steen, Vannatta, & Liu, 2017). Group therapy challenges can be compounded by factors that may impact group functioning, such as self-protective walls that may hinder disclosure of individual and familial issues by African American girls and the complex nature of intersecting identities for the girls (Stark-Rose, Livingston-Sacin, Merchant, & Finley, 2012).

Even with these challenges, group therapy approaches can yield positive impacts for African American girls, given the existence of core desires for supportive relationships. Relational-cultural theories point to the importance of relationships that contribute to healthy development and are characterized by mutual empowerment and mutual empathy (Comstock et al., 2008; Jordan & Hartling, 2002). For girls who are at critical phases of discovery about themselves, group therapy can serve as a safe space for exploring questions and concerns with peers through supportive facilitation by a therapist. Such outlets may be of particular importance for African American adolescent girls, who are often navigating through negative societal and community messages that can have harmful impacts on healthy development. The issues previously noted concerning the adultification of African American girls contributes to negative messaging and can have deleterious effects on a range of outcomes, including educational achievement, leadership opportunities, juvenile justice contact, and responses to trauma and violence victimization (Epstein et al., 2017).

Culturally Responsive Group Treatment and Intervention

African American adolescent girls, especially those in marginalized communities and the juvenile justice system, are often underrepresented in research on group therapy and other therapy approaches (Caldwell et al., 2016). The lower levels of research correlate directly with lower levels of tested interventions and specific adaptations of existing interventions to address unique cultural considerations of African American girls and other underrepresented groups (Steen et al., 2017). Given the critical role of ethnic and racial identity in African American adolescent girls' development, attention to culturally competent interventions that build resiliency for girls to avoid stereotypical perceptions often put forth by society (Tatum, 1997). In a meta-analysis of mental health interventions that had cultural adaptations, Griner and Smith (2006) found the culturally adapted programs to be four times as effective as universal programs without adaptations. One example of this type of program can be seen with the Sisters of Nia intervention (Belgrave, Cherry, Butler, & Townsend, 2008). This 15-session program developed for middle school and high school African American girls embeds cultural traditions into interventions, with a focus on the principles of Kwanzaa. An evaluation study of the Sisters of Nia program found that middle school girls in an intervention group were significantly more likely to have increased racial identity and decreases in relational aggression compared with a control group (Belgrave et al., 2004).

Importance of Trustworthy, Culturally Informed Facilitators
The complex lived experiences that many African American girls bring to group therapeutic settings speak to the critical need for skilled facilitators who can build trust with the group participants and effectively speak to unique cultural considerations for participants. Such culturally informed approaches speak to the importance of therapists working with African American girls to understand the collective African American experience that is influenced by historic and systemic racism and disparate conditions (Parham, 2002). The APA (2007) *Guidelines for Psychological Practice With Girls and Women* discuss the need for psychologists to recognize and use information about oppression, privilege, and identity development in contextual frameworks at varying socioecological levels. The APA (2017) *Multicultural Guidelines* provide further related guidance for psychologists in terms of their self-examination of explicit and implicit biases that may influence their attitudes, beliefs, and perceptions. This is often most successfully achieved through facilitators who are perceived by girls as credible on the basis of their lived experiences or, at a minimum, an ability to genuinely relate to the experiences through shared cultural or socioeconomic backgrounds (Gilligan, 1991). Equally important is therapy grounded in recognizing the positive factors for African American girls to encourage their positive development and facilitate them to thrive. Using supportive factors, such as religious support and communalism, have shown promise as contributing factors for positive youth development among African American girls (Gooden & McMahon, 2016).

Organizations such as the Association of Black Psychologists and the Community Healing Network have encouraged the use of consciousness-raising interventions in group formats through their Emotional Emancipation Initiative to address "the lie of Black inferiority and the emotional legacies of enslavement and racism" (Association of Black Psychologists, n.d., para. 1). This initiative has several awareness-raising activities, including emotional emancipation circles, which encourage the use of storytelling to aid in the understanding of historical events on current emotional functioning and the provision of strategies for effectively challenging this emotional baggage propagated by the broader society.

Building Trust Among Group Members

Basic group dynamics come into play with group therapy, with continuity of membership playing an important role with group functioning. However, attrition for such groups may prove to be higher among high-risk African American girls. In a small pilot study of an adapted expressive group therapy, Stuart and Tuason (2008) found that attrition of participants often stemmed from issues such as conflict among participants and lack of transportation. The lack of trust among girls' peers may be linked to trauma impacts on challenges with trust for disclosure within group settings. Facilitators can play a large role in creating a safe place for girls to be vulnerable with sharing fears. The curriculum *It's a Girl Thang* provides guidance in its curricula implementation regarding a few key factors in developing groups, including (a) establishment of rules and consequences, (b) clarity on guidelines and limitations of confidentiality (including reporting), and (c) the schedule of the topics each week on the importance of structure (Bell-Gadsby, Clark, & Hunt, 2006). Bell-Gadsby and colleagues (2006) further noted the importance of control, connection, and meaning among group members, especially when there are co-occurring issues such as trauma and substance use.

Understanding the Impacts of Co-Occurring Issues in Group Dynamics

Therapy with African American girls is often complicated by the presence of multiple issues, many stemming from trauma and maladaptive coping behaviors such as substance use, risky sexual behavior, and eating disorders (Steen et al., 2017). The following case vignette continues our understanding of Tasha's experience with group therapy and provides an example of how complex experiences may impact therapy for her individually and among a group of girls in a juvenile justice setting, with notable use of storytelling in the therapeutic approach.

The Struggle Continues: Tasha's Group Experience

Despite making some strides and evidencing some improvement in her behavior, Tasha had a serious lapse of judgment, which resulted in her being sent to the county detention center. It was Week 4 of a 10-week therapy group for girls in the detention center. There were eight African American girls in the group, and the therapist was an Afro Caribbean woman. The therapist felt good about the rapport she developed with the eight girls in her group. Because of the nature of detention centers, there was some attrition during the first 3 weeks of the group, with four girls getting released from the detention center to their homes—which left the eight remaining girls. The presenting problems for the girls in the group ranged from conduct disorders and depression to risky sexual activity and substance abuse.

During one of the sessions, the therapist decided to use storytelling for the activity. Storytelling builds on the oral tradition of African Americans by which history was passed down orally through stories. Each group member had to share a short story about her favorite memory. As the young women shared their stories, it became clear to the therapist that each story was framed in the context of trauma. Tasha described her favorite memory as taking place a couple of years earlier, when she was 12. Her father was released from prison after being incarcerated for 10 years. She shared how much she had disliked going to visit him when he was incarcerated. She described the smell of the facility and how scared she was as she went through the gates of the facility. After describing the fun things she and her father did after he returned home, she concluded her story by saying the regular nightmares she used to have about the prison had finally gone away but had returned since she had been in the detention center.

Sadly, when many of the other girls described their favorite memories, they had a similar tone of happiness within the context of trauma. Although the presenting problem for each girl did not include posttraumatic stress disorder, it became clear to the therapist that this diagnosis was a co-occurring disorder for all of them. The therapist made efforts, however, to reinforce the strength and resilience of each girl in being able to find positive aspects with their experiences, and they discussed the ways that they were working to understand and grow from them. For example, Tasha commented on choices she made with certain friends who were not the best influences for her, which impacted her ability to be with her family. She also proudly talked about her improved relationship and better communication with her mother and grandmother, a renewed interest in keeping her grades up, and the fact that she had begun thinking about working on her relationship with her father and possibly sharing some of her artwork, which he had always encouraged her to do.

OVERARCHING CONSIDERATIONS

African American girls' demonstration of resiliency in the face of context and situations that are not optimal for thriving provide ongoing evidence of their amazing "girl power." It is critical that therapeutic approaches, whether individual, family, or group based, consider community and systemic challenges faced by girls, on top of the normal stressors experienced during adolescent development. Given low rates of treatment seeking and high rates of attrition for mental health treatment among African American adolescents as a whole, it is essential that issues of cultural mistrust and cultural incongruity with the therapist and client are addressed. It is important to note that this incongruency is not just about race and ethnicity considerations but one of understanding the complex social and system-level challenges faced by marginalized African American adolescent girls and an ability to appropriately reframe and recognize girls' coping mechanisms as strengths.

African American girls thrive, even when the high level of risk factors surrounding them would predict otherwise. However, it is imperative that resources and support for truly nurturing their mental and behavioral health continue to develop, including strategies for increasing accessibility and use of treatment. The touchpoints of individual, family, and group therapy can serve as facilitators of resiliency building but must be rooted in culturally relevant care by practitioners. We propose the following overarching considerations with therapeutic approaches with African American girls.

- Practitioners must continue to explore and understand the significant role of trauma on the mental health of African American girls. Traumatic experiences can manifest in behavior that impacts treatment engagement and decision making and subsequent behaviors that may cyclically affect future trauma exposure. Being aware of the masking that occurs in the form of other behaviors is critical when building trust among African American girls and ensuring a holistic treatment approach.

- Effectively working with African American girls hinges on understanding their multiple identities and social groups that they represent, whether they are embraced or not. This includes explicating how these representations of girls may be experienced at different social-ecological levels, both intrapersonally and interpersonally, and building resiliency skills to thrive even with discriminatory messaging that may be experienced. In its 2008 report, the APA Task Force on Resilience and Strength in Black Children and Adolescents reinforced the importance of reframing the negativity that is often used to characterize African American children and adolescents to shift toward positive views that highlight their resiliency and strength. Their recommendations for focus on identity, emotional, social, cognitive, and physical health development are common areas of needed focus for adolescents; however, as they noted, these developmental priorities have to be considered within the context of African American children and adolescents, and both boys' and girls' unique cultural experiences. Therapists should consider these developmental areas in their work with African American girls and how girls' strengths are nurtured for ongoing development in these areas.

- Practitioners working with African American girls need cross-cultural education and ongoing strategies for self-awareness regarding potential unconscious and implicit biases that can shape interpretation and understanding of girls' behavior. As noted in the *Multicultural Guidelines* (APA, 2017),

  > Psychologists aspire to recognize and understand that as cultural beings, they hold attitudes and beliefs that can influence their perceptions of and interactions with others as well as their clinical and empirical conceptualizations. As such, psychologists strive to move beyond conceptualizations rooted in categorical assumptions, biases, and/or formulations based on limited knowledge about individuals and communities. (p. 4)

- Therapist self-awareness and a culturally informed approach with African American girls can contribute to the raised awareness of the girls themselves. Interventions that focus on increasing girls' knowledge and awareness of existing stereotypes, providing positive affirmation strategies that discount these stereotypes for the girls, and providing a safe context that allows for exploration of the challenging messages aid in building the resiliency of girls to potential negative effects of pervasive stereotypical views.

- The term *African American* is often used globally to represent diverse groups of girls, including African American, African Caribbean, Continental African, and other distinct African descending groups. The even greater scarcity of studies with these subgroups increases challenges with a full understanding of unique counseling needs that may arise (e.g., the impacts of unique cultural and immigration experiences on girls). Each group has distinct cultural and historical experiences that must be considered with care and appropriate adaptations that meet the need of these diverse groups. Therapists must take the time to understand the heritage of girls and how this history impacts their worldview and can serve as positive anchors for the therapeutic approach.

- Stigma related to mental health treatment seeking, low levels of treatment initiation, and high attrition rates among African American girls are ongoing barriers to effective mental health care. Practitioners must continue to heed empirically grounded recommendations for increases in mental health literacy for both youth and adult populations, but we must also embrace innovative approaches to reaching African American girls through community, medical, educational, and other accessible contexts.

- Practitioners should also recognize the important role that spirituality plays for many African Americans. Girls and their caregivers, who may be resistant to traditional treatment, may be more receptive to a therapist who is spiritually grounded and/or provides spiritually based therapy. As Frame and Williams (1996) described,

> African American culture is rich with religious and spiritual traditions and practices. The prominence of the African American church, the importance of Biblical themes such as liberation and freedom, the centrality of music from indigenous African rhythms to the Negro Spirituals, to blues, soul, jazz, and rap are all aspects of African American spirituality that largely have been ignored in traditional approaches to counseling with this population. (p. 16)

CONCLUSION

African American girls represent a resilient group that holds promise for facilitating understanding of thriving even when faced with systemic barriers. Although the focus on mental health care for African American girls has increased to some extent, the need for effective therapeutic techniques that are culturally appropriate remain. The variability among African American girls and other girls of African descent continues to be overlooked, with insufficient attention not only to unique historical contexts of these girls but also the multiple identities that shape engagement and response to treatment. To facilitate the needed ongoing evolution of therapists' understanding of effective treatment approaches with African American girls, research and practice must continue to grow our understanding of evidence-based approaches that are centered on positive youth development and an ultimate goal of reducing mental health disparities for African American girls.

REFERENCES

Abdullah, A. S. (1998). Mammy-ism: A diagnosis of psychological misorientation for women of African descent. *Journal of Black Psychology, 24*, 196–210. https://dx.doi.org/10.1177/00957984980242009

Aldwin, C. M. (2007). *Stress, coping, and development: An integrative perspective* (2nd ed.). New York, NY: Guilford Press.

American Psychological Association. (2007). *Guidelines for psychological practice with girls and women.* Retrieved from https://www.apa.org/practice/guidelines/girls-and-women.aspx

American Psychological Association. (2017). *Multicultural guidelines: An ecological approach to context, identity, and intersectionality.* Retrieved from www.apa.org/about/policy/multicultural-guidelines.pdf

American Psychological Association, Task Force on Resilience and Strength in Black Children and Adolescents. (2008). *Resilience in African American children and adolescents: A vision for optimal development.* Retrieved from https://www.apa.org/pi/families/resources/resiliencerpt.pdf

American Psychological Association, Task Force on the Sexualization of Girls. (2007). *Report of the APA Task Force on the Sexualization of Girls.* Retrieved from https://www.apa.org/pi/women/programs/girls/report-full.pdf

Annamma, S. A., Anyon, Y., Joseph, N. M., Farrar, J., Greer, E., Downing, B., & Simmons, J. (2016). Black girls and school discipline: The complexities of being overrepresented and understudied. *Urban Education.* http://dx.doi.org/10.1177/0042085916646610

Assari, S., & Caldwell, C. H. (2017). Mental health service utilization among Black youth; Psychosocial determinants in a national sample. *Children, 4,* 40. http://dx.doi.org/10.3390/children4050040

Association of Black Psychologists. (n.d.). *The emotional emancipation initiative.* Retrieved from https://www.abpsi.org/EEC.html

Banks, D., & Kyckelhahn, T. (2011). *Characteristics of suspected human trafficking incidents, 2008–2010.* Retrieved from https://www.bjs.gov/content/pub/pdf/cshti0810.pdf

Baquet, D. (2017, November 29). On therapy, politics, marriage, the state of rap, and being a Black man in Trump's America: Jay-Z and Dean Baquet. *The New York Times Style Magazine.* Retrieved from https://www.nytimes.com/interactive/2017/11/29/t-magazine/jay-z-dean-baquet-interview.html

Becvar, D. S., & Becvar, R. J. (2009). *Family therapy: A systemic integration* (7th ed.). New York, NY: Pearson.

Belgrave, F. Z., Cherry, V. R., Butler, D. S., & Townsend, T. (2008) *Sisters of NIA: A cultural enrichment program to empower African American girls.* Champagne, IL: Research Press.

Belgrave, F. Z., Reed, M. C., Plybon, L. E., Butler, D. S., Allison, K. W., & Davis, T. (2004). An evaluation of Sisters of Nia: A cultural program for African American girls. *Journal of Black Psychology, 30,* 329–343. http://dx.doi.org/10.1177/0095798404266063

Bell-Gadsby, C., Clark, N., & Hunt, S. (2006). *It's a girl thang! A manual on creating girl groups.* Vancouver, Canada: McCreary Youth Foundation.

Bent-Goodley, T. B. (2004). Perceptions of domestic violence: A dialogue with African American women. *Health & Social Work, 29,* 307–316. http://dx.doi.org/10.1093/hsw/29.4.307

Billingsley, A. (1992). *Climbing Jacob's ladder: The enduring legacy of African-American families.* New York, NY: Simon & Schuster.

Biro, F. M., Huang, B., Crawford, P. B., Lucky, A. W., Striegel-Moore, R., Barton, B. A., & Daniels, S. (2006). Pubertal correlates in black and white girls. *The Journal of Pediatrics, 148,* 234–240. http://dx.doi.org/10.1016/j.jpeds.2005.10.020

Black, B. M., Chido, L. M., Preble, K. M., Weisz, A. N., Yoon, J. S., Delaney-Black, V., Kernsmith, P., & Lewandowski, L. (2015). Violence exposure and teen dating: Violence among African American youth. *Journal of Interpersonal Violence, 30,* 2174–2195. https://dx.doi.org/10.1177/0886260514552271

Boyd-Franklin, N. (1989). *Black families in therapy: A multisystems approach.* New York, NY: Guilford Press

Boyd-Franklin, N. (1991). Recurrent themes in the treatment of African-American women in group psychotherapy. *Women & Therapy, 11,* 25–40. http://dx.doi.org/10.1300/J015V11N02_04

Breland-Noble, A. M., Burriss, A., & Poole, H. K. (2010). Engaging depressed African American adolescents in treatment: Lessons from the AAKOMA PROJECT. *Journal of Clinical Psychology, 66,* 868–879. http://dx.doi.org/10.1002/jclp.20708

Brown, S. P., Lipford-Sanders, J., & Shaw, M. (1995). *Kujichagulia*-uncovering the secrets of the heart: Group work with African-American women on predominantly Caucasian campuses. *The Journal for Specialists in Group Work, 20,* 151–158. http://dx.doi.org/10.1080/01933929508411339

Brown, T. L., Linver, M. R., & Evans, M. (2010). The role of gender in the racial and ethnic socialization of African American adolescents. *Youth & Society, 41,* 357–381. http://dx.doi.org/10.1177/0044118X09333665

Brunson, R. K., & Miller, J. (2006). Gender, race, and urban policing: The experience of African American youths. *Gender & Society, 20,* 531–552. http://dx.doi.org/10.1177/0891243206287727

Caldwell, C. H., Assari, S., & Breland-Noble, A. M. (2016). The epidemiology of mental disorders in African American children and adolescents. In A. M. Breland-Noble, C. S. Al-Mateen, & N. N. Singh (Eds.), *Handbook of mental health in African American youth* (pp. 3–20). Zurich, Switzerland: Springer International. http://dx.doi.org/10.1007/978-3-319-25501-9_1

Centers for Disease Control and Prevention. (2016). *Welcome to WISQARS.* Retrieved from http://www.cdc.gov/injury/wisqars/index.html

Centers for Disease Control and Prevention. (2018). *Youth Risk Behavior Survey data summary & trends report, 2007–2017.* Retrieved from https://www.cdc.gov/healthyyouth/data/yrbs/pdf/trendsreport.pdf

Child Welfare Information Gateway. (2016). *Racial disproportionality and disparity in child welfare.* Washington, DC: U.S. Department of Health and Human Services, Children's Bureau.

Cloitre, M. (1998). Sexual revictimization: Risk factors and prevention. In V. M. Follette, J. L. Ruzek, & F. R. Abueg (Eds.), *Cognitive-behavioral therapies for trauma* (pp. 278–304). New York, NY: Guilford Press.

CNN. (2018, January 20). *Jay-Z: Therapists should be in schools* [Video file]. Retrieved from https://www.cnn.com/videos/cnnmoney/2018/01/27/jay-z-mental-health-therapy-sot-van-jones-show.cnn

Collins, P. H. (2000). *Black feminist thought: Knowledge, consciousness, and the politics of empowerment* (2nd ed.). New York, NY: Routledge.

Comstock, D. L., Hammer, T. R., Strentzsch, J., Cannon, K., Parsons, J., & Salazar, G., II. (2008). Relational-cultural theory: A framework for bridging relational, multicultural, and social justice competencies. *Journal of Counseling & Development, 86,* 279–287. http://dx.doi.org/10.1002/j.1556-6678.2008.tb00510.x

Connell, C. (2010). Multicultural perspectives and considerations within structural family therapy: The premises of structure, subsystems, and boundaries. *Insight: Rivier Academic Journal, 6*(2), 1–6.

Cramer-Azima, F. J. (2002). Group psychotherapy for children and adolescents. In M. Lewis (Ed.), *Child and adolescent psychiatry: A comprehensive textbook* (3rd ed., pp. 1032–1036). Philadelphia, PA: Lippincott Williams Wilkins.

Crenshaw, K. W. (1991). Mapping the margins: Intersectionality, identity politics, and violence against women of color. *Stanford Law Review, 43,* 1241–1299. http://dx.doi.org/10.2307/1229039

Crenshaw, K. W., Ritchie, A. J., Anspach, R., Gilmer, R., & Harris, L. (2015). *Say her name: Resisting police brutality against Black women.* Retrieved from https://static1.square-space.com/static/53f20d90e4b0b80451158d8c/t/560c068ee4b0af26f72741df/1443628686535/AAPF_SMN_Brief_Full_singles-min.pdf

DeFreitas, S. C., Crone, T., DeLeon, M., & Ajayi, A. (2018). Perceived and personal mental health stigma in Latino and African American college students. *Frontiers in Public Health, 6*(49). http://dx.doi.org/10.3389/fpubh.2018.00049

Donovan, R. A. (2007). To blame or not to blame: Influences of target race and observer sex on rape blame attribution. *Journal of Interpersonal Violence, 22,* 722–736. http://dx.doi.org/10.1177/0886260507300754

Drake-Burnette, D., Garrett-Akinsanya, B., & Bryant-Davis, T. (2016). Womanism, creativity, and resistance: Making a way out of "No Way." In T. Bryant-Davis & L. Comas-Díaz (Eds.), *Womanist and mujerista psychologies: Voices of fire, acts of courage* (pp. 173–193). Washington, DC: American Psychological Association. http://dx.doi.org/10.1037/14937-008

Edwards, A. L., & Few-Demo, A. L. (2016). African American maternal power and the racial socialization of preschool children. *Sex Roles, 75,* 56–70. http://dx.doi.org/10.1007/s11199-016-0633-y

Epstein, R., Blake, J., & González, T. (2017). *Girlhood interrupted: The erasure of Black girls' childhood.* Retrieved from http://dx.doi.org/10.2139/ssrn.3000695

Faryna, E. L., & Morales, E. (2000). Self-efficacy and HIV-related risk behaviors among multiethnic adolescents. *Cultural Diversity and Ethnic Minority Psychology, 6,* 42–56. http://dx.doi.org/10.1037/1099-9809.6.1.42

Federal Interagency Forum on Child and Family Statistics. (2018). *America's children: Key national indicators of well-being, 2018.* Washington, DC: U.S. Government Printing Office.

Feiring, C., Rosenthal, S., & Taska, L. (2000). Stigmatization and the development of friendship and romantic relationships in adolescent victims of sexual abuse. *Child Maltreatment, 5,* 311–322. http://dx.doi.org/10.1177/1077559500005004003

Flores, R. (2016). The determinants of health: Neighborhood characteristics, obesity and the mental health of African-American adolescent girls. *Open Journal of Social Sciences, 4,* 126–136. http://dx.doi.org/10.4236/jss.2016.412012

Frame, M., & Williams, C. (1996). Counseling African Americans: Integrating spirituality into therapy. *Counseling and Values, 41,* 16–28.

Fredrickson, B. L., & Roberts, T.-A. (1997). Objectification theory: Toward understanding women's lived experiences and mental health risks. *Psychology of Women Quarterly, 21,* 173–206. https://dx.doi.org/10.1111/j.1471-6402.1997.tb00108.x

Freyd, J. J. (1996). *Betrayal trauma: The logic of forgetting childhood abuse.* Cambridge, MA: Harvard University Press.

Garland, A. F., Lau, A. S., Yeh, M., McCabe, K. M., Hough, R. L., & Landsverk, J. A. (2005). Racial and ethnic differences in utilization of mental health services among high-risk youths. *The American Journal of Psychiatry, 162,* 1336–1343. http://dx.doi.org/10.1176/appi.ajp.162.7.1336

Gershoff, E. T. (2002). Corporal punishment by parents and associated child behaviors and experiences: A meta-analytic and theoretical review. *Psychological Bulletin, 128,* 539–579. http://dx.doi.org/libproxy.lib.unc.edu/10.1037/0033-2909.128.4.539

Gershoff, E. T., Lansford, J. E., Sexton, H. R., Davis-Kean, P., & Sameroff, A. J. (2012). Longitudinal links between spanking and children's externalizing behaviors in a national sample of White, Black, Hispanic, and Asian American families. *Child Development, 83,* 838–843. http://dx.doi.org/10.1111/j.1467-8624.2011.01732.x

Gilligan, C. (1991). Women's psychological development: Implications for psychotherapy. In C. Gilligan, A. Rogers, & D. Tolman (Eds.), *Women, girls, and psychotherapy: Reframing resistance.* Binghamton, NY: Haworth Press.

Gillum, T. L. (2002). Exploring the Link between stereotypic images and intimate partner violence in the African American community. *Violence Against Women, 8,* 64–86. http://dx.doi.org/10.1177/10778010222182946

Gooden, A. S., & McMahon, S. D. (2016). Thriving among African-American adolescents: Religiosity, religious support, and communalism. *American Journal of Community Psychology, 57,* 118–128. http://dx.doi.org/10.1002/ajcp.12026

Gordon, M. K. (2008). Media contributions to African American girls' focus on beauty and appearance: Exploring the consequences of sexual objectification. *Psychology of Women Quarterly, 32,* 245–256. http://dx.doi.org/10.1111/j.1471-6402.2008.00433.x

Graves, K., Kaslow, N., & Frabutt, J. (2010). A culturally-informed approach to trauma, suicidal behavior, and overt aggression in African American adolescents. *Aggression and Violent Behavior, 15,* 36–41. http://dx.doi.org/10.1016/j.avb.2009.07.014

Greene, B. (1994). African American women: Derivations of racism and sexism in psychotherapy. In E. Toback & B. Russ (Eds.), *Sexism and racism: Challenges to genetic explanations of diversity* (pp. 122–139). New York, NY: Feminist Press.

Griner, D., & Smith, T. B. (2006). Culturally adapted mental health intervention: A meta-analytic review. *Psychotherapy: Theory, Research, Practice, Training, 43,* 531–548. http://dx.doi.org/10.1037/0033-3204.43.4.531

Haen, C., & Aronson, S. (2017). *Handbook of child and adolescent group therapy.* New York, NY: Routledge.

Harrell, S. P., & Rowe, D. M. (2014). Clinical applications with African Americans. In D. W. Sue, M. E. Gallardo, & H. A. Neville (Eds.), *Case studies in multicultural counseling and therapy* (pp. 3–20). Hoboken, NY: Wiley.

Harris, K. M., Gordon-Larsen, P., Chantala, K., & Udry, J. R. (2006). Longitudinal trends in race/ethnic disparities in leading health indicators from adolescence to young adulthood. *Archives of Pediatrics & Adolescent Medicine, 160,* 74–81. http://dx.doi.org/10.1001/archpedi.160.1.74

Harris, T. M., & Hill, P. S. (1998). Waiting to "exhale" or "breath(ing) again": A search for identity, empowerment, and love in the 1990's. *Women & Language, 21,* 9–20.

Harrison, A. O., Wilson, M. N., Pine, C. J., Chan, S. Q., & Buriel, R. (1990). Family ecologies of ethnic minority children. *Child Development, 61,* 347–362. http://dx.doi.org/10.1111/j.1467-8624.1990.tb02782.x

Hill, C. P. (2000). *Black feminist thought: Knowledge, consciousness, and the politics of empowerment*. New York, NY: Routledge.

Hughes, D., & Chen, L. (1997). When and what parents tell children about race: An examination of race-related socialization among African American families. *Applied Developmental Science, 1*, 200–214. http://dx.doi.org/10.1207/s1532480xads0104_4

Hughes, D., & Chen, L. (1999). The nature of parents' race-related communications to children: A developmental perspective. In L. Balter & C. S. Tamis-Lemonda (Eds.), *Child psychology: A handbook of contemporary issues* (pp. 467–490). Philadelphia, PA: Psychology Press.

Hughes, D., Rodriguez, J., Smith, E. P., Johnson, D. J., Stevenson, H. C., & Spicer, P. (2006). Parents' ethnic-racial socialization practices: A review of research and directions for future study. *Developmental Psychology, 42*, 747–770. http://dx.doi.org/10.1037/0012-1649.42.5.747

Johnson, O., Gilbert, K., & Ibrahim, H. (2018). *Race, gender, and the contexts of unarmed fatal interactions with police*. Retrieved from https://cpb-us-w2.wpmucdn.com/sites.wustl.edu/dist/b/1205/files/2018/02/Race-Gender-and-Unarmed-1y9md6e.pdf

Joinson, C., Heron, J., Lewis, G., Croudace, T., & Araya, R. (2011). Timing of menarche and depressive symptoms in adolescent girls from a UK cohort. *The British Journal of Psychiatry, 198*, 17–23, 1–2. http://dx.doi.org/10.1192/bjp.bp.110.080861

Jordan, J. V., & Hartling, L. M. (2002). New developments in relational-cultural theory. In M. Ballou & L. S. Brown (Eds.), *Rethinking mental health and disorders: Feminist perspectives* (pp. 48–70). New York, NY: Guilford Press.

Keenan, K., Culbert, K. M., Grimm, K. J., Hipwell, A. E., & Stepp, S. D. (2014). Timing and tempo: Exploring the complex association between pubertal development and depression in African American and European American girls. *Journal of Abnormal Psychology, 123*, 725–736. http://dx.doi.org/10.1037/a0038003

Keenan, K., & Hipwell, A. E. (2005). Preadolescent clues to understanding depression in girls. *Clinical Child and Family Psychology Review, 8*, 89–105. http://dx.doi.org/10.1007/s10567-005-4750-3

Kerr, C., Hoshino, J., Sutherland, J., Parashak, S. T., & McCarley, L. L. (2008). *Family art therapy: Foundations of theory and practice*. New York, NY: Routledge/Taylor & Francis.

Kilpatrick, D. G., Resnick, H. S., Ruggiero, K. J., Conoscenti, L. M., & McCauley, J. (2007). *Drug-facilitated, incapacitated, and forcible rape: A national study*. Retrieved from https://www.ncjrs.gov/pdffiles1/nij/grants/219181.pdf

Kilpatrick, D. G., Ruggiero, K. J., Acierno, R., Saunders, B. E., Resnick, H. S., & Best, C. L. (2003). Violence and risk of PTSD, major depression, substance abuse/dependence, and comorbidity: Results from the National Survey of Adolescents. *Journal of Consulting and Clinical Psychology, 71*, 692–700. http://dx.doi.org/10.1037/0022-006X.71.4.692

Laszloffy, T. A., & Hardy, K. V. (2000). Uncommon strategies for a common problem: Addressing racism in family therapy. *Family Process, 39*, 35–50. http://dx.doi.org/10.1111/j.1545-5300.2000.39106.x

Lewis, J. A., Mendenhall, R., Harwood, S. A., & Huntt, M. B. (2016). "Ain't I a woman?" Perceived gendered racial microaggressions experienced by Black women. *The Counseling Psychologist, 44*, 758–780. https://dx.doi.org/10.1177/0011000016641193

Lewis, J. A., & Neville, H. A. (2015). Construction and initial validation of the gendered racial microaggressions scale for Black women. *Journal of Counseling Psychology, 62,* 289–302. http://dx.doi.org/10.1037/cou0000062

Loeb, T. B., Williams, J. K., Carmona, J. V., Rivkin, I., Wyatt, G. E., Chin, D., & Asuan-O'Brien, A. (2002). Child sexual abuse: Associations with the sexual functioning of adolescents and adults. *Annual Review of Sex Research, 13,* 307–345.

McCann, L., & Pearlman, A. (1990). Vicarious traumatization: A framework for understanding the psychological effects of working with victims. *Journal of Traumatic Stress, 3,* 131–149. http://dx.doi.org/10.1007/BF00975140

McHale, J. (2011). Assessing coparenting. In J. McHale & K. Lindahl (Eds.), *Coparenting: A conceptual and clinical examination of family systems* (pp. 149–170). Washington, DC: American Psychological Association.

Miech, R. A., Johnston, L. D., O'Malley, P. M., Bachman, J. G., Schulenberg, J. E., & Patrick, M. E. (2017). *Monitoring the future: National survey results on drug use, 1975–2016: Vol. I. Secondary school students.* Retrieved from http://www.monitoringthefuture.org/pubs/monographs/mtf-vol1_2017.pdf

Miller, E. B. (1994). Musical intervention in family therapy. *Music Therapy, 12*(2), 39–57. http://dx.doi.org/10.1093/mt/12.2.39

Miller, L. M., Southam-Gerow, M. A., & Allin, R. B., Jr. (2008). Who stays in treatment? Child and family predictors of youth client retention in a public mental health agency. *Child & Youth Care Forum, 37,* 153–170. http://dx.doi.org/10.1007/s10566-008-9058-2

Miranda, D. (2013). The role of music in adolescent development: Much more than the same old song. *International Journal of Adolescence and Youth, 18*(1), 5–22. http://dx.doi.org/10.1080/02673843.2011.650182

Murry, V. M., Heflinger, C. A., Suiter, S. V., & Brody, G. H. (2011). Examining perceptions about mental health care and help-seeking among rural African American families of adolescents. *Journal of Youth and Adolescence, 40,* 1118–1131. http://dx.doi.org/10.1007/s10964-010-9627-1

Nemesh, B. (2017). Family-based music therapy: From dissonance to harmony. *Nordic Journal of Music Therapy, 26,* 167–184. http://dx.doi.org/10.1080/08098131.2016.1144638

Norris, F. H. (1992). Epidemiology of trauma: Frequency and impact of different potentially traumatic events on different demographic groups. *Journal of Consulting and Clinical Psychology, 60,* 409–418. http://dx.doi.org/10.1037/0022-006X.60.3.409

Oldfield, A., Bell, K., & Pool, J. (2012). Three families and three music therapists: Reflections on short term music therapy in child and family psychiatry. *Nordic Journal of Music Therapy, 21,* 250–267. http://dx.doi.org/10.1080/08098131.2011.640436

Parham, T. A. (2002). Counseling models for African Americans. In T. A. Parham (Ed.), *Counseling persons of African descent* (pp. 100–118). Thousand Oaks, CA: Sage.

Paulozzi, L. J., Saltzman, L. E., Thompson, M. P., & Holmgreen, P. (2001). Surveillance for homicide among intimate partners—United States, 1981–1998. *Morbidity and Mortality Weekly Report, 50,* 1–15.

Perilla, J. L., Norris, F. H., & Lavizzo, E. A. (2002). Ethnicity, culture, and disaster response: Identifying and explaining ethnic differences in PTSD. *Journal of Social and Clinical Psychology, 21,* 20–45. http://dx.doi.org/10.1521/jscp.21.1.20.22404

Peterson, S. H., Wingood, G. M., DiClemente, R. J., Harrington, K., & Davies, S. (2007). Images of sexual stereotypes in rap videos and the health of African

American female adolescents. *Journal of Women's Health, 16*, 1157–1164. http://dx.doi.org/10.1089/jwh.2007.0429

Phillips, J. (2015). Black girls and the (im)possibilities of a victim trope: The intersectional failures of legal and advocacy interventions in the commercial sexual exploitation of minors in the United States. *UCLA Law Review, 62*, 1642–1675.

Roberts, D. F., Henriksen, L., & Foehr, U. G. (2009). Adolescence, adolescents, and media. In R. M. Lerner & L. Steinberg (Eds.), *Handbook of adolescent psychology: Vol. 2. Contextual influences on adolescent development* (3rd ed., pp. 314–344). Hoboken, NJ: Wiley.

Robillard, A. (2012). Music videos and sexual risk in African American adolescent girls: Gender, power and the need for media literacy. *American Journal of Health Education, 43*, 93–103. http://dx.doi.org/10.1080/19325037.2012.10599224

Sanders, J. L., & Bradley, C. (2005). Multiple-lens paradigm: Evaluating African American girls and their development. *Journal of Counseling and Development, 83*, 299–304. http://dx.doi.org.libproxy.lib.unc.edu/10.1002/j.1556-6678.2005.tb00347

Shechtman, Z. (2007). *Group counseling and psychotherapy with children and adolescents: Theory, research and practice.* New York, NY: Routledge.

Sherman, F. T., & Grace, L. G. (2011). The system response to the commercial sexual exploitation of girls. In F. T. Sherman & F. H. Jacobs (Eds.), *Juvenile justice: Advancing research, policy, and practice* (pp. 331–351). Hoboken, NJ: Wiley.

Shorter-Gooden, K. A. (2009). Therapy with African American men and women. In H. A. Neville, M. Tynes, & S. O. Utsey (Eds.), *Handbook of African American psychology* (pp. 445–458). Thousand Oaks, CA: Sage.

Silverman, J. G., Raj, A., & Clements, K. (2004). Dating violence and associated sexual risk and pregnancy among adolescent girls in the United States. *Pediatrics, 114*, e220–e225. http://dx.doi.org/10.1542/peds.114.2.e220

Stark-Rose, R. M., Livingston-Sacin, T. M., Merchant, N., & Finley, A. C. (2012). Group counseling with United States minority groups: A 25-year content analysis. *Journal for Specialists in Group Work, 37*, 277–296. http://dx.doi.org/10.1080/01933922.2012.690831

Steen, S., Vannatta, R., & Liu, X. (2017). Cultural considerations in group work: Implications for school and mental health settings. In C. Haen & S. Aronson (Eds.), *Handbook of child and adolescent group therapy* (pp. 255–265). New York, NY: Routledge.

Stephens, D. P., & Phillips, L. D. (2005). Integrating Black feminist thought into conceptual frameworks of African American adolescent women's sexual scripting processes. *Sexualities, Evolution & Gender, 7*, 37–55. http://dx.doi.org/10.1080/14616660500112725

Stuart, K. S., & Tuason, T. G. (2008). Expressive group therapy with at-risk African American adolescent girls. *International Journal of Adolescence and Youth, 14*, 135–159. http://dx.doi.org/10.1080/02673843.2008.9747999

Tarrant, M., North, A. C., & Hargreaves, D. J. (2000). English and American adolescents' reasons for listening to music. *Psychology of Music, 28*, 166–173. http://dx.doi.org/10.1177/0305735600282005

Task Force on Trafficking of Women and Girls. (2014). Report of the Task Force on Trafficking of Women and Girls. Washington, DC: American Psychological Association. Retrieved from http://www.apa.org/pi/women/programs/trafficking/report.aspx

Tatum, B. (1997). *"Why are all the Black kids sitting together in the cafeteria?" And other conversations about race.* New York, NY: Basic Books.

Thomas, A. (2017, April). Promoting culturally affirming parenting in African-American parents: Positive parenting in African-American families. *CYF News*. Retrieved from https://www.apa.org/pi/families/resources/newsletter/2017/04/african-american-parents.aspx

Thompson, M. P., Kaslow, N. J., Kingree, J. B., Rashid, A., Puett, R., Jacobs, D., & Matthews, A. (2000). Partner violence, social support, and distress among inner-city African American women. *American Journal of Community Psychology, 28*, 127–143. http://dx.doi.org/10.1023/A:1005198514704

Thompson, V. L. S., Bazile, A., & Akbar, M. (2004). African Americans' perceptions of psychotherapy and psychotherapists. *Professional Psychology: Research and Practice, 35*, 19–26. http://dx.doi.org/10.1037/0735-7028.35.1.19

Townsend, T. G. (2002). The impact of self-components on sexual attitudes among African American pre-adolescent girls. *Sex Roles, 47*, 11–20. http://dx.doi.org/10.1023/A:1020675518819

Townsend, T. G., Jones Thomas, A., Neilands T. B., & Jackson, T. R. (2010). I'm no Jezebel, I am young, gifted, and Black: Identity, sexuality, and Black girls. *Psychology of Women Quarterly, 34*, 273–285. http://dx.doi.org/10.1111/j.1471-6402.2010.01574.x

Underwood, L., Stewart, S. E., & Castellanos, A. M. (2007). Effective practices for sexually traumatized girls: Implications for counseling and education. *International Journal of Behavioral Consultation and Therapy, 3*, 403–419. http://dx.doi.org/10.1037/h0100815

U.S. Census Bureau. (2016). *QuickFacts: People*. Retrieved from https://www.census.gov/quickfacts/fact/table/US/PST045218

U.S. Census Bureau. (2018). *Race*. Retrieved from https://www.census.gov/topics/population/race/about.html

U.S. Department of Education Office for Civil Rights. (2014). *Civil rights data collection data snapshot: School discipline*. Retrieved from https://www2.ed.gov/about/offices/list/ocr/docs/crdc-discipline-snapshot.pdf

Victims of Trafficking and Violence Protection Act of 2000. Pub. L. No. 106-386 [H.R. 3244] (2000).

Voisin, D. R. (2007). The effects of family and community violence exposure among. *Journal of Social Work Education, 43*, 51–66. http://dx.doi.org/10.5175/JSWE.2007.200400473

Waller, M. R. (2012). Cooperation, conflict, or disengagement? Coparenting styles and father involvement in fragile families. *Family Process, 51*, 325–342. http://dx.doi.org/10.1111/j.1545-5300.2012.01403.x

Waller, M. R., & Emory, A. D. (2014). Parents apart: Differences between unmarried and divorcing parents in separated families. *Family Court Review, 52*, 686–703. http://dx.doi.org/10.1111/fcre.12121

Ward, E. C., Wiltshire, J. C., Detry, M. A., & Brown, R. L. (2013). African American men and women's attitude toward mental illness, perceptions of stigma, and preferred coping behaviors. *Nursing Research, 62*, 185–94. http://dx.doi.org/10.1097/NNR.0b013e31827bf533

Westcott, K. (2015). Race, criminalization, and historical trauma in the United States: Making the case for a new justice framework. *Traumatology, 21*, 273–284. http://dx.doi.org/10.1037/trm0000048

Whaley, A. L. (2003). Cognitive-cultural model of identity and violence prevention for African American youth. *Genetic, Social, and General Psychology Monographs, 129*, 101–151.

Wiemann, C. M., Agurcia, C. A., Berenson, A. B., Volk, R. J., & Rickert, V. I. (2000). Pregnant adolescents: Experiences and behaviors associated with physical assault by an intimate partner. *Maternal and Child Health Journal, 4*, 93–101. http://dx.doi.org/10.1023/A:1009518220331

Wilkins, E., Whiting, J., Watson, M., Russon, J., & Moncrief, A. M. (2013). Residual effects of slavery: What clinicians need to know. *Contemporary Family Therapy, 35*, 14–28. http://dx.doi.org/10.1007/s10591-012-9219-1

Wilson, H. W., Donenberg, G. R., & Emerson, E. (2014). Childhood violence exposure and the development of sexual risk in low-income African American girls. *Journal of Behavioral Medicine, 37*, 1091–1101. http://dx.doi.org/10.1007/s10865-014-9560-y

Wilson, H. W., Woods, B. A., Emerson, E., & Donenberg, G. R. (2012). Patterns of violence exposure and sexual risk in low-income, urban African American girls. *Psychology of Violence, 2*, 194–207. http://dx.doi.org/10.1037/a0027265

Wingood, G. M., DiClemente, R. J., McCree, D. H., Harrington, K., & Davies, S. L. (2001). Dating violence and the sexual health of black adolescent females. *Pediatrics, 107*, e72. http://dx.doi.org/10.1542/peds.107.5.e72

Wintersteen, M. B., Mensinger, J. L., & Diamond, G. S. (2005). Do gender and racial differences between patient and therapist affect therapeutic alliance and treatment retention in adolescents? *Professional Psychology: Research and Practice, 36*, 400–408. http://dx.doi.org/10.1037/0735-7028.36.4.400

Yancy, G., & Jones, J. (Eds.). (2012). *Pursuing Trayvon Martin: Historical contexts and contemporary manifestations of racial dynamics.* Lanham, MD: Lexington Books.

Zillmann, D., & Gan, S. (1997). Musical taste in adolescence. In J. Hargreaves & A. C. North (Eds.), *The social psychology of music* (pp. 161–187). New York, NY: Oxford University Press.

4 ASIAN AMERICAN ADOLESCENT GIRLS

Navigating Stress Across Multiple Contexts

PRATYUSHA TUMMALA-NARRA AND EUN JEONG YANG

It is estimated that one in 10 youth in the United States will be of Asian origin by 2060 (Arora, Wheeler, Fisher, & Barnes, 2017). The Asian population in the United States grew significantly, approximately 72%, from 11.9 million to 20.4 million between 2000 and 2015, placing this group as the fastest growing among any racial and ethnic group in the United States (Pew Research Center, 2018). Asian Americans encompass diverse backgrounds with respect to national origin (or parents' national origin), culture, language, religion, social class, and experiences of immigration, and there are growing numbers of multiracial Asian Americans who identify with multiple racial, cultural, and/or religious backgrounds. In addition, there are numerous ethnic and national origins among Asian Americans, with Chinese, Indian, and Filipino Americans as the three largest Asian American subgroups, followed by Vietnamese, Korean, and Japanese Americans, with regard to population size (Pew Research Center, 2018).

Although different subgroups of Asian American adolescents (e.g., Bangladeshi, Cambodian, Chinese, Filipino, Indian, Japanese, Korean, Vietnamese) have distinct experiences of growing up and living in the United States, they share some common experiences as a function of being racial

http://dx.doi.org/10.1037/0000140-005
Multicultural Feminist Therapy: Helping Adolescent Girls of Color to Thrive,
T. Bryant-Davis (Editor)

minorities (Arora et al., 2017). Growing mental health concerns among these adolescents coexist with the pervasiveness of the model minority stereotype. The term *model minority* first emerged in the United States in the mid-1960s. It describes the image of Asian immigrants as successful ethnic minorities who realize the "American dream" by working hard and remaining silent or passive in the face of challenging circumstances and racial discrimination (Petersen, 1966; Alvarez, Juang, & Liang, 2006; Wong, Lai, Nagasawa, & Lin, 1998). Although the stereotype has somewhat evolved over the last few decades, the present-day version still retains an essential conceptualization of Asian Americans as highly successful academically, economically, and socially because of attributes such as intelligence, perseverance, diligence, hard work, and a belief in meritocracy (Yoo, Miller, & Yip, 2015). It also reflects the belief that Asian Americans experience minimal to no psychological distress and far fewer social, economic, or political barriers to success compared with other minority groups (Chao, Chiu, & Lee, 2010; Leong & Okazaki, 2009). Relatedly, psychological conceptualizations of the experiences of Asian American adolescents have either homogenized their experiences or contributed to the neglect of mental health problems and culturally informed interventions, and their lived experiences remain largely invisible in mainstream U.S. society.

In this chapter, we explore Asian American adolescent girls' experiences, particularly those of girls between ages 13 to 18 years, as situated in and driven by the broader U.S. context and the immigrant context. We recognize that Asian Americans are a highly diverse population within the United States, with important implications for the lived experiences of adolescents. Although the scope of this chapter does not allow for a detailed exploration of the experiences of girls from specific ethnic and religious groups, we are interested in highlighting experiences that may be shared by Asian American girls across different ethnic and religious backgrounds. Specifically, we focus on (a) mental health issues and barriers to receiving help; (b) acculturative stress and exposure to violence; (c) negotiation of identity; and (d) multicultural, feminist approaches to individual and group psychotherapy and community-based interventions. It is important to note that the experiences of Asian American adolescent girls have been understudied in psychology, and as such, this chapter includes a review of research that is largely nongendered (e.g., Asian American youth), with additional consideration given to literature relating to the specific experiences of adolescent girls. We recognize the complexity of individual and collective experiences that shape stress and resilience among adolescent girls from different Asian American backgrounds. As such, we provide two case illustrations highlighting how Asian American adolescent girls experience and cope with stress and negotiate their identities and relationships from a strength-based perspective. We also provide recommendations for therapists working with Asian American adolescent girls in psychotherapy.

MENTAL HEALTH CONCERNS

There has been growing evidence that Asian American adolescent girls are at high risk of depression, anxiety, eating disorders, substance abuse, and suicide (Nadal, Wong, Sriken, Griffin, & Fujii-Doe, 2015; S. Sue, Cheng, Saad, & Chu, 2012). A majority of studies comparing mental health and educational outcomes across immigrant generations indicate a phenomenon known as the *immigrant paradox*, where second and later generation Asian Americans have worse mental health (e.g., depression, anxiety, substance abuse) and educational outcomes compared with the first generation (Lau, Tsai, Shih, Liu, Hwang, & Takeuchi, 2013). These findings suggest differences in the ways that stress is experienced across immigrant generations. Asian Americans' mental health issues remain significantly understudied relative to other ethnic groups, and there is still limited knowledge about the prevalence of mental health problems among Asian Americans (S. Sue et al., 2012). In addition, Asian Americans are a diverse group with differences in factors such as national origin, ethnicity, socioeconomic status, migration history, and acculturation. As such, there are subgroup differences in the prevalence of mental disorders among Asian American populations (e.g., S. Sue et al., 2012). This heterogeneity of Asian American groups makes it challenging to draw conclusions about the prevalence of mental health problems among Asian Americans.

However, some research has suggested a greater prevalence of psychological distress among some subgroups, such as refugees and their children, with a higher degree of traumatic stress (American Psychological Association, 2012). Filipino adolescents have been found to experience higher levels of depressive symptomatology, suicidal ideation, and substance abuse compared with White adolescents and other Asian American adolescents (J. R. Javier, Lahiff, Ferrer, & Huffman, 2010). It is important to consider that different Asian American subgroups face unique challenges concerning migration history, premigration context, circumstances of migration, documentation status, and postmigration reception. For example, the history of colonization in the Philippines by the United States has been thought to contribute to a colonial mentality that is internalized, with implications for psychological oppression experienced by some Filipino immigrants in the United States (J. R. Javier et al., 2014; Nadal & Monzones, 2010). These premigration sources of stress can have an ongoing impact in the process of acculturation and psychological well-being among immigrants and later generations. For some Asian immigrants, threats of deportation and stress related to the lack of documentation or ambiguous documentation status pose ongoing psychological distress. As such, mental health concerns among Asian American subgroups should be understood within broader sociocultural contexts, including both premigration and postmigration experiences.

Depression and Suicidality

Asian American adolescents tend to experience higher levels of depressive symptomatology compared with White adolescents (Young, Fang, & Zisook, 2010), and Asian American girls have reported higher levels of depressive symptoms than Asian American boys (Otsuki, 2003). Strikingly, studies examining rates of suicide among White, African American, Latinx, and Asian adolescents and young adults in the United States have found that Asian American girls and women between ages 15 and 24 years have been found to have the highest rate of completed suicides compared with all other racial and ethnic groups (Arora et al., 2017; Centers for Disease Control and Prevention, 2014).

Anxiety

Results from research concerning the prevalence of anxiety disorders among Asian Americans are mixed. Asian American youth have been consistently found to report higher levels of general anxiety and social anxiety compared with White European American peers (e.g., Lau, Fung, Wang, & Kang, 2009; Okazaki, Liu, Longworth, & Minn, 2002). Yet, prevalence estimates of anxiety disorders among Asian Americans are lower than rates for other racial and ethnic groups in the United States, according to national epidemiologic studies (Asnaani, Richey, Dimaite, Hinton, & Hofmann, 2010). Anxiety among Asian American adolescents remains significantly understudied (H. Liu, Lieberman, Stevens, Auerbach, & Shankman, 2017). Most studies about anxiety among Asian Americans have included college student samples, and there is a paucity of research with adolescents. Scholars have called for more studies on anxiety among Asian American adolescents in relation to sociocultural variables, such as racially motivated peer discrimination, acculturation, and affect valuation (H. Liu et al., 2017).

Eating Disorders

In much of the psychological literature, eating and body image issues have been thought to primarily impact affluent European American girls and women (Smart & Tsong, 2014). Although there is considerable literature on the etiology and treatment of eating disorders, Asian American women were rarely included in research until recently (Smart, Tsong, Mejía, Hayashino, & Braaten, 2011). Research on eating disorders among Asian American women is far less thorough and has yielded mixed findings. For example, some studies have suggested that Asian American women have less body dissatisfaction than White women (Nouri, Hill, & Orrell-Valente, 2011), whereas others have indicated that Asian American women report body dissatisfaction at levels higher than or equivalent to that of young White women and experience similar adverse outcomes, including negative affect and disordered eating (Cummins & Lehman, 2007; Forbes & Frederick, 2008). Although eating disorders among Asian Americans are still not well understood, scholars concur that Asian American women are clearly at risk (Smart & Tsong, 2014). A meta-analysis by Wildes, Emery, and Simons (2001) concluded that Asian Americans had equal or greater rates of disturbed eating compared with White Americans. Despite reporting similar rates of eating disorder symptoms to White Americans, Asian Americans are less likely to be referred for evaluation of eating disorders, possibly due to their smaller body size and being stereotyped as a model minority group (Kawamura, 2012). Further, emerging empirical literature points to the relevance of racial discrimination as a risk factor for disordered eating among racial and ethnic minority women (Cheng, 2014; Velez, Campos, & Moradi, 2015).

Substance Abuse

In spite of the popular notion of Asian Americans as a model minority group, Asian American adolescent girls face an increased risk of substance use (Fang & Schinke, 2013). Trend statistics of secondary school students have suggested that Asian American girls have the largest increase of alcohol, marijuana, and stimulant use from eighth to 12th grade, compared with girls with other ethnic backgrounds (Wallace et al., 2003). Binge drinking among Asian American adolescent girls, as well as the prevalence of alcohol abuse among young Asian American females, has been continuously increasing (Grant et al., 2004; Hahm, Lahiff, & Guterman, 2004). Literature has suggested that increased acculturation (Choi & Lahey, 2006), low self-esteem (Otsuki, 2003), and depressive mood (Fang, Barnes-Ceeney, & Schinke, 2011) are the risk factors for Asian American adolescent girls' substance use. Family-level factors such as family functioning, parental monitoring, parent–child communication, and parent–child relationships have also been found to impact substance use among Asian American adolescent girls (Fang et al., 2011).

BARRIERS TO TREATMENT AND RISK FACTORS

It is well documented that Asian Americans use mental health services at lower rates than other racial and ethnic groups (e.g., Eisenberg, Golberstein, & Gollust, 2007; J. E. Kim & Zane, 2016). Linguistic barriers, economic challenges, immigration status, cultural and/or religious beliefs concerning psychological distress and healing, concerns about breaches in confidentiality and privacy, lack of access to culturally informed practitioners, shame, stigma, and experiences of racism are all thought to shape the decision to seek help (Chowbey, 2017; J. E. Kim & Zane, 2016; P. Y. Kim, Kendall, & Cheon, 2017). Some research indicates that higher levels of acculturation are associated with positive attitudes about seeking professional help (Fung & Wong, 2007). However, many Asian American adolescents are reluctant to share their psychological distress with their parents and other family members because they fear burdening others with their concerns. In some cases, adolescents decide not to share their concerns when they perceive that their parents will not understand or relate to the source of their stress. Indeed, many Asian American parents may not be prepared to identify psychological distress experienced by their children unless the distress reaches a level of crisis (e.g., suicidality).

In addition, expressions of mental health symptomology may be somatic, and as such, adolescents may attend to the physical nature of symptoms and may not consider psychological intervention to be helpful (Goldston et al., 2008). Adolescents may also prefer to seek out informal supports such as a religious figure, extended family member, or a friend to cope with mental health issues. They may also draw support from engaging in indigenous healing practice and religious traditions. For example, in some Indian American families, the practice of meditation, yoga, prayer, and Ayurvedic and homeopathic medicine is preferred as a way to approach sadness, anxiety, and other emotional concerns. Other healing approaches, such as herbal medicine, may be used among families with origins in various parts of Asia, such as China, Japan, Vietnam, and Tibet. Although some adolescents and their families may use these forms of healing, it is important to consider that most Asian American adolescents and their caregivers are unaware of how to access culturally informed mental health services, and the problem of recognizing psychological distress may be intensified by the internalization of the model minority stereotype and the minimization of psychological distress and stress related to sociocultural oppression (e.g., racism; Zhou, Siu, & Xin, 2009). In the following sections, we describe some risk factors related to acculturative stress and traumatic stress, all of which contribute to mental health concerns and challenges in accessing appropriate help. We also explore the implications of these concerns for the negotiation of identity.

Acculturative Stress

Acculturation experiences are gendered, as evident in differential expectations of girls and boys within ethnic and religious communities and within mainstream U.S. society (Qin, 2009). Due to their social position factors such as race, ethnicity, gender, English proficiency, and immigrant or refugee background, Asian American adolescent girls have distinct acculturation experiences in various contexts (i.e., family, school, peer groups, ethnic and religious communities). These separate contexts are not isolated from each other but interact with each other across time (Marks, Ejesi, McCullough, & García Coll, 2014; Qin, 2009) and influence the developmental trajectories and mental health concerns among Asian American adolescent girls.

Although acculturation offers opportunities for positive growth for Asian American girls, it can also contribute to stress. For racial minority immigrant-origin girls and women, racism, sexism, homophobia, ableism, and classism contribute to acculturative stress. Although there are numerous types of acculturative stress faced by Asian American adolescent girls, we highlight racial, ethnic, and religious discrimination, language barriers, socioeconomic status, and family expectations and intergenerational conflicts.

Racial, Ethnic, and Religious Discrimination

In spite of the popular notion that Asian American youth experience less intense racism and racial discrimination compared with other racial and ethnic minority groups, researchers have demonstrated that Asian American adolescents experience overt and implicit racism inside as well as outside of school settings (Tummala-Narra, Deshpande, & Kaur, 2016). Asian American children and adolescents are frequently bullied in U.S. schools (Tummala-Narra et al., 2016), and in fact, peer discrimination against Asian Americans has been found to occur with more frequency than that targeting other racial and ethnic minorities (Miller, Kim, Chen, & Alvarez, 2012). The racism that Asian American adolescents face manifests in various behaviors, including name-calling, racial or ethnic teasing, bullying, social rejection, vandalism of homes and places of worship, and physical violence (Alvarez & Juang, 2010). Studies have documented the association between racial, ethnic, and religious discrimination, including microaggressions and negative mental health outcomes among Asian American youth, including depression, anxiety, substance abuse, disordered eating, and suicidal ideation (Chang, Wong, Liu, & Tran, 2017; Cheng, Lin, & Cha, 2015; P. Y. Kim et al., 2017; Nadal et al., 2015).

Discrimination experiences in adolescence are especially problematic because this is a critical period when youth explore and develop their identities through interactions with others and are increasingly sensitive and attuned to others' perceptions of them (Sirin & Fine, 2008). As such, developmental transitions such as that from middle school to high school and from high school to college can be characterized by heightened awareness of racial, religious, and ethnic identities and experiences of marginalization and isolation. For Asian American girls who are biracial or multiracial or adopted by parents of an ethnic or racial background different from their own, experiences of discrimination are often directed by people both within Asian American and mainstream U.S. contexts (Crane, 2013; R. M. Lee, 2010).

It is important to note that the model minority stereotype is pervasive, with one study reporting over 99% of Asian American adolescents having had some encounter with being stereotyped as a model minority (Thompson & Kiang, 2010). For Asian American girls, the interaction of race and gender stereotypes results in distinct stereotypes including the China doll, geisha girl, lotus blossom, dragon lady, and tiger mom (Chang et al., 2017). The *China doll* and *geisha girl* stereotypes portray Asian women and girls as subservient and dependent. The *lotus blossom* image depicts Asian women as sexually pleasing to men and servile. The *dragon lady* stereotype depicts Asian women as exotic and manipulative, and the *tiger mom*, as controlling and relentless. These stereotypes about Asian American females reflect extreme types of characteristics such as being overly feminine, subservient (e.g., China doll), or castrating (e.g., dragon lady). These stereotypes are also highly sexualized, exoticized, and objectified, and they stand in contrast to other stereotypes of Asian American girls as quiet and nerdy. Stereotypes also vary across different Asian American subgroups. For example, stereotypes of South Asian girls can range from those reflecting exoticization and sexualization to images of these girls being unattractive, hairy, and smelly. South Asian girls are also often typed as passive, weak, oppressed, hyper-religious, or associated with terrorism. Muslim adolescent girls further contend with harassment and violence when they are marked as the other and the terrorist for wearing hijab or other religious symbols (Singh, 2009; Tummala-Narra et al., 2016). Studies have indicated that discrimination against Muslim adolescents in U.S. school settings by peers and teachers, in addition to that experienced in public spaces, is a cause of significant distress among these adolescents (Aroian, 2012; Sirin & Fine, 2008). The loss of sense of safety in school settings is especially daunting, considering the importance of peer and adult relationships in developing a sense of belonging in broader U.S. society.

In the context of gendered racism (Essed, 1991), Asian American adolescent girls face unique pressures to conform to racial and gender stereotypes (D. W. Sue, Bucceri, Lin, Nadal, & Torino, 2007). For example, Asian American girls are exposed to mainstream cultural ideals of beauty that reflect White middle class and Western typologies of appearance (e.g., slim build, light skin tone, tall height, long limbs, large breasts, blonde hair; Capodilupo & Forsyth, 2014). Asian American girls and women often strive to match the appearance ideals, which are mostly unachievable, to manage the fear of being racially singled out and the pressure to assimilate (Smart & Tsong, 2014). This may influence body dissatisfaction and disordered eating (S. J. Javier & Belgrave, 2015). Skin color, hair texture, and eyelid shape all become matters of conflict and stress for many Asian American girls who contend with negative familial and peer messages. In addition, physical characteristics, such as skin color, body shape, and eyelid shape, may be an explicit focus of criticism and hostility for girls experiencing interpersonal violence where the perpetrator devalues certain aspects of a girl's body, reifying gendered stereotypes. Attempts to cope with conflicts related to skin color and eyelid shape, in particular, are manifested in some girls' and women's attempts to lighten their skin tone through lotions and creams and to alter upper eyelid shape through surgery (M. R. Lee & Thai, 2015; Tran, Cheng, Netland, & Miyake, 2017; Tummala-Narra, 2007).

Language

Low levels of English proficiency of Asian American students in middle school have been linked to stereotyping, discriminatory experiences, and depressive symptoms (S. Y. Kim, Wang, Deng, Alvarez, & Li, 2011). A qualitative study of Asian American adolescents also revealed that adolescents were harassed by peers at school because of their English language skills and their nonstandard American accent (Qin, Way, & Mukherjee, 2008). Many first-generation immigrants report experiencing high levels of stress related to their own limited English language proficiency or that of their parents (Tummala-Narra, 2016; Zhang, Hong, Takeuchi, & Mossakowski, 2012). Even for second and later generation immigrants, it may be difficult to speak English like a native English speaker when a different language is spoken at home (Zhang et al., 2012).

Lower levels of English proficiency are also believed to be an important marker of "perpetual foreigner" status (Qin, 2009). It is important to note that language issues can also encompass the process of naming. Many Asian American girls have both ethnic heritage names and Anglicized names. At times, these names are chosen by their parents, and other times, girls and boys select their own Anglicized names. The experience of carrying two or more names is connected with acculturation, creating new identities, and efforts to eliminate problems with others' pronunciation of their ethnic heritage names (Tummala-Narra, 2016).

Socioeconomic Status

A common misconception regarding the socioeconomic status of Asian Americans is that Asian American families are generally well-adjusted and do not experience financial hardships compared with families from other racial and ethnic minority backgrounds. Federal reports do suggest that Asian American households report a relatively high median income (U.S. Census Bureau, 2011). These same reports, however, indicate that almost 12% of Asian American families live below the poverty line. This rate is similar to the rates among non-Hispanic Whites (U.S. Census Bureau, 2017). There is significant diversity within the Asian American population, and family socio-economic status depends on various factors, including parental education level, country of origin, reasons for immigration, and refugee or citizenship status (Kiang, Andrews, Stein, Supple, & Gonzalez, 2013). Importantly, some Asian subgroups (e.g., Cambodians, Hmong, Laotians) tend to face significant financial difficulties and stress (Leong, Park, & Kalibatseva, 2013).

Family Expectations and Intergenerational Conflicts

Many Asian American children and adolescents experience high levels of academic expectations from their parents because securing success and stability in broader U.S. society is a primary goal for immigrant parents. Qin (2009) pointed out that although many Chinese American parents perceive their parental role as working hard to provide for the economic and educational needs for their children, children may, in fact, long for their parents' emotional presence and support. This contrast in expectations can play a role in children's and adolescents' experiences of emotional disconnection from their parents.

In addition, research has suggested that Asian American girls face more complex challenges related to gender roles at home than Asian American boys. Asian immigrants, in coping with separation from a familiar cultural environment, often idealize the traditional family value system and gender roles of origin in their family environments (Mahalingam & Leu, 2005). Research has demonstrated that compared with their brothers, immigrant girls tend to be expected to complete more domestic chores and have more responsibilities at home, such as cooking, child care, translating, and advocating in financial, medical, and legal transactions (Suárez-Orozco & Qin, 2006). Asian American immigrant and refugee parents tend to have higher expectations for their daughters to embody traditional ideas than for their sons and monitor their daughters more than sons (Qin, 2009). For example, parents place stricter control over their daughters' activities outside the home compared with those of their sons and place more restrictions in daughters' dating, clothing styles, and makeup (Qin, 2009).

Intergenerational conflict within the family has been identified as a major contributor to psychological distress for Asian American youth, including low self-esteem, anxiety, somatization, and depression (Inman, 2006; Leu, Walton, & Takeuchi, 2011; D. J. Nguyen, Kim, Weiss, Ngo, & Lau, 2018). Conflicts in family relationships and loss of face, or the fear of losing a sense of social integrity or status within interpersonal relationships, have also been associated with Asian American adolescents' depression and alcohol use (Fang & Schinke, 2011; Kalibatseva, Leong, Ham, Lannert, & Chen, 2017). In addition, conflicts can arise because of linguistic and communication barriers between Asian American parents and adolescents (Tummala-Narra et al., 2016). In some cases, individuals within a family have different immigration status, with children being unaware of their parents', siblings', or their own undocumented status (American Psychological Association, 2012). In the present sociopolitical climate, fears of deportation for undocumented immigrants from Asian countries are heightened, contributing to additional stress within the family.

Intergenerational conflicts often coexist with family dynamics characterized by a sense of support, connection, and interdependence. Studies with Asian American adolescents have indicated that parental emotional support protects against anxiety and depressive symptoms (Arora et al., 2017; Han & Lee, 2011). Parental and family support can also facilitate adolescents' sense of connection and pride in their cultural and religious heritage, fostering self-esteem (Chang, Han, Lee, & Qin, 2015). Many Asian American adolescents perceive their parents as experiencing challenges in acculturation and make efforts to help their parents with both cultural and language acculturation. In such cases, adolescents experience the ability to help their parents as both a source of self-esteem and as a source of stress (P. V. Nguyen, 2008). Intergenerational conflict should be considered with an understanding of the interconnection between stress and resilience. When adolescents help their parents with translating both linguistically and culturally, they can feel burdened and at the same time feel pride in being able to provide support to their parents.

Collective and Interpersonal Violence

Many Asian American adolescent girls and their family members are exposed to a variety of traumatic experiences. With respect to political trauma, one poignant example is the experience of many Southeast Asian Americans. Various Southeast Asian groups began migrating to the United States in substantial numbers after the conclusion of the Vietnam War in 1975 and related political turmoil in surrounding countries. Thus, most Southeast

Asian Americans are either refugees or children of refugees, who have a migration history distinct from other Asian Americans. Studies have indicated higher rates of posttraumatic stress disorder, depression, and other mental illness among Southeast Asian American populations (Marshall, Schell, Elliott, Berthold, & Chun, 2005). Children of Southeast Asian refugees tend to experience higher levels of depressive symptoms, lower self-esteem, and disproportionately high rates of delinquency (Sangalang & Gee, 2015). Parental experiences of collective trauma can adversely affect family relationships and mental health of children and adolescents (Field, Muong, & Sochanvimean, 2013; Sangalang, Jager, & Harachi, 2017). Research has suggested that although Southeast Asian American students tend to be perceived by the larger society through the lens of the model minority stereotype (Reyes, 2007), they often endure lower expectations from teachers and school authorities, producing another stereotype of "problem minority" (Reyes, 2007).

Other Asian American subgroups have faced collective trauma in the United States, which impacts current generations of Asian American adolescents. For example, it is important to consider the collective traumas faced by Japanese Americans (e.g., internment camps, incarceration) during World War II, and its effects on subsequent generations of Japanese Americans (Nagata, Kim, & Nguyen, 2015). A poignant example of racial trauma in the 1980s was the murder of Vincent Chen in Michigan (in 1982) by two White men who beat him to death with a baseball bat after verbally assaulting him with racial slurs. In more recent years, post-9/11, South Asian Americans, particularly Sikhs and others perceived to be Muslims and terrorists, have been targets of discrimination, verbal assaults, physical violence, and murder (Ahluwalia & Alimchandani, 2013; Inman, Tummala-Narra, Kaduvettoor-Davidson, Alvarez, & Yeh, 2015). It is important to note that collective trauma experienced by Asian Americans is largely unpublicized and invisible within the mainstream American context. Yet, these forms of racial trauma have significant intrapsychic and interpersonal consequences, leaving Asian American adolescents living with apprehension, fear, and marginalization.

In addition to collective trauma, many Asian American girls and women face interpersonal violence. A majority of studies with Asian American women have focused on domestic violence and intimate partner violence. It is estimated that 20% of Asian American women report experiencing partner violence in their lifetime, approximately 57% of Asian American college students indicate experiencing psychological abuse by a partner, and 15% report experiencing sexual violence (T. Q. Nguyen et al., 2016). According to some estimates of interpersonal violence among South Asian communities in the United States, over 75% of women report intimate partner violence or domestic violence (Mahapatra & Dinitto, 2013; Raj & Silverman, 2007). In one study with South Asians in the United States (Robertson, Chaudhary Nagaraj, & Vyas, 2016), approximately 25% of women reported experiencing sexual abuse in childhood (Robertson et al., 2016). In addition, a significant number of people subject to sex trafficking and forced labor comprise Asian origin girls and women (Bryant-Davis & Tummala-Narra, 2017). These estimates signify a public health crisis concerning violence against women and girls in Asian American communities and the problem of children and adolescents witnessing violence in their homes. It has been noted that a patriarchal structure in Asian immigrant homes contributes to stigma and silence concerning sexual and physical violence and to challenges in recognizing trauma and accessing adequate help (Singh, 2009; Tummala-Narra et al., 2016). This is especially problematic because family and peer support is critical to recovery from traumatic stress.

Negotiation of Identity

Asian American adolescent girls' identity development takes place in the context of acculturation and acculturative stress, such as that related to discrimination, sexism, stereotyping, conflicting values between home and school, and possible language and financial barriers. Researchers have underscored the importance of bicultural identity in psychological well-being and suggested that immigrant-origin youth engage in developing a positive bicultural identity with a connection with the heritage culture as well as with the mainstream context (Tummala-Narra & Sathasivam-Rueckert, 2016). The navigation across different cultural contexts can be especially challenging in the case of biracial and multiracial and/or adopted adolescent girls and girls who identify as lesbian, bisexual, queer, transgender, or gender nonconforming because they may face marginalization both within and outside their ethnic and/or religious communities (Chong & Kuo, 2015; Crane, 2013).

Eng and Han (2000) described *racial melancholia* as an experience common to many Asian Americans as they negotiate challenges of being seen as a racial other, even when they have been born and raised in the United States. Specifically, they suggested that the model minority stereotype dismisses the reality of discrimination experienced by Asian Americans and becomes a "melancholic mechanism" (Eng & Han, 2000, p. 673). The internalization of the model minority stereotype serves to bring visibility to Asian Americans in the mainstream context under the guise of "positive" stereotype and at the same time diminishes the possibility of the American dream by marginalizing Asian Americans as the racial other. As such, Eng and Han emphasized the importance of recognizing this dilemma of the model minority notion and of mourning the loss of the ideal of Whiteness, which is unattainable for Asian Americans.

Such dilemmas concerning race and ethnicity intersect with other aspects of social location and identity such as gender, sexual orientation, social class, language, immigration status, sexual orientation, religion, and dis/ability. Asian American girls engage in identity work that encompasses multiple, intersecting aspects of sociocultural location and experience. They often operate within in-between or hyphenated spaces where they may feel connected and disconnected with any one particular context at varying times. The complex matrix of identity and intersectionality can involve a deep sense of pride in one's cultural heritage, movement away from one's cultural heritage, and other spaces in which girls explore their identities. Identity development is also dynamic and continues to be negotiated across the life span, shaped by relationships, life transitions, losses, traumatic experiences, and exposure to new sociocultural perspectives (Tummala-Narra, 2016). Increasingly, social media has played an important role in identity development as adolescents play with different aspects of their experience, often within spaces where they evaluate and are evaluated by others. Adolescent girls may experience hostility from others in these spaces but may also feel empowered to create and express new identities. The technological age has posed new possibilities for exploring intersectional identity and for developing connections with other Asian American adolescents who may have shared experiences.

Ethnic and religious communities can play an important role in Asian American girls' identities. Approximately 73% of Asian Americans identify with a religion, and 32% attend services at least once a week (Pew Research Center, 2012). In many Asian American immigrant communities, religious organizations provide sources of social support, opportunities for leadership, a sense of belonging, and resources that help individuals overcome the loss of social status and belonging resulting from immigration. Religious involvement also provides second and later generation Asian American adolescents with opportunities to sustain ethnic and religious identity through maintaining networks with those who share a common history and facilitates a sense of connectedness with one's cultural group (Davis & Kiang, 2016).

It is important to recognize that there are intragroup differences among Asian American subgroups with regard to the role of religion and spirituality (Davis & Kiang, 2016). For example, some Asian American families routinely engage with a religious and/or spiritual community that is a source of strength and resilience, whereas others actively disengage with religion due to past experiences of religious persecution or trauma. Although many adolescent girls find ways to engage in and draw emotional strength from spirituality, for some girls, heritage spiritual and religious beliefs can conflict with messages in mainstream U.S. society. For the latter group, the task of developing a spirituality that is strength based within a broader context with contrasting messages can be especially challenging (Ibrahim & Dykeman, 2011; Singh, 2009).

THERAPEUTIC CONSIDERATIONS AND RECOMMENDATIONS FOR THERAPISTS

The underutilization of mental health services in part results from the lack of services that are sensitive to the sociocultural and linguistic needs of Asian American girls and women (Kallivayalil, 2007; Tummala-Narra, 2016). In addressing the problem of underutilization and the inadequate access to mental health services and interventions, multicultural feminist frameworks present an important alternative to traditional Western European American therapeutic models.

One of the premises of feminist therapy is that problems are rooted in social, political, and cultural contexts. Feminist therapy views disempowerment and the consequences of powerlessness as central sources of emotional distress and behavioral dysfunction and has the goal of empowerment of clients (Brown, 2010). The feminist model of distress suggests that repeated encounters with overt and covert oppression, bias, and stereotyping create disempowerment and problematic self-schemata for individuals (Brown, 2010). Feminist therapy attempts to accomplish its goal of empowerment through several specific strategies, including the development of an egalitarian relationship, reframing of psychopathology into distress and dysfunction, gender role analysis and gender role intervention, assertiveness training, and taking social actions. Feminist therapy has gone through a number of significant transformations from the 1960s onward and has been criticized for neglecting the role of sociocultural factors such as race, ethnicity, language, social class, dis/ability, sexual orientation, religion, histories of colonization, and experiences of emigration and dislocation. Feminist multicultural scholars have, in response, proposed multicultural feminist therapy models that are more attentive to the realities of the diversity and complexity of women's experiences (Comas-Díaz, 2000). For many Asian American women, racism is a more powerful, visible, and day-to-day experience than sexism. However, the oppression of girls and women within some Asian American patriarchal cultures remains potent because many of these communities are based on a structural hierarchy of gender, age, generation, and well-defined gender roles (Kallivayalil, 2007). As such, it is essential to integrate both feminism and multiculturalism in working with Asian American adolescent girls and recognize the complexity of gender, culture, race, and other aspects of experience, such as sexual orientation, language, immigration status, religion, dis/ability, and social class, in their lives (Kallivayalil, 2007).

Literature in the 1990s concerning feminist therapy interventions with Asian women was largely conceptual, suggesting that feminist work can be inherently contradictory to Asian values. These perspectives suggest that Asian cultures based on collectivism and vertical hierarchy within families are incompatible with the assumptions and practices of feminist interventions that focus on self-assertion, autonomy, and individualism (Yick, 2001). Some South Asian scholars (Goel, 2005) also suggested that indoctrinated gender roles are rooted in long-respected myths and traditions. The self-sacrificial, interdependent role that has been prescribed to women for generations makes it less likely for girls and women to embrace interventions focused on autonomy and self-determination. The values inherent to psychotherapy are thought to reflect European, Western, and imperialist colonial influence, and women espousing these values may be perceived as not authentically identified with their South Asian heritage (Goel, 2005). Thus, therapists working with Asian American women might be concerned that the principles advocated by Western feminists can pose a threat to Asian cultural values and traditions, such as patriarchy, collectivism, and filial piety, and to traditional gender-role expectations. Furthermore, therapists may fear that encouraging female clients to question discrimination, oppression, and violence may cause even greater pain and create even more intense conflicts that jeopardize their positions within their own families and communities. As such, scholars have cautioned that some Asian cultural values may not be congruent with the aims of White feminist ideology and approaches to psychotherapy (Kallivayalil, 2007).

It is important to note that these tensions have promoted the idea that Asian women would respond to "practical approaches" of therapy and would not respond to insight-oriented therapeutic interventions (Preisser, 1999). Other scholars have suggested that the practitioner should use solution-focused approaches, provide more directive and less insight-based forms of interventions, and teach skills and practices that provide immediate symptom relief early on (Hsieh & Bean, 2014; Ting & Hwang, 2007). For example, Ting and Hwang (2007) suggested that therapists can gain credibility by presenting themselves as expert authority figures who can help the clients resolve their problems because many Asian cultures place greater importance on hierarchical relationships, social structure, and respect for authority figures.

However, other psychologists have challenged these overgeneralizations of Asian American women and girls and instead have developed multicultural feminist therapy with Asian American girls and women, emphasizing girls' and women's individual needs, relationships, and broader sociocultural contexts

(Chin, 2007; Crane, 2013; Patel, 2007). In their view, feminist and multicultural approaches to psychotherapy can be integrated with other approaches (e.g., humanistic, psychodynamic, cognitive behavior). Multicultural feminist scholars have emphasized the role of therapists' understanding of the client's sociocultural context and the examination of their own cultural history and its impact on the therapeutic relationship and have challenged the ways in which traditional theories have been conceptualized and implemented in psychotherapy (Crane, 2013; Hays, 2016; Tummala-Narra, 2016). These theorists have worked toward creating new spaces to explore the diverse experiences of Asian American adolescent girls and women. Although scholarship in this area encompasses various approaches to psychotherapy with specific subgroups of Asian American women, in the following sections, we highlight some of the ways in which scholars have advanced new conceptualizations of multicultural feminist interventions. We refer the reader to Appendix 4.1 for some recommendations for relevant activities developed from a multicultural, feminist lens that may be helpful in psychotherapy.

Individual Psychotherapy

Feminist multicultural theorists have challenged White, European American–centered models of psychotherapy by presenting womanist and *mujerista* frameworks, where women's indigenous cultural narratives and perspectives lie at the root of voice, empowerment, and therapeutic healing and change (Bryant-Davis & Comas-Diaz, 2016). A number of scholars have challenged White, European American–centered models of psychotherapy specifically with Asian American women. Jean Lau Chin (2007) argued that empowering Asian American girls and women to meet the cultural ideals of White women is neither culturally competent nor feminist. For example, assertiveness training, a strategy commonly used in Western feminist therapy to help girls and women to speak their voices, may not be appropriate for some Asian American girls and women if the therapist does not consider the different ways in which assertiveness is defined, valued, and demonstrated in a particular cultural context. Chin suggested that to empower girls and women in the Asian American community, it is imperative to replace negative, stereotypic images of Asian American girls and women with powerful images, including ancient mythological images. In Chin's perspective, the negative stereotypes of the exotic China doll and the passive, sexualized, self-effacing, and obedient Asian wife shift to other extreme images of the dragon lady and tiger mom when a girl or woman becomes assertive. Chin argued that therapists should help clients challenge these negative stereotypes without obliterating girls' and women's cultural values. To achieve this, she recommended that therapists use positive and powerful images from the client's heritage culture. For example, she suggested that reviving an ancient mythological image of a powerful woman warrior in China, where matriarchal social order preceded Confucian patriarchy, as a helpful path to empowering Chinese American girls and women.

Navsaria and Petersen (2007) noted the lack of attention to the role of spirituality and religion in the psychological well-being of Asian Indian and Indian American girls and women, specifically from Hindu backgrounds. They proposed that developing a psychotherapy model relevant to Hindu religion and culture can help girls and women explore issues of power and become empowered while remaining connected to their Hindu, Indian heritage and context. They suggested that the Hindu concept of Shakti, the spiritual feminine of procreative power who is a gentle protector and fierce warrior, would provide a more familiar agent of change for many clients. In this view, Shakti's dual nature is relevant to the dichotomous roles maintained by Hindu girls and women living in the United States. At the same time, the power of this Hindu goddess stands in contrast to many Indian girls' and women's experiences in patriarchal family systems (Singh, 2009). Navsaria and Petersen recommended incorporating Shakti in psychotherapy because it can provide a more familiar frame of discussing issues of power and control and help the client explore identity and expand and exert her choices. Diya Kallivayalil (2007) further elaborated on feminist therapy with South Asian girls and women in the United States. She emphasized the importance of the therapist and the client considering the role of patriarchy in women's and girl's experiences of constraint and/or traumatic experience. As such, feminist approaches with South Asian women and girls have increasingly attempted to address the complexity of power and constraint and strength and vulnerability, particularly within family contexts.

Reiko Homma-True (2017), a Japanese American psychologist, has written about her integrative approach to psychotherapy with Asian American girls and women, which integrates concepts from different traditions, such as psychodynamic therapy, cognitive behavior therapy, somatic therapy, and mindfulness meditation. She, among other scholars (Crane, 2013; Porter, 2015; Tummala-Narra et al., 2016), emphasized the diversity among Asian American girls and women with respect to race, ethnicity, acculturation, immigration history, educational backgrounds, and parental attitudes toward gender roles, as well as the role of interdependence and independence in the psychological lives of girls and women. Such diversity requires close attention to the particular sociocultural context of a client as it intersects with individual family history and circumstances.

Natalie Porter (2015) has written about the importance of feminist therapy engaging with some ways in which Asian American girls and women may adopt views of being superior with respect to their family values in contrast to White women in the United States. She proposed that the attempt to idealize patriarchy in the family structure may be shaped by a desire to "set themselves apart from White women and from the dominant culture's version of who they are" (Porter, 2015, p. 211). Although this position may provide a sense of pride in connection to cultural heritage, it can also serve to minimize women's and girl's needs within their families. In some cases, the inclusion of family members in psychotherapy with adolescent girls can help facilitate improved understanding and communication regarding family dynamics, family expectations, and psychological distress and for girls to develop ways to express their experiences and needs to their loved ones (Tummala-Narra, 2016).

Leilani Crane (2013) further explored the intersections of identity among multiracial Asian American adolescent girls and women. She highlighted that "whether or not the multiracial client specifically names identity issues as a concern in her life, she does consider identity, sense of self, and sense of self-efficacy salient in all treatment concerns" (Crane, 2013, pp. 275–276). Crane noted that multiracial girls and women are overlooked on interpersonal and institutional levels when their parents' experiences of immigration and acculturation are left unexplored. As multiracial Asian American girls and women are often perceived to have ambiguous physical features, they may experience conflicts with regard to developing a sense of belonging in any one particular context. Crane recommended that therapists attend to their own racial, cultural, and gender-related attitudes and values as they work with multiracial girls and women to expand a sense of agency, choice, and self-acceptance.

Multicultural feminist scholars emphasize consideration of the therapist's role in working with Asian American girls and women. Specifically, they value therapists' self-examination with regard to their sociocultural histories, gender socialization, social location, and life circumstances in relation to that of the client. The therapeutic relationship has been conceptualized as mirroring broader social structures and inequities, as evident in differences in power and privilege (Bryant-Davis & Comas-Díaz, 2016; Tummala-Narra, 2016). Multicultural feminist therapy involves the consideration of the relational dynamics between the client and the therapist that may reproduce social injustice (e.g., microaggressions) and the therapist's ability to engage in an honest exploration of these dynamics. It is also important that the therapist clearly assess her or his knowledge of the client's sociocultural background and context and work toward gaining such knowledge throughout the course of psychotherapy. It has been noted that techniques such as gender role analysis and power analysis can help clients to develop critical consciousness (Brown, 2010). However, it is critical that these techniques be guided with the assumption that sexism, racism, homophobia, and other forms of sociocultural oppression occur not only within one's ethnic and religious communities but also within broader U.S. society (Patel, 2007; Tummala-Narra, 2016).

Case Illustrations of Individual Psychotherapy[1]

Gita

Gita is a 14-year-old Indian American cisgender girl who was born in the United States. Both her parents were born in an urban area in India and moved to the United States to pursue job opportunities shortly after getting married. Her parents are practicing Hindus who are active in their temple and their ethnic community, primarily composed of Tamil-speaking Asian Indians. Gita had been close to her parents during her early childhood, but in the past 3 years she had become more withdrawn. She no longer confided in her parents or her older sister. In middle school, Gita's academic performance and her engagement in school declined, and she experienced increasing anxiety. Her mother, after seeking consultation from a primary care physician, urged Gita to meet with a therapist. Gita agreed to see a therapist but was concerned about whether she would be able to trust a therapist with details of her personal life. Further, she was worried about working with an Indian American therapist who she thought may have negative feelings or opinions about her.

In the initial session, Gita talked briefly about her experiences at home and school and asked me (PT-N, her therapist) whether I grew up in the United States. When I told her that I was born in India and raised primarily in the United States, she expressed relief that I had spent most of my childhood and adolescence in the United States. She stated, "I don't think I can really talk to someone like my mom or dad because they don't understand what it's like for kids here." In our initial sessions, Gita said that she cared deeply for her family but that she found it difficult to share details about her personal life with them. Specifically, she did not tell her family about her experiences of being harassed at school, when some of her peers would call her "an ugly foreigner" or "terrorist girl." These experiences felt extremely hurtful to her, and although she had friends who witnessed some of these incidents, they did little to actively speak back to the classmates who bullied her. Over the next several months, Gita revealed to me that she is queer and that she had not

---

[1] The details of the case studies have been changed to preserve the anonymity of the individuals involved.

come out to her parents or her sister. In fact, she was terrified to tell anyone about her sexual identity.

The therapeutic process involved attending to Gita's anxiety about her emotional safety at both her school and home. Initially, we focused on relaxation and breathing exercises in sessions, and then later Gita began to write in a journal about her feelings regarding her school and home experiences. As she connected more with these feelings, our conversations in psychotherapy shifted to her feelings about being constrained by others' expectations of her and her concern that I too may have expectations of her. In one session, I commented, "I wonder if you are worried that I too may have demands and expectations of you." She responded, "I feel like that with everyone. I don't want to let anyone down." Gita felt that she had to hide aspects of herself to be whoever other people needed her to be. She shifted from one context to the next without awareness of how this experience of shifting impacted her well-being. We increasingly spoke about how she felt the burden of managing my feelings about her struggles in psychotherapy. I was aware of the stigma concerning the issue of sexual identity in the Indian American community and felt concerned about how she may experience me and specifically how my Indian background may be associated with this stigma. I said to her, "It must be hard at times to tell me about your life and trust that I will be able to hear whatever you say and not feel burdened by it. It can be challenging to talk with another Indian person about your sexual identity." She expressed her relief in these moments and told me that she found it difficult to talk openly about her sexual identity in Indian and non-Indian contexts and that she wanted to try to trust someone else because it was too much of a burden to stay silent. She gradually spoke in more detail about her anxiety and sadness.

In subsequent sessions, Gita spoke about how she took pride in her academic work but resented her parents' high expectations of her and her sister. She did not want to be defined by her academic accomplishments and felt as though her parents would be ashamed of her if she did not achieve academically. Her fears of bringing shame to her family were most heightened when she thought about coming out as a queer person. At the same time, she resented not being able to be herself openly. She both dreaded and wished that she could be the first girl in her Indian community to come out and help other girls who were struggling with coming out to their families. She wanted to stay connected with her Indian community and her Hindu temple as a queer Hindu Indian American girl, an identity that was "forbidden." In one session, Gita said, "I want to be okay with myself. I actually am, but I don't think I can tell my parents, and then I have to deal with their reaction to me. I want to scream sometimes, just, like, tell everyone in my family and the temple that this is fine. It's normal, and I'm fine. It's not a sin."

Over the next several months, Gita, although remaining anxious, began to consider talking with her parents and her sister about her sexual identity. In sessions, she engaged in role plays with me as a way of preparing for her initial set of conversations with her family. She felt that it was important for her to come out to her family because she did not yet feel safe enough to come out to her friends at school. Gita worried that she would be bullied even more severely if people at school knew that she is queer. She eventually came out to her parents and sister, each of whom had their own set of reactions. They joined Gita in several sessions with me to better understand her experience and to talk about their sense of confusion and disappointment. These sessions also created a space for Gita to share her disappointment, sadness, anxiety, and isolation and for her family to engage more genuinely with each other.

This case description offers a glimpse into my work with Gita, illustrating how intersectional experiences across different sociocultural contexts (e.g., home, school), racism, heterosexism, and homophobia, and the dynamics of immigration can shape identity, relational conflicts, and emotional well-being. The case further illustrates Gita's resilience as she engages actively in her healing through her journal writing and through her willingness to imagine new possibilities for how she relates to others. Specifically, over the course of psychotherapy, by working through her conscious and unconscious fears of disclosing her experiences of self and others to me, she considered the possibility of not having to only present herself to others in the ways that they expected from her. Rather, she began to imagine having a sense of choice and agency in her life.

Ava

Ava is a biracial, heterosexual 17-year-old cisgender girl coping with posttraumatic stress after being raped by a boyfriend. She sought psychotherapy after disclosing to her mother that she had been raped. Ava's mother was born in Vietnam and fled by boat to the United States following the Vietnam War and met her husband (Ava's father) in the United States. Ava's father is a White Irish American man whose extended family is close to Ava. Throughout Ava's childhood, she interacted mostly with her father's family and learned about her mother's family through listening to stories from her mother. Ava's mother lost most of her family members, including her parents and siblings, in the war and had coped with depression for several years throughout Ava's childhood. There was tension between Ava's parents throughout her upbringing, and at several points, Ava worried that her parents would divorce. However, her parents, in more recent years, worked to resolve their conflicts with each other. Ava began dating a boy when she was 16 years old, and several months later, the boy raped her while they attended a party. Ava did not seek any medical care, although she had bruising in her genital area. She initially did not tell anyone about being raped and over the next several weeks and months became increasingly anxious and depressed. She had difficulty falling asleep, often had nightmares, and began to withdraw from interacting with her friends. When she brought up her distress with her boyfriend, he denied that he had raped her. A few weeks later, she ended the relationship. Her mother, after recognizing these changes in Ava, asked her whether something had happened to her. It was at this point Ava revealed that she had been raped.

In her initial session with me (PT-N), Ava expressed feeling sad and stated, "I don't know if I'll ever be myself again." She trusted her boyfriend and worried that she did something to cause the rape. She also doubted her judgment concerning her choice of a boyfriend. She stated, "I feel disgusting. I hate thinking about it and what he did. My body feels gross." Our work focused on her traumatic stress, including her negative feelings about her body and her distrust of boys. We also discussed her feelings about others' reactions to her rape. At school, some of her peers blamed her for ending the relationship with her boyfriend because they were unaware of the rape. At home, her mother was supportive in listening to her but did not know how to help her cope with the trauma. Her father was angry about the rape and told Ava that he did not want her to date boys. Other people's reactions contributed to Ava feeling as though she was somehow responsible for what happened. She stated in one session, "I am supposed to know how to deal with this. No one else knows how to deal with it. I'm alone." Her self-blame was often located within her feelings of "disgust" with herself and her body.

Over the course of our work, I asked her to tell me more about her feelings about her body. She gradually revealed that she had never been comfortable with her body and, more generally, her physical appearance and that being raped made her feel even more unattractive and undesirable than previously. She stated, "I was always seen as this Asian girl, even though I'm also White. No one in my school wants to date an Asian girl." Even though Ava interacted primarily with her father's side of the family and all her friends are White, others had typically perceived her as Asian because of her physical resemblance to her mother. She often fantasized about looking more like her paternal aunts and cousins and her friends at school. At the same time, she felt guilty about these fantasies because she was deeply connected with her mother. Ava shared that she felt angry when she heard people in her school or in social media denigrate how Asian women looked. She stated, "I hate hearing, 'Look at that Asian girl with the small eyes,' or 'I bet that Asian girl would listen to her man and do whatever he wants her to do.' It really bothers me, really pisses me off." Ava struggled with these messages, which came primarily from White people. Although she identified as both Vietnamese and White, in her early teens, she wanted to feel more accepted by some of her White peers. When she met her boyfriend, who is White, she had hoped that this relationship would help with her sense of belonging and acceptance in school. His betrayal left her feeling confused and isolated.

In the course of our work together, Ava, at times, asked me questions about my experiences. For instance, in our 4th month of working together, she asked whether I had ever been a target of racism. She posed this question in the context of our discussion regarding her own experiences of racism. I responded by telling her that I had experienced racism as well and asked her to share her reactions to my response. Ava told me that she was not surprised by my response and that she knew that South Asian women too face racism. She continued to talk about her anger toward injustice against girls and women of color, including racism directed toward her mother, and later about her feelings of guilt about being White and her feelings of anger about not being seen as both White and Vietnamese. She said, "The only people who seem to see that I am both are my parents and maybe now you." This was a critical moment when Ava could begin to experience her racial identity more fully. Our work then shifted to a discussion of how she could imagine that being biracial could be a positive force in her life, rather than something that was only painful. She continued to work through her complex feelings concerning her rape and her experiences of race both within and outside her family. She eventually decided to talk more openly with her parents and some of her close friends about these feelings. Toward the end of our work, Ava told me that she wanted to find ways to prevent date rape. She became active in a local network for adolescent girls focused on personal safety and empowerment. Ava continued to cope with her feelings of sadness concerning her rape and at the same time felt that she had a growing voice in her life.

Ava's case illustrates how many multiracial Asian American girls cope with discrimination and/or alienation in multiple familial and sociocultural contexts. Her traumatic experience not only caused severe psychological stress but also deepened her concerns about her body image and her sense of belonging in White racial contexts. Her experiences of interpersonal violence and racism further contributed to feelings of invisibility, specifically that others only saw one of her racial backgrounds. As such, it was critical that psychotherapeutic work recognized the impact of these racialized experiences and her rape on her relational life and psychological well-being and the unique ways in which she negotiated stress.

Group Psychotherapy

Traditional group psychotherapy approaches focused on self-disclosure, verbalization, confrontation, conflict resolution, individuation, and autonomy may not be appealing to some Asian American girls and women and can lead to disengagement or premature termination (Y. Liu, Tsong, & Hayashino, 2007). Y. Liu and colleagues (2007) developed culturally specific group counseling for Asian American girls and women integrating multicultural and feminist perspectives. In their group work with Asian American female college students, facilitators strived to build egalitarian relationships with clients. Facilitators honored clients' multiple cultural identities and lived experiences rather than presenting themselves as authority figures who help group members resolve cultural conflicts. To foster openness and trust in the group, facilitators used self-disclosures related to their gender, ethnicity, and culture. With two Asian American female college student groups, they observed central themes such as stigma of seeking psychotherapy, bicultural identities and their impact on interpersonal relationships including family relationships, experiences with racism and sexism in work and school settings, and internalized racism, including discomfort with their ethnic features and feelings of dislike toward Asian immigrants who had recently arrived in the United States. The group was able to provide validation from shared experiences and feelings and became a resource for students to discuss how to work through intergenerational conflicts with parents. The group also provided the opportunity to promote understanding of their concerns within the broader context of culture, race, gender, and society. Although the group members were able to connect with each other relatively quickly, facilitators observed tensions and conflicts among the students due to the differences in acculturation levels, generational status, socioeconomic status, and religion. Feminist multicultural approaches attend to these tensions and draw on strengths of individual group members and the interpersonal connections among group members to facilitate and shift the process toward empowerment for both the individual client and the group.

It is important to recognize that first-generation immigrants have distinctive experiences from later generation immigrants (Cheng et al., 2015; C. M. Liu & Suyemoto, 2016; Miller et al., 2012). As such, psychotherapeutic approaches should consider the unique experiences of Asian American adolescent girls from different immigrant generations. Literature concerning group psychotherapy approaches with first-generation Asian Americans has noted distinct ways in which women and girls may present and discuss their psychological distress. For example, S. Kim (2013) introduced group music therapy with first-generation Korean immigrant women that integrated culturally informed music therapy with feminist therapy. S. Kim noted that it is not encouraged in Korean custom to outwardly or freely express oneself in a group, especially when there is an authority figure present. Thus, Korean clients may appear to be submissive, remote, reluctant to share, or to not fully engage in group work (S. Kim, 2013). In the 6-month-long group therapy with Korean immigrant women, S. Kim helped group members use music, including Korean folk songs that were familiar to them, as a medium to express their homesickness and loneliness, struggles with cultural adjustments, issues of gender roles, and racism and discrimination. Group members reported, "We don't like to express our inner self, but through music, we are able to be expressive without concerning out pride." Many Korean traditional folk songs express traditional Korean women's pain, suffering, and sorrow, as well as their resilience (S. Kim, 2006). These songs convey the collective feeling of *Han*, a Korean term for "deep sorrow and anger that grow from the accumulated experiences of oppression" (E. H. Kim, 1995, p. 160). As group members developed egalitarian relationships not only with other members but also with the therapist, they began to voice themselves, take on more leadership roles, and reported feeling acknowledged, respected, empowered, and more confident.

Psychoeducation and Activism

A key aspect of multicultural feminist approaches involves psychoeducation that can be engaged in multiple forms of clinical and community-based interventions. Education and outreach can be particularly important in helping Asian American girls and women identify psychological distress and access adequate help in coping with this distress. School-based interventions can offer an increased understanding of the impact of stereotyping and discrimination on adolescents' psychosocial adjustment and academic life and the role of family dynamics, including parental expectations, in adolescent girls' well-being. Various scholars have written about the use of family-based interventions to increase awareness of mental health problems such as depression, anxiety, psychosis, and suicide among Asian American parents (Fang & Schinke, 2013; Kennedy, Schepp, & Rungruangkonkit, 2008). These interventions emphasize the importance of education regarding the nature and course of different mental health problems, connections among group members, the use of interpreters to facilitate clear linguistic and cultural communication, skills for coping with stress, and the recognition of cultural differences and similarities in group members' experiences (Kennedy et al., 2008).

Family- and group-based interventions are thought to be critical for Asian American girls and women, particularly in reducing their sense of isolation and marginalization. Some family-based interventions have also been used effectively for preventive purposes, such as those focused on substance use prevention, where Asian American adolescent girls and their mothers engage in developing the strength of their relationships through more effective communication (Fang & Schinke, 2013). Other family- and group-based interventions with Asian American parents aim to develop trust and engagement in coping with dilemmas of parenting in a new cultural context where parenting norms stand in contrast to those in their heritage cultures (Lau, Fung, & Yung, 2010; D. J. Nguyen et al., 2018). Each of these interventions emphasizes the importance of families and communities gaining knowledge, recognizing the needs of children and adolescents, addressing the problem of stigma, and developing skills to support their families.

Another important way in which Asian American communities engage in psychoeducation is through women's collectives. Most often, women's collectives form through women and girls informally sharing experiences of cultural adjustment in the United States. At times, collectives have been formed as a way of challenging silence and stigma within ethnic and religious communities, where certain issues such as violence against women are viewed as taboo topics. For example, Saheli (see https://saheliboston.org/), a women's organization based in the Boston area, developed through informal discussions among South Asian women who shared with each other experiences of immigration and parenting. This group has grown into a collective that offers support for women facing domestic violence, help with legal services, and economic empowerment for South Asian women. We emphasize the significance of informal sources of support such as women's collectives because these are often the spaces in which Asian American girls and women gain access to resources that are critical for their safety and well-being.

Asian American girls and women have also been increasingly active in advocating for the rights of undocumented immigrants, Deferred Action for Childhood Arrivals recipients, and women's reproductive rights. More recently, Asian American social and political youth groups and organizations, based in centers of worship, educational settings, and local, nonreligious communities, have provided spaces for Asian American girls to engage in social and political activism and leadership development. It is important to recognize that although Asian American girls often face significant pressure concerning academic performance and caring for others in their families, access to these opportunities for civic engagement and leadership offers new possibilities for empowerment and connection with others both within and outside their ethnic and religious communities.

Recommendations for Therapists

The following recommendations consider the diversity, strength, and resilience of Asian American adolescent girls. They also consider the challenges they face concerning their safety, well-being, identity, and relational life across multiple cultural contexts. As such, these recommendations attend to the complexity of Asian American girls' lived experiences (Tummala-Narra, 2016).

Attend to Family Immigration History and Dynamics

It is important for the therapist to learn about a girl's and/or her family's migration history, along with immigration status, if she is comfortable disclosing this to the therapist. The current sociopolitical climate concerning immigration policy warrants careful attention to immigration status. At times, crisis intervention may be most appropriate for girls and family members who are facing deportation or fear that one or more family members or friends may be deported. Further, learning about the premigration context can help the therapist and client to better understand the process of acculturation in the United States (Cheng et al., 2015). The family migration history can also inform family dynamics and interactions, including intergenerational conflicts. At times, it may be helpful to include family members in psychotherapy sessions as a way to facilitate more effective communication within the family and work through interpersonal conflicts. Such inclusion of family may help parents, siblings, and other relatives to identify girls' emotional distress and strategies to support healing (Lau et al., 2010; Zhou et al., 2009).

Listen for the Complexity of Narrative Concerning Acculturation and Identity

Therapists can achieve a more complete understanding of girls' acculturation experiences by inquiring about girls' experiences at home, school, workplaces, and social spaces, including social media. These are all spaces in which girls develop their identities and relationships and can potentially recognize both conflicts and opportunities unique to each space or context. It is also important to attend to how girls negotiate contradictory or conflicting messages concerning gender roles that they may receive from others in each of these contexts (Tummala-Narra, 2016). The negotiation of acculturative stress involves both strategies that can be adaptive, fostering resilience, and strategies that can pose further conflict and stress. Attending to clients' cultural narratives also encompasses the ways in which they conceptualize feminism. Asian American girls' conceptualization of feminism may be distinct from that of mainstream feminist views and typically remains invisible in mainstream contexts. Therefore, the therapist can play a critical role in helping the client explore and voice her conceptualization of feminism and its role in her life.

Use a Strength-Based Lens That Recognizes the Intertwined Nature of Resilience and Stress

Resilience from a multicultural feminist lens is multidimensional and culturally embedded (Bryant-Davis & Comas-Díaz, 2016; Chin, 2007). As such, therapists should consider how resilience may be conceptualized by girls and by significant people in their lives, such as parents, caregivers, teachers, friends, and extended family. At times, what is considered resilience in one context may contrast with conceptualizations of resilience in another context. These differences can pose stress but also offer new possibilities for empowerment as girls explore their ability to engage with different aspects of their identities. It is important that therapists recognize that adolescent girls' stress is often intertwined with resilience as they find new ways to navigate across multiple cultural contexts. Further, therapists should inquire about cultural symbols and narratives that are meaningful and empowering to girls. For example, for some Muslim girls, wearing the hijab is an act that stands against and rejects sexual objectification (Patel, 2007). Some girls may be empowered through engaging in consciousness-raising and social action in their ethnic and/or religious communities or the mainstream context. Others may find strength in artistic creation, academic pursuits, participation in sports, and leadership development. Hence, therapists must remain open to and explore various forms of resilience and empowerment that are personally meaningful to adolescent girls.

Attend to Language and Expression of Emotional Distress

Therapists should attend to the use and meanings of English and heritage language in psychotherapy. Specifically, they can explore the role of bilingualism or multilingualism and ethnic heritage names and Anglicized names in girls' experiences of themselves and their interactions with family and friends. Because different languages hold different emotional experiences (Akhtar, 2011; Tummala-Narra, 2016), it would be helpful to inquire about whether speaking in a specific language holds different meanings. Further, therapists should consider that girls in psychotherapy may express emotional distress in ways that are congruent with expressions of distress within their families and ethnic communities. For example, it may be more culturally congruent for some families that psychological distress is communicated through somatic symptoms rather than verbal expression. In these cases, therapists should inquire about how girls and their family members experience and communicate distress.

Recognizing the Role of Social Oppression and Trauma

It is critical that therapists recognize the role of discrimination and trauma rooted in gender, race, immigration status, language, sexual orientation, social class, religion, and disability on girls' lives and that they initiate an inquiry into discriminatory and racialized experiences in psychotherapy. The negative impact of stereotyping and discrimination on identity and psychological well-being can be profound, and as such, therapists should be prepared to challenge negative messages and images of Asian American girls and women and help girls navigate stereotyping and discrimination (Chin, 2007; P. Y. Kim et al., 2017; Yoo et al., 2015). In addition, therapists should recognize how intersecting forms of social oppression rooted in patriarchy, such as gendered racism, sexism, classism, heterosexism, and ableism, in ethnic and religious communities impact girls' internal and relational lives. It is also essential that therapists explore the role of interpersonal violence and collective violence experienced by girls and their family members (Bryant-Davis, Chung, & Tillman, 2009). Therapists can help girls explore ways of coping with discrimination and trauma with a consideration of different conceptualizations of trauma and recovery within multiple contexts (e.g., home, ethnic and/or religious community, school, peer group, social media community).

Engage in Self-Examination

Therapists must engage in reflection concerning their life histories and socialization concerning gender, race, immigration, language, sexual orientation, religion, social class, and disability throughout their careers. Because the therapeutic relationship can mirror broader social dynamics (e.g., through transference and countertransference), the therapist has to be able to recognize when she or he may collude with racist, sexist, heterosexist, classist, and ableist notions about girls and women or dismiss the role of sociocultural issues in girls' experiences (Bryant-Davis & Comas Díaz, 2016; Patel, 2007; Yi, 2014). Therapists should also examine their worldviews concerning their understanding of pathology and resilience and develop the willingness and ability to consider worldviews that contrast from these worldviews. A personal commitment to diversity and the recognition that engaging in multicultural learning is a lifelong process is essential to developing an ability to listen to the client's cultural narrative (Tummala-Narra, 2016).

CONCLUSION

Asian American adolescent girls are a diverse group of individuals with myriad life experiences rooted in cultural, linguistic, and religious heritage; premigration family histories; and postmigration experiences. They experience acculturative stress in ways that are uniquely tied to their racial, ethnic, linguistic, and religious backgrounds in the context of living in the United

States. Racialized perceptions of Asian American adolescent girls influence how girls negotiate acculturative stress and identity and experience psychological well-being. It is important to note that many Asian American girls cope with trauma and mental health concerns that are either invisible to others or remain unidentified until these concerns reach crisis levels. Multicultural feminist approaches that closely examine the full complexity of adolescent girls' experiences are critical to formulating interventions that address their stress across multiple contexts (e.g., families, schools, broader U.S. sociopolitical context, social media) and how they negotiate resilience in the face of this stress. Resilience should be conceptualized with an understanding of the importance of girls' connection to their families and communities and to their sense of agency in developing their multicultural and/or multiracial identities.

APPENDIX 4.1: SPECIFIC ACTIVITIES RECOMMENDED FOR THERAPISTS

"MASK" ACTIVITY: INDIVIDUAL AND GROUP THERAPY

The purpose of this activity is to provide clients a chance to identify the stereotypes, prejudice, and bias they experience as well as to express who they believe they really are. Provide your clients with an art therapy mask and let them choose among the male, female, or neutral versions. You can easily find and print out various types of mask drawings online. Have various art tools available such as pens, colored pencils, markers, and crayons. Ask your clients to use the front of the mask to depict how they believe others see them through the use of drawings, symbols, or just words if they do not feel comfortable with their art skills. On the back of the mask, ask them to write down how they see themselves, especially in ways that differ from the front of the mask. Allow your clients to share and discuss the masks. Ask clients to read out loud what they wrote about how they see themselves (e.g., "I am . . .") on the back of the mask. (See https://www.therapistaid. com/therapy-worksheet/art-therapy-masks for more information.)

"ASIAN AMERICAN WOMEN LEADERS" ACTIVITY: INDIVIDUAL AND GROUP THERAPY

The goal of this activity is to help clients identify Asian American female role models or identify positive and powerful images of Asian American women who have drawn strength from their Asian cultural heritage as well as from the dominant U.S. culture. Help each of your clients find an Asian American woman leader who can inspire them. Encourage clients to find more information about those women's life stories. Share life stories and discuss how race, gender, immigrant background, and other social position factors, as well as their bicultural or multicultural and/or multiracial identities, have been impacting their lives.

"MY FULLEST NAME" ACTIVITY: INDIVIDUAL GROUP THERAPY

The goal of this activity is to help clients to reflect on their identities related to their names and share aspects of their backgrounds (e.g., culture, ethnicity, language). Ask clients to write out their full names and tell stories related to their names. Many Asian American girls have ethnic heritage names and English names, and therefore, it would be helpful to explore these different names. The therapist can encourage participants to share any meanings, cultural significance, specific ancestors, or any background stories relevant to their names. (See Goldbach, 2017, for more information.) Therapists can ask clients the following questions to facilitate the process:

- Who gave you your name(s)? Do you know any background stories about why they gave you the name(s)?
- Do you know the ethnic origin of your name(s)?
- Do you have any nicknames? If so, how did you get them? What is your preferred name?

"IDENTITY WHEEL" ACTIVITY

The purpose of the identity wheel activity is to encourage clients to identify and reflect on their various identities. First, ask your clients to write down all aspects of their identities (e.g., race, ethnicity, age, occupation, religion, gender, languages, sexual orientation, socioeconomic background, dis/ability, immigration background). Help them create a pie chart that depicts these aspects of identity. Ask clients to make the size of each part of the pie related to how much they are aware of each identity on a daily basis. Encourage them to discuss each of their identities on the pie chart. (See http://schd.ws/ hosted_files/2016uppermidwestcivicengagements/5e/06_23_PersonalIdentity

WheelExercise_592.pdf for more information.) Therapists can ask the following questions to facilitate conversations:

- Which identities are you more aware of?
- Which identities are the targets of prejudice and discrimination? Which identities are privileged and advantaged?
- Which identities do you take for granted and not think about often?

REFERENCES

Ahluwalia, M. K., & Alimchandani, A. (2013). A call to integrate religious communities into practice: The case of Sikhs. *The Counseling Psychologist, 41,* 931–956. http://dx.doi.org/10.1177/0011000012458808

Akhtar, S. (2011). *Immigration and acculturation: Mourning, adaptation, and the next generation.* New York, NY: Jason Aronson.

Alvarez, A. N., & Juang, L. P. (2010). Filipino Americans and racism: A multiple mediation model of coping. *Journal of Counseling Psychology, 57,* 167–178. http://dx.doi.org/10.1037/a0019091

Alvarez, A. N., Juang, L., & Liang, C. T. H. (2006). Asian Americans and racism: When bad things happen to "model minorities." *Cultural Diversity and Ethnic Minority Psychology, 12,* 477–492. http://dx.doi.org/10.1037/1099-9809.12.3.477

American Psychological Association, Presidential Task Force on Immigration. (2012). *Crossroads: The psychology of immigration in the new century.* Retrieved from http://www.apa.org/topics/immigration/report.aspx

Aroian, K. J. (2012). Discrimination against Muslim American adolescents. *The Journal of School Nursing, 28,* 206–213. http://dx.doi.org/10.1177/1059840511432316

Arora, P. G., Wheeler, L. A., Fisher, S., & Barnes, J. (2017). A prospective examination of anxiety as a predictor of depressive symptoms among Asian American early adolescent youth: The role of parent, peer, and teacher support and school engagement. *Cultural Diversity and Ethnic Minority Psychology, 23,* 541–550. http://dx.doi.org/10.1037/cdp0000168

Asnaani, A., Richey, J. A., Dimaite, R., Hinton, D. E., & Hofmann, S. G. (2010). A cross-ethnic comparison of lifetime prevalence rates of anxiety disorders. *Journal of Nervous and Mental Disease, 198,* 551–555. http://dx.doi.org/10.1097/NMD.0b013e3181ea169f

Brown, L. S. (2010). *Feminist therapy.* Washington, DC: American Psychological Association.

Bryant-Davis, T., Chung, H., & Tillman, S. (2009). From the margins to the center: Ethnic minority women and the mental health effects of sexual assault. *Trauma, Violence, & Abuse, 10,* 330–357. http://dx.doi.org/10.1177/1524838009339755

Bryant-Davis, T., & Comas-Díaz, L. (Eds.). (2016). *Womanist and* mujerista *psychologies: Voices of fire, acts of courage.* Washington, DC: American Psychological Association. http://dx.doi.org/10.1037/14937-000

Bryant-Davis, T., & Tummala-Narra, P. (2017). Cultural oppression and human trafficking: Exploring the role of racism and ethnic bias [Special issue]. *Women & Therapy, 40,* 152–169. http://dx.doi.org/10.1080/02703149.2016.1210964

Capodilupo, C. M., & Forsyth, J. M. (2014). Consistently inconsistent: A review of the literature on eating disorders and body image among women of color. In M. L. Miville & A. D. Ferguson (Eds.), *Handbook of race-ethnicity and gender in psychology* (pp. 343–359). New York, NY: Springer. http://dx.doi.org/10.1007/978-1-4614-8860-6_16

Centers for Disease Control and Prevention. (2014). *Leading causes of death in females, 2014* (current listing). Retrieved from https://www.cdc.gov/women/lcod/2014/asian-pacific/

Chang, T.-F., Han, E.-J., Lee, J.-S., & Qin, D. B. (2015). Korean American adolescent ethnic-identity pride and psychological adjustment: Moderating effects of parental support and school environment. *Asian American Journal of Psychology, 6,* 190–199. http://dx.doi.org/10.1037/aap0000016

Chang, T. K., Wong, Y. J., Liu, T., & Tran, K. (2017). Asian American female college students' subjective femininity conceptualizations: Using a mixed-methods approach. *Journal of Multicultural Counseling and Development, 45,* 260–275. http://dx.doi.org/10.1002/jmcd.12077

Chao, M. M., Chiu, C., & Lee, J. S. (2010). Asians as the model minority: Implications for US Governments policies. *Asian Journal of Social Psychology, 13,* 44–52. http://dx.doi.org/10.1111/j.1467-839X.2010.01299.x

Cheng, H. (2014). Disordered eating among Asian/Asian American women. *The Counseling Psychologist, 42,* 821–851. http://dx.doi.org/10.1177/0011000014535472

Cheng, H., Lin, S., & Cha, C. H. (2015). Perceived discrimination, intergenerational family conflicts, and depressive symptoms in foreign-born and U.S.-born Asian American emerging adults. *Asian American Journal of Psychology, 6,* 107–116. http://dx.doi.org/10.1037/a0038710

Chin, J. L. (2007). Psychotherapy for Asian American woman warriors. *Women & Therapy, 30,* 7–16. http://dx.doi.org/10.1300/J015v30n03_02

Choi, Y., & Lahey, B. B. (2006). Testing the model minority stereotype: Youth behaviors across racial and ethnic groups. *Social Service Review, 80,* 419–452. http://dx.doi.org/10.1086/505288

Chong, V., & Kuo, B. C. (2015). Racial identity profiles of Asian-White biracial young adults: Testing a theoretical model with cultural and psychological correlates. *Asian American Journal of Psychology, 6,* 203–212. http://dx.doi.org/10.1037/aap0000022

Chowbey, P. (2017). Women's narratives of economic abuse and financial strategies in Britain and South Asia. *Psychology of Violence, 7,* 459–468. http://dx.doi.org/10.1037/vio0000110

Comas-Díaz, L. (2000). An ethnopolitical approach to working with people of color. *American Psychologist, 55,* 1319–1325. http://dx.doi.org/10.1037/0003-066X.55.11.1319

Crane, L. S. (2013). Multiracial daughters of Asian immigrants: Identity and agency. *Women & Therapy, 36,* 268–285. http://dx.doi.org/10.1080/02703149.2013.797776

Cummins, L. H., & Lehman, J. (2007). Eating disorders and body image concerns in Asian American women: Assessment and treatment from a multicultural and feminist perspective. *Eating Disorders, 15,* 217–230. http://dx.doi.org/10.1080/10640260701323474

Davis, R. F., III, & Kiang, L. (2016). Religious identity, religious participation, and psychological well-being in Asian American Adolescents. *Journal of Youth and Adolescence, 45*, 532–546. http://dx.doi.org/10.1007/s10964-015-0350-9

Eisenberg, D., Golberstein, E., & Gollust, S. E. (2007). Help-seeking and access to mental health care in a university student population. *Medical Care, 45*, 594–601. http://dx.doi.org/10.1097/MLR.0b013e31803bb4c1

Eng, D. L., & Han, S. (2000). A dialogue on racial melancholia. *Psychoanalytic Dialogues, 10*, 667–700. http://dx.doi.org/10.1080/10481881009348576

Essed, P. (1991). *Understanding everyday racism.* Newbury Park, CA: Sage.

Fang, L., Barnes-Ceeney, K., & Schinke, S. P. (2011). Substance use behavior among early-adolescent Asian American girls: The impact of psychological and family factors. *Women & Health, 51*, 623–642. http://dx.doi.org/10.1080/03630242.2011.616575

Fang, L., & Schinke, S. P. (2011). Alcohol use among Asian American adolescent girls: The impact of immigrant generation status and family relationships. *Journal of Ethnicity in Substance Abuse, 10*, 275–294. http://dx.doi.org/10.1080/15332640.2011.623484

Fang, L., & Schinke, S. P. (2013). Two-year outcomes of a randomized, family-based substance use prevention trial for Asian American adolescent girls. *Psychology of Addictive Behaviors, 27*, 788–798. http://dx.doi.org/10.1037/a0030925

Field, N. P., Muong, S., & Sochanvimean, V. (2013). Parental styles in the intergenerational transmission of trauma stemming from the Khmer Rouge regime in Cambodia. *American Journal of Orthopsychiatry, 83*, 483–494. http://dx.doi.org/10.1111/ajop.12057

Forbes, G. B., & Frederick, D. A. (2008). The UCLA body project II: Breast and body dissatisfaction among African, Asian, European, and Hispanic American college women. *Sex Roles, 58*, 449–457. http://dx.doi.org/10.1007/s11199-007-9362-6

Fung, K., & Wong, Y. L. (2007). Factors influencing attitudes towards seeking professional help among East and Southeast Asian immigrant and refugee women. *International Journal of Social Psychiatry, 53*, 216–231. http://dx.doi.org/10.1177/0020764006074541

Goel, R. (2005). Sita's Trousseau: Restorative justice, domestic violence, and South Asian culture. *Violence Against Women, 11*, 639–665. http://dx.doi.org/10.1177/1077801205274522

Goldbach, J. (2017, October 25). *Diversity toolkit: A guide to discussing identity, power and privilege.* Retrieved from https://msw.usc.edu/mswusc-blog/diversity-workshop-guide-to-discussing-identity-power-and-privilege/#name

Goldston, D. B., Molock, S. D., Whitbeck, L. B., Murakami, J. L., Zayas, L. H., & Hall, G. C. (2008). Cultural considerations in adolescent suicide prevention and psychosocial treatment. *American Psychologist, 63*, 14–31. http://dx.doi.org/10.1037/0003-066X.63.1.14

Grant, B. F., Dawson, D. A., Stinson, F. S., Chou, S. P., Dufour, M. C., & Pickering, R. P. (2004). The 12-month prevalence and trends in *DSM–IV* alcohol abuse and dependence: United States, 1991–1992 and 2001–2002. *Drug and Alcohol Dependence, 74*, 223–234. http://dx.doi.org/10.1016/j.drugalcdep.2004.02.004

Hahm, H. C., Lahiff, M., & Guterman, N. B. (2004). Asian American adolescents' acculturation, binge drinking, and alcohol- and tobacco-using peers. *Journal of Community Psychology, 32*, 295–308. http://dx.doi.org/10.1002/jcop.20002

Han, M., & Lee, M. (2011). Risk and protective factors contributing to depressive symptoms in Vietnamese American college students. *Journal of College Student Development, 52*, 154–166. http://dx.doi.org/10.1353/csd.2011.0032

Hays, P. A. (2016). *Addressing cultural complexities in practice: Assessment, diagnosis, and therapy*. Washington, DC: American Psychological Association. http://dx.doi.org/10.1037/14801-000

Homma-True, R. (2017). Feminist psychology and psychotherapy: A personal journey. *Women & Therapy, 40*, 427–441. http://dx.doi.org/10.1080/02703149.2017.1241584

Hsieh, A. L., & Bean, R. A. (2014). Understanding familial/cultural factors in adolescent depression: A culturally-competent treatment for working with Chinese American families. *American Journal of Family Therapy, 42*, 398–412. http://dx.doi.org/10.1080/01926187.2014.884414

Ibrahim, F. A., & Dykeman, C. (2011). Counseling Muslim Americans: Cultural and spiritual assessments. *Journal of Counseling & Development, 89*, 387–396. http://dx.doi.org/10.1002/j.1556-6676.2011.tb02835.x

Inman, A. G. (2006). South Asian women: Identities and conflicts. *Cultural Diversity and Ethnic Minority Psychology, 12*(2), 306–319. http://dx.doi.org/10.1037/1099-9809.12.2.306

Inman, A. G., Tummala-Narra, P., Kaduvettoor-Davidson, A., Alvarez, A. N., & Yeh, C. J. (2015). Perceptions of race-based discrimination among first-generation Asian Indians in the United States. *The Counseling Psychologist, 43*, 217–247. http://dx.doi.org/10.1177/0011000014566992

Javier, J. R., Lahiff, M., Ferrer, R. R., & Huffman, L. C. (2010). Examining depressive symptoms and use of counseling in the past year among Filipino and non-Hispanic White adolescents in California. *Journal of Developmental and Behavioral Pediatrics, 31*, 295–303. http://dx.doi.org/10.1097/DBP.0b013e3181dbadc7

Javier, J. R., Supan, J., Lansang, A., Beyer, W., Kubicek, K., & Palinkas, L. A. (2014). Preventing Filipino mental health disparities: Perspectives from adolescents, caregivers, providers, and advocates. *Asian American Journal of Psychology, 5*, 316–324. http://dx.doi.org/10.1037/a0036479

Javier, S. J., & Belgrave, F. Z. (2015). An examination of influences on body dissatisfaction among Asian American college females: Do family, media, or peers play a role? *Journal of American College Health, 63*, 579–583. http://dx.doi.org/10.1080/07448481.2015.1031240

Kalibatseva, Z., Leong, F. T. L., Ham, E. H., Lannert, B. K., & Chen, Y. (2017). Loss of face, intergenerational family conflict, and depression among Asian American and European American college students. *Asian American Journal of Psychology, 8*, 126–133. http://dx.doi.org/10.1037/aap0000067

Kallivayalil, D. (2007). Feminist therapy: Its use and implications for south Asian immigrant survivors of domestic violence. *Women & Therapy, 30*, 109–127. http://dx.doi.org/10.1300/J015v30n03_09

Kawamura, K. Y. (2012). Asian American body images. In T. F. Cash & L. Smolak (Eds.), *Body image: A handbook of science, practice, and prevention* (2nd ed., pp. 229–236). New York, NY: Guilford Press.

Kennedy, M. G., Schepp, K. G., & Rungruangkonkit, S. (2008). Experiences of Asian American parents in a group intervention for youth with schizophrenia. *Journal of Child and Adolescent Psychiatric Nursing, 21,* 220–227. http://dx.doi.org/10.1111/j.1744-6171.2008.00138.x

Kiang, L., Andrews, K., Stein, G. L., Supple, A. J., & Gonzalez, L. M. (2013). Socioeconomic stress and academic adjustment among Asian American adolescents: The protective role of family obligation. *Journal of Youth and Adolescence, 42,* 837–847. http://dx.doi.org/10.1007/s10964-013-9916-6

Kim, E. H. (1995). Home is where the Han is. In K. Mehuron & G. Percesepe (Eds.), *Free spirits: Feminist philosophers on culture* (pp. 160–173). Englewood Cliffs, NJ: Prentice Hall.

Kim, J. E., & Zane, N. (2016). Help-seeking intentions among Asian American and White American students in psychological distress: Application of the health belief model. *Cultural Diversity and Ethnic Minority Psychology, 22,* 311–321. http://dx.doi.org/10.1037/cdp0000056

Kim, P. Y., Kendall, D. L., & Cheon, H. S. (2017). Racial microaggressions, cultural mistrust, and mental health outcomes among Asian American college students. *American Journal of Orthopsychiatry, 87,* 663–670. http://dx.doi.org/10.1037/ort0000203

Kim, S.-A. (2006). Feminism and music therapy in Korea. In S. Hadley (Ed.), *Feminist perspectives on music therapy* (pp. 127–156). Gilsum, NH: Barcelona.

Kim, S.-A. (2013). Re-discovering voice: Korean immigrant women in group music therapy. *The Arts in Psychotherapy, 40,* 428–435. http://dx.doi.org/10.1016/j.aip.2013.05.005

Kim, S. Y., Wang, Y., Deng, S., Alvarez, R., & Li, J. (2011). Accent, perpetual foreigner stereotype, and perceived discrimination as indirect links between English proficiency and depressive symptoms in Chinese American adolescents. *Developmental Psychology, 47,* 289–301. http://dx.doi.org/10.1037/a0020712

Lau, A. S., Fung, J., Wang, S. W., & Kang, S. M. (2009). Explaining elevated social anxiety among Asian Americans: Emotional attunement and a cultural double bind. *Cultural Diversity and Ethnic Minority Psychology, 15,* 77–85. http://dx.doi.org/10.1037/a0012819

Lau, A. S., Fung, J. J., & Yung, V. (2010). Group parent training with immigrant Chinese families: Enhancing engagement and augmenting skills training. *Journal of Clinical Psychology, 66,* 880–894. http://dx.doi.org/10.1002/jclp.20711

Lau, A. S., Tsai, W., Shih, J., Liu, L. L., Hwang, W. C., & Takeuchi, D. T. (2013). The immigrant paradox among Asian American women: Are disparities in the burden of depression and anxiety paradoxical or explicable? *Journal of Consulting and Clinical Psychology, 81,* 901–911. http://dx.doi.org/10.1037/a0032105

Lee, M. R., & Thai, C. J. (2015). Asian American phenotypicality and experiences of psychological distress: More than meets the eyes. *Asian American Journal of Psychology, 6,* 242–251. http://dx.doi.org/10.1037/aap0000015

Lee, R. M. (2010). Parental perceived discrimination as a postadoption risk factor for internationally adopted children and adolescents. *Cultural Diversity and Ethnic Minority Psychology, 16,* 493–500. http://dx.doi.org/10.1037/a0020651

Leong, F., Park, Y. S., & Kalibatseva, Z. (2013). Disentangling immigrant status in mental health: Psychological protective and risk factors among Latino and Asian American immigrants. *American Journal of Orthopsychiatry, 83,* 361–371. http://dx.doi.org/10.1111/ajop.12020

Leong, F. T. L., & Okazaki, S. (2009). History of Asian American psychology. *Cultural Diversity and Ethnic Minority Psychology, 15,* 352–362. http://dx.doi.org/10.1037/a0016443

Leu, J., Walton, E., & Takeuchi, D. (2011). Contextualizing acculturation: Gender, family, and community reception influences on Asian immigrant mental health. *American Journal of Community Psychology, 48*, 168–180. http://dx.doi.org/10.1007/s10464-010-9360-7

Liu, C. M., & Suyemoto, K. L. (2016). The effects of racism-related stress on Asian Americans: Anxiety and depression among different generational statuses. *Asian American Journal of Psychology, 7*, 137–146. http://dx.doi.org/10.1037/aap0000046

Liu, H., Lieberman, L., Stevens, E. S., Auerbach, R. P., & Shankman, S. A. (2017). Using a cultural and RDoC framework to conceptualize anxiety in Asian Americans. *Journal of Anxiety Disorders, 48*, 63–69. http://dx.doi.org/10.1016/j.janxdis.2016.09.006

Liu, Y., Tsong, Y., & Hayashino, D. (2007). Group counseling with Asian American women. *Women & Therapy, 30*, 193–208. http://dx.doi.org/10.1300/J015v30n03_14

Mahalingam, R., & Leu, J. (2005). Culture, essentialism, immigration and representations of gender. *Theory & Psychology, 15*, 839–860. http://dx.doi.org/10.1177/0959354305059335

Mahapatra, N., & Dinitto, D. M. (2013). Help-seeking behaviors of South Asian women experiencing domestic violence in the United States. *Partner Abuse, 4*, 295–313. http://dx.doi.org/10.1891/1946-6560.4.3.295

Marks, A. K., Ejesi, K., McCullough, M. B., & García Coll, C. (2014). Developmental implications of discrimination. In R. Lerner (Ed.), *Handbook of child psychology and developmental science* (7th ed., Vol. 3, pp. 1–42). Hoboken, NJ: Wiley.

Marshall, G. N., Schell, T. L., Elliott, M. N., Berthold, S. M., & Chun, C. A. (2005, August 3). Mental health of Cambodian refugees 2 decades after resettlement in the United States. *JAMA, 294*, 571–579. http://dx.doi.org/10.1001/jama.294.5.571

Miller, M. J., Kim, J., Chen, G. A., & Alvarez, A. N. (2012). Exploratory and confirmatory factor analyses of the Asian American Racism-Related Stress Inventory. *Assessment, 19*, 53–64. http://dx.doi.org/10.1177/1073191110392497

Nadal, K. L., & Monzones, J. (2010). Filipino Americans and neuropsychology. In D. Fujii (Ed.), *The neuropsychology of Asian Americans* (pp. 47–70). Boca Raton, FL: Taylor & Francis.

Nadal, K. L., Wong, Y., Sriken, J., Griffin, K., & Fujii-Doe, W. (2015). Racial microaggressions and Asian Americans: An exploratory study of within-group differences and mental health. *Asian American Journal of Psychology, 6*, 136–144. http://dx.doi.org/10.1037/a0038058

Nagata, D. K., Kim, J. H., & Nguyen, T. U. (2015). Processing cultural trauma: Intergenerational effects of the Japanese American incarceration. *Journal of Social Issues, 71*, 356–370. http://dx.doi.org/10.1111/josi.12115

Navsaria, N., & Petersen, S. (2007). Finding a voice in Shakti. *Women & Therapy, 30*, 161–175. http://dx.doi.org/10.1300/J015v30n03_12

Nguyen, D. J., Kim, J. J., Weiss, B., Ngo, V., & Lau, A. S. (2018). Prospective relations between parent-adolescent acculturation conflict and mental health symptoms among Vietnamese American adolescents. *Cultural Diversity and Ethnic Minority Psychology, 24*, 151–161. http://dx.doi.org/10.1037/cdp0000157

Nguyen, P. V. (2008). Perceptions of Vietnamese fathers' acculturation levels, parenting styles, and mental health outcomes in Vietnamese American adolescent immigrants. *Social Work*, *53*, 337–346. http://dx.doi.org/10.1093/sw/53.4.337

Nguyen, T. Q., Bandeen-Roche, K., German, D., Nguyen, N. T., Bass, J. K., & Knowlton, A. R. (2016). Negative treatment by family as a predictor of depressive symptoms, Life satisfaction, suicidality, and tobacco/alcohol use in Vietnamese sexual minority women. *LGBT Health*, *3*, 357–365. http://dx.doi.org/10.1089/lgbt.2015.0017

Nouri, M., Hill, L. G., & Orrell-Valente, J. K. (2011). Media exposure, internalization of the thin ideal, and body dissatisfaction: Comparing Asian American and European American college females. *Body Image*, *8*, 366–372. http://dx.doi.org/10.1016/j.bodyim.2011.05.008

Okazaki, S., Liu, J. F., Longworth, S. L., & Minn, J. Y. (2002). Asian American–White American differences in expressions of social anxiety: A replication and extension. *Cultural Diversity and Ethnic Minority Psychology*, *8*, 234–247. http://dx.doi.org/10.1037/1099-9809.8.3.234

Otsuki, T. A. (2003). Substance use, self-esteem, and depression among Asian American adolescents. *Journal of Drug Education*, *33*, 369–390. http://dx.doi.org/10.2190/RG9R-V4NB-6NNK-37PF

Patel, N. R. (2007). The construction of South Asian-American womanhood: Implications for counseling and psychotherapy. *Women & Therapy*, *30*, 51–61. http://dx.doi.org/10.1300/J015v30n04_05

Petersen, W. (1966, January 9). Success story: Japanese-American style. *New York Times Magazine*, pp. 20–43.

Pew Research Center. (2012). *Asian Americans: A mosaic of faiths*. Retrieved from http://www.pewforum.org/2012/07/19/asian-americans-a-mosaic-of-faiths-overview/

Pew Research Center. (2018). *Key facts about Asian Americans, a diverse and growing population*. Retrieved from http://www.pewresearch.org/fact-tank/2017/09/08/key-facts-about-asian-americans/

Porter, N. (2015). The butterfly dilemma: Asian women, Whiteness, and heterosexual relationships. *Women & Therapy*, *38*, 207–219. http://dx.doi.org/10.1080/02703149.2015.1059182

Preisser, A. B. (1999). Domestic violence in South Asian communities in America. *Violence Against Women*, *5*, 684–699. http://dx.doi.org/10.1177/10778019922181437

Qin, D. B. (2009). Being "good" or being "popular": Gender and ethnic identity negotiations of Chinese immigrant adolescents. *Journal of Adolescent Research*, *24*, 37–66. http://dx.doi.org/10.1177/0743558408326912

Qin, D. B., Way, N., & Mukherjee, P. (2008). The other side of the model minority story: The familial and peer challenges faced by Chinese American adolescents. *Youth & Society*, *39*, 480–506. http://dx.doi.org/10.1177/0044118X08314233

Raj, A., & Silverman, J. G. (2007). Domestic violence help-seeking behaviors of South Asian battered women residing in the U.S. *International Review of Victimology*, *14*, 143–170. http://dx.doi.org/10.1177/026975800701400108

Reyes, A. (2007). *Language, identity, and stereotype among Southeast Asian American youth: The other Asian*. Mahwah, NJ: Erlbaum.

Robertson, H. A., Chaudhary Nagaraj, N., & Vyas, A. N. (2016). Family violence and child sexual abuse among South Asians in the US. *Journal of Immigrant and Minority Health, 18*, 921–927. http://dx.doi.org/10.1007/s10903-015-0227-8

Sangalang, C. C., & Gee, G. C. (2015). Racial discrimination and depressive symptoms among Cambodian American adolescents: The role of gender. *Journal of Community Psychology, 43*, 447–465. http://dx.doi.org/10.1002/jcop.21696

Sangalang, C. C., Jager, J., & Harachi, T. W. (2017). Effects of maternal traumatic distress on family functioning and child mental health: An examination of Southeast Asian refugee families in the U.S. *Social Science & Medicine, 184*, 178–186. http://dx.doi.org/10.1016/j.socscimed.2017.04.032

Singh, A. A. (2009). Helping South Asian immigrant women use resilience strategies in healing from sexual abuse: A call for a culturally relevant model. *Women & Therapy, 32*, 361–376. http://dx.doi.org/10.1080/02703140903153229

Sirin, S. R., & Fine, M. (2008). *Muslim American youth: Understanding hyphenated identities through multiple methods.* New York: New York University Press.

Smart, R., & Tsong, Y. (2014). Weight, body dissatisfaction, and disordered eating: Asian American women's perspectives. *Asian American Journal of Psychology, 5*, 344–352. http://dx.doi.org/10.1037/a0035599

Smart, R., Tsong, Y., Mejía, O. L., Hayashino, D., & Braaten, M. E. (2011). Therapists experiences treating Asian American women with eating disorders. *Professional Psychology: Research and Practice, 42*, 308–315. http://dx.doi.org/10.1037/a0024179

Suárez-Orozco, C., & Qin, D. B. (2006). Gendered perspectives in psychology: Immigrant origin youth. *The International Migration Review, 40*, 165–198. http://dx.doi.org/10.1111/j.1747-7379.2006.00007.x

Sue, D. W., Bucceri, J., Lin, A. I., Nadal, K. L., & Torino, G. C. (2007). Racial micro-aggressions and the Asian American experience. *Cultural Diversity and Ethnic Minority Psychology, 13*, 72–81. http://dx.doi.org/10.1037/1099-9809.13.1.72

Sue, S., Cheng, J. K. Y., Saad, C. S., & Chu, J. P. (2012). Asian American mental health: A call to action. *American Psychologist, 67*, 532–544. http://dx.doi.org/10.1037/a0028900

Thompson, T. L., & Kiang, L. (2010). The model minority stereotype: Adolescent experiences and links with adjustment. *Asian American Journal of Psychology, 1*, 119–128. http://dx.doi.org/10.1037/a0019966

Ting, J. Y., & Hwang, W. (2007). Eating disorders in Asian American Women. *Women & Therapy, 30*, 145–160. http://dx.doi.org/10.1300/J015v30n03_11

Tran, A. G. T. T., Cheng, H. L., Netland, J. D., & Miyake, E. R. (2017). Far from fairness: Prejudice, skin color, and psychological functioning in Asian Americans. *Cultural Diversity and Ethnic Minority Psychology, 23*, 407–415. http://dx.doi.org/10.1037/cdp0000128

Tummala-Narra, P. (2007). Skin color and the therapeutic relationship. *Psychoanalytic Psychology, 24*, 255–270. http://dx.doi.org/10.1037/0736-9735.24.2.255

Tummala-Narra, P. (2016). *Psychoanalytic theory and cultural competence in psychotherapy.* Washington, DC: American Psychological Association. http://dx.doi.org/10.1037/14800-000

Tummala-Narra, P., Deshpande, A., & Kaur, J. (2016). South Asian adolescents' experiences of acculturative stress and coping. *American Journal of Orthopsychiatry, 86*, 194–211. http://dx.doi.org/10.1037/ort0000147

Tummala-Narra, P., & Sathasivam-Rueckert, N. (2016). The experience of ethnic and racial group membership among immigrant-origin adolescents. *Journal of Adolescent Research, 31*, 299–342. http://dx.doi.org/10.1177/0743558415592178

U.S. Census Bureau. (2011). *Quick facts*. Retrieved from https://www.census.gov/quickfacts/fact/table/US/RHI425217#RHI425217

U.S. Census Bureau. (2017). *Income and poverty in the United States: 2016*. Retrieved from https://www.census.gov/content/dam/Census/library/publications/2017/demo/P60-259.pdf

Velez, B. L., Campos, I. D., & Moradi, B. (2015). Relations of sexual objectification and racist discrimination with Latina women's body image and mental health. *The Counseling Psychologist, 43*, 906–935. http://dx.doi.org/10.1177/0011000015591287

Wallace, J. M., Jr., Bachman, J. G., O'Malley, P. M., Schulenberg, J. E., Cooper, S. M., & Johnston, L. D. (2003). Gender and ethnic differences in smoking, drinking and illicit drug use among American 8th, 10th and 12th grade students, 1976–2000. *Addiction, 98*, 225–234. http://dx.doi.org/10.1046/j.1360-0443.2003.00282.x

Wildes, J. E., Emery, R. E., & Simons, A. D. (2001). The roles of ethnicity and culture in the development of eating disturbance and body dissatisfaction: A meta-analytic review. *Clinical Psychology Review, 21*, 521–551. http://dx.doi.org/10.1016/S0272-7358(99)00071-9

Wong, P., Lai, C. F., Nagasawa, R., & Lin, T. (1998). Asian Americans as a model minority: Self-perceptions and perceptions by other racial groups. *Sociological Perspectives, 41*, 95–118. http://dx.doi.org/10.2307/1389355

Yi, K. (2014). From no name to birth of integrated identity: Trauma-based cultural dissociation in immigrant women and creative integration. *Psychoanalytic Dialogues, 24*, 37–45. http://dx.doi.org/10.1080/10481885.2014.870830

Yick, A. G. (2001). Feminist theory and status inconsistency theory. *Violence Against Women, 7*, 545–562. http://dx.doi.org/10.1177/10778010122182596

Yoo, H. C., Miller, M. J., & Yip, P. (2015). Validation of the internalization of the Model Minority Myth Measure (IM-4) and its link to academic performance and psychological adjustment among Asian American adolescents. *Cultural Diversity and Ethnic Minority Psychology, 21*, 237–246. http://dx.doi.org/10.1037/a0037648

Young, C. B., Fang, D. Z., & Zisook, S. (2010). Depression in Asian-American and Caucasian undergraduate students. *Journal of Affective Disorders, 125*, 379–382. http://dx.doi.org/10.1016/j.jad.2010.02.124

Zhang, W., Hong, S., Takeuchi, D. T., & Mossakowski, K. N. (2012). Limited English proficiency and psychological distress among Latinos and Asian Americans. *Social Science & Medicine, 75*, 1006–1014. http://dx.doi.org/10.1016/j.socscimed.2012.05.012

Zhou, Z., Siu, C. R., & Xin, T. (2009). Promoting cultural competence in counseling Asian American children and adolescents. *Psychology in the Schools, 46*, 290–298. http://dx.doi.org/10.1002/pits.20375

5

LATINA ADOLESCENT GIRLS AT THE CULTURAL BORDERLANDS

LILLIAN COMAS-DÍAZ

Are Latino-Americans white? Black? Other? Illegal aliens from Mars?
Or are we the very face of America?
—Raquel Cepeda, *Bird of Paradise, How I Became Latina*

Latina adolescents are a heterogeneous and resilient group that exhibits both strengths and challenges while living in the cultural borderlands. Their lived experiences emphasize the need for an intersectional perspective during psychological treatment. This chapter provides essential information to psychologists, clinicians in training, and educators to help them understand Latina adolescents' mental health needs. It presents a cultural borderlands lens to identify Latina youths' strengths and psychological challenges. Gendered racism, cultural discrepancy, negative stereotypes, socioeconomic challenges, and immigration history, among other challenges, are discussed, alternating with gendered cultural resilience. Finally, this chapter examines Latina community programs and multicultural feminist psychotherapy that promote empowerment, well-being, and thriving among Latina youth.

http://dx.doi.org/10.1037/0000140-006
Multicultural Feminist Therapy: Helping Adolescent Girls of Color to Thrive,
T. Bryant-Davis (Editor)

A case study illustrates the application of multicultural feminist therapy, specifically a *mujerista* psychotherapy.

BACKGROUND AND CONTEXT: LIVING IN THE CULTURAL BORDERLANDS

The Latinx population is one of the largest ethnic minority groups in the United States. The term *Latinx* is a gender-neutral concept that goes beyond binary gender identifications, such as Latino (male) and Latina (female), and encompasses lesbian, gay, bisexual, transgender, and queer identities (McAlister, 2016; Santos, 2017). In this chapter, the term *Latinx* refers to the entire Latinx community, whereas Latina youth designates Latina adolescent girls between the ages of 13 and 19 years (Garcia & Lindgren, 2009). The Latinx population is projected to reach 119 million, or 29% of the total U.S. population, by 2060 (U.S. Census Bureau, 2017). The largest Latinx groups in the United States are people of Mexican ancestry, who mostly reside in the southwestern states. Puerto Ricans constitute the second largest group, and they tend to populate the eastern part of the country, including Florida. A significant number of Cuban Americans, Dominicans, and Central and South Americans add to the Latinx mosaic. Although the Latinx are the second largest minority group in the United States, a recent reduction in Latinx immigration and a declining birth rate among Latinas has restrained this population's growth (Krogstad, 2016b). Nonetheless, the Latinx comprise a significant portion of the country's future workforce and leadership. Because most of the Latinx are young (U.S. Census Bureau, 2017), this trend is expected to continue.

As previously indicated, the Latinx population is heterogeneous and diverse. However, what unifies most Latinx individuals is that they share common roots in Latin America, the Iberian Peninsula, and/or Africa. To illustrate, the Latinx may have Native American, European, and/or African ancestry. Indeed, one fourth of all Latinx self-identify as having African ancestry (Afro Latinx and/or Afro Caribbean) and/or roots in Latin America (Pew Research Center, 2014). Some Latinx may speak Spanish (with regional idiomatic differences), Portuguese, English, Spanglish, a Native American language such as Mayan, or a combination of these languages. Likewise, numerous Latinx blend Native American, European, and African traditions and practice a syncretism of Christianity with Native American and African beliefs. Even though the majority of Latinx are Christians, there are about 200,000 who are Jewish (Markoe, 2016), and the Latinx Muslim population is increasing (Pew Research Center, 2017).

About 6% of U.S. Muslims are Latinx (Padgett, 2013), and most of them are Latinas (Martin, 2006). About 35% of Latinx in the United States reported being foreign born in 2014 (Pew Research Center, 2014). Regardless of nativity, Latina adolescents straddle at least two cultures: Latinx culture and the dominant U.S. culture. Numerous Latina youth grow up in a culture different from their immigrant relatives' culture. Although Latina adolescents share similarities with Latina women, they confront specific cultural and developmental realities. Regardless of place of birth, these young Latinas tend to culturally adapt faster than their parents and their adult Latina peers (U.S. Census Bureau, 2017). Most Latina adolescents use English as their preferred language, even though many speak Spanish and/or Spanglish with their relatives. As a consequence, they develop a need to adapt to diverse and conflicting cultural influences.

Gloria Anzaldua's (1987) theory of borderlands (*la frontera*) is instrumental in understanding Latina youth in the United States. The concept of borderlands goes beyond physical location to include cultural, psychological, conceptual, sociopolitical, and spiritual spheres. According to the borderlands theory, Latinas inhabit in-between cultures, where they are seen as the other. Therefore, they develop their identities in cultural contexts with contradictory messages about what it means to be Latina. Consequently, visible U.S. Latinas become inner exiles in their own country. The combined experience of stress, discrimination, and oppression exposes Latina adolescents to health and psychological vulnerabilities (Cardemil, Kim, Pinedo, & Miller, 2005).

Like African American girls who are sexualized and dehumanized before puberty (Epstein, Blake, & Gonzalez, 2017), many Latina adolescents become sexually objectified and adultified. *Adultification* refers to the perception of girls of color as being more independent, hypersexualized, and knowledgeable about adult topics and thus requiring less protection, nurturance, and support compared with White girls (Epstein et al., 2017). Adolescent girls who are sexually objectified are susceptible to eating disorders, low self-esteem, and depression (American Psychological Association [APA], Task Force on the Sexualization of Girls, 2007). Moreover, they experience negative consequences in public systems such as education, child welfare, and legal juvenile justice. Because many Latina girls achieve puberty at an earlier age than White girls (Ruiz & Sanchez Korrol, 2006), they are exposed to more sexual objectification. Even more, LatiNegras (Afro Latinas) face a multitude of negative stereotypes associated with being Black females (Comas-Díaz, 1994). Research has shown that Latina teens with darker skin color in the United States had negative self-perceptions, felt unattractive, and wanted their skin color to be lighter (Telzer & Vazquez Garcia, 2009).

Although living in the borderlands may place Latina youth at risk, it paradoxically may protect their well-being. Inhabiting the cultural borderlands nurtures a border thinking, a borderlands consciousness, and an intersectional identity that embraces gender, ethnic, phenotypic, linguistic, emotional, location, and sociopolitical contexts (Anzaldua, 1987). Such an identity helps to transform vulnerabilities into strengths. According to Anzaldua, a borderlands consciousness helps Latinas acquire an awareness of power dynamics that helps them navigate power differentials. Notably, living at the borderlands infuses a type of perception—*la facultad*—a spiritual intuition that allows Latinas to see accurately through people, dynamics, events, and systems (Anzaldua, 1987). When Latina youth are able to connect with their *facultad*, they view it as a spiritual gift and begin to recover their gendered cultural strengths to cope with psychological vulnerabilities and enhance their sense of well-being. Latina youths' development of *la facultad* seems consistent with the outsider within concept. According to Collins (1986), an *outsider within* status relates to how African American women (and other women of color) engage in creativity while being marginalized within the dominant cultural environment. Similarly, many Latina youth use their outsider within status to engage in creative ways of coping with cultural challenges. The next section presents Latina adolescents' strengths while living in the cultural borderlands.

CULTURAL STRENGTHS

Most Latinx families have an intrinsic resilience (Bermudez & Mancini, 2013). Despite their exposure to adversity and traumatic circumstances, many Latina youth survive and thrive. Indeed, not all aversive experiences interrupt individuals' capacity to thrive (Bonanno, 2004). Thus, many Latina youth have an inherent cultural resilience (Gómez et al., 2014). *Cultural resilience* refers to a host of strengths, values, and practices that promote coping mechanisms, adaptive reactions, and functional coping strategies for traumatic oppression (Elsass, 1992). Traditional Latin American values can serve as protective factors that facilitate Latinx coping with challenging experiences (Holleran & Waller, 2003). Although these values are strongest among the most recent immigrants, many Latinx families endorse traditional values that nurture a cultural resilience (Parra-Cardona, Bulock, Imig, Villaruel, & Gold, 2006). Equally important, Latinx religiosity and spirituality offer a source of hope and resilience, particularly during adverse experiences (Hunter-Hernández, Costas-Muñíz, & Gany, 2015). Moreover, Latinx families' religious involvement has been associated with strong social networks and civic engagement (APA, 2017). Certainly, spirituality provides Latinas with a positive path for coping with health and illness (Jurkowski, Kurlanska, & Ramos, 2010). In addition to their gendered and cultural resilience, many Latina youth have cultural wealth.

Cultural Wealth

The concept of *cultural wealth* refers to a compilation of knowledge, skills, behaviors, and abilities that communities of color have to cope with and resist racism and other forms of oppression (Yosso, 2006). Yosso (2005) coined this concept to apply a strength-based framework to understand students of color. According to this perspective, there are six forms of cultural wealth: (a) aspirational, (b) linguistic, (c) familial, (d) social (including peers and social contacts), (d) navigational (ability to navigate social institutions), and (e) resistance (historical legacy of resistance; Yosso, 2005).

Cultural *aspirational wealth* is exemplified by the numerous Latina adolescents who aim to thrive due to their family history of immigration and/or displacement. Many Latina youth believe they will achieve their family's dreams (Ceja, 2004). Therefore, they aspire to attend college for both themselves and their relatives who have supported them throughout their life. According to the Pew Research Center (A. Flores, 2017), the Latinx high school dropout rate has decreased significantly during the past decade. Indeed, more Latinx youth are attending college, particularly community college (Krogstad, 2016a). Moreover, many Latinx youth work part-time to support their education (Fry & Taylor, 2013). Therefore, aspirational wealth nurtures resilience among Latinx youth so they may achieve their educational dreams (Kanagala, Rendón, & Nora, 2016). For instance, Gómez and her associates (2014) studied Latinx youths' assets that help them overcome discriminatory low expectations, improve sexual decision making, and develop educational aspirations. The researchers found that although most Latinx desired to attend college, their perceived discrimination by teachers was associated with a lower likelihood of attending college. On the basis of these findings, Gómez and colleagues recommended the reframing of Latinx youths' negative educational expectations, a recognition of their resilience, and the urgent need to address the structural factors underlying inequalities affecting this population.

Linguistic ability, another cultural wealth, is manifested among young Latinas through their linguistic aptitude to code switch due to bilingualism, incipient bilingualism, and/or use of Spanglish. Even if Latina teens use English as their preferred language, they acquire an ability to code switch that extends beyond the linguistic realm. For example, bilingual Latinx adolescents develop an ability to communicate in multiple and diverse environments (Kanagala et al., 2016). Moreover, their linguistic wealth is enriched with the storytelling tradition prevalent among many Latinx communities (Gort, 2012).

Notably, Latinx family resilience enhances the mental health of children and adolescents (Romero-Marin & Garcia Vázquez, 2012). Latinx *family cultural wealth* entails the values of *familismo*, cohesion, collectivism, interdependence, and *personalismo*. Although *familismo* (strong connectivity to the family) is expressed in close, supportive, warm, and affectionate family relationships, *personalismo* focuses on developing positive relationships with others (Ayón & Aisenberg, 2010). For instance, research has shown that Latinx child-rearing practices frequently value family support over developing individualistic self-reliance (Tacón & Caldera, 2001). Indeed, a study found that Latinx adolescents' reports of positive family functioning (defined as balanced family cohesion and flexibility) were associated with a decreased rate of externalizing problems and an increased level of global self-worth (Kapke, Grace, Gerdes, & Lawton, 2017). Moreover, because of *familismo*, Latina youths' aspirations are influenced and shared by family members (Gonzalez, Stein, & Huq, 2013). In this vein, Latinx parental involvement at the high school level has been linked to students' sense of belonging in school and teachers' higher expectations for students (Kuperminc, Darnell, & Alvarez-Jimenez, 2008). Therefore, Latina adolescents' aspirational goals are collectivistic and extend beyond the individual to include family and community.

Many Latina youth learn *social wealth* through gendered cultural socialization. In particular, Latinx collectivistic values of mutual care and community ethnic pride help reinforce young Latinas' social wealth. In other words, Latina adolescents learn lessons from the experiences, realities, and social networks of other Latinx. To this end, Latina youth make use of their social networks in their communities to circumnavigate systemic barriers.

Latinx *navigational wealth* helps Latina teens fulfill their academic aspirations. Latinx students who engaged in extracurricular activities and volunteerism, even though they experienced risk factors, reported the highest levels of resilience (W. Perez, Espinoza, Ramos, Coronado, & Cortes, 2009). Consistent with this finding, cultural wealth facilitates Latina youths' perseverance and fosters their determination, self-reliance, and self-confidence to achieve goals and dreams. Without a doubt, young Latinas' cultural wealth enhances their positive ethnic–racial identity.

Positive Ethnic–Racial Identity

Like other ethnic minority persons, Latina youths have an individual and a collective cultural resilience. In my clinical practice I have observed that in spite of adversity, many Latina youth have thrived while maintaining strong positive gendered and ethnocultural identities. Positive ethnic–racial identity is associated with positive global self-esteem among youth of color (APA, 2017). By the time Latinas reach adolescence, most of them have developed a grounded ethnic–racial identity shaped by living in the cultural borderlands. Indeed, Latina adolescents' assets such as healthy self-esteem, high aspirations for the future, and effective communication skills have been linked to positive sexual health outcomes, including making responsible decisions about sex (Gómez et al., 2014). Moreover, as part of their gendered socialization, Latina adolescents are taught to take care of others. Rather than engaging in self-sacrificing behavior, many Latina youth transform this cultural mandate into mutual care, an activity that enhances their sense of well-being (Comas-Díaz, 2013). Research has shown that positive ethnic identification is associated with life satisfaction, high self-esteem, and reduced mental distress among most Latinx youth (Torres, 2010). Furthermore, a strong ethnic identity mitigates the perception of discrimination, as well as depressive reactions due to discrimination (Rivas-Drake et al., 2014; Umaña-Taylor & Updegraff, 2007).

Living in the cultural borderlands, many Latina adolescents endorse a bicultural and/or multicultural identity. Research has shown that a bicultural identity can protect children facing adversity by allowing them to draw on the resources and supportive outlets of the two cultures (Smokowski & Bacallao, 2011). Moreover, biculturalism has been associated with optimal functioning for children, including lower depression and better academic and interpersonal adjustment (Berger Cardoso & Thompson, 2010). Sadly, notwithstanding their cultural resilience and wealth, numerous Latina adolescents face serious mental health challenges.

RISK FACTORS AND MENTAL HEALTH CONCERNS

Many Latinas bear multiple family responsibilities during childhood, adolescence, and adulthood. Moreover, they are exposed to the intersection of racism, sexism, xenophobia, classism, and other forms of oppression. Certainly, perceived discrimination affects the health of people of color (Todorova, Falcón, Lincoln, & Price, 2010). Studies have indicated that Latinx immigrants tend to have better health than U.S.-born Latinx. This phenomenon has been labeled the *Hispanic health paradox* (Morales, Lara, Kington, Valdez, & Escarce, 2002). Unfortunately, the Hispanic health paradox does not extend to the immigrant's offspring, whose health tends to be poorer than that of their parents. The dominant society's ethnic discrimination seems to be responsible for the U.S. Latinx's decline in health status. Discriminatory experiences increase Latina adolescents' vulnerability to mental health problems. For instance, Garcia and Lindgren (2009) researched Latinx teens' and their parents' perspectives regarding adolescent mental health stressors. They found that both sets of participants identified discrimination, immigration, and familial disconnection as factors conducive to mental health problems among Latinx adolescents. Moreover, the scholarly literature has identified depression, suicidal attempts, eating disorders, and posttraumatic stress disorders among numerous Latina youth (Alegria et al., 2007; Céspedes & Huey, 2008; Chesin & Jeglic, 2012; E. Flores, Tschann, Dimas, Pasch, & de Groat, 2010; Zayas & Pilat, 2008). The following section offers a discussion of young Latinas' main psychological problems.

Depression

Depression is a serious problem among many Latina youth. To illustrate, Céspedes and Huey (2008) found that compared with males, Latina adolescents reported greater differences in traditional gender role beliefs between themselves and their parents, coupled with higher levels of depression. In addition, the researchers found that gender role discrepancy was linked to higher youth depression, whereby family dysfunction increased this relationship. In another study, Latina adolescents reported experiencing more depressive symptoms in the prior month than males of any other adolescent group (Garcia, Skay, Sieving, Naughton, & Bearinger, 2008). What is more, U.S.-based research indicated that compared with other teens, Latina youth had higher rates of major depressive disorder (Gonzales, Deardorff, Formoso, Barr, & Barrera, 2006). Sadly, depression is a risk factor for suicide, the third leading cause of death among adolescents. Unfortunately, many depressed Latina adolescents engage in suicidal attempts.

Suicide Attempts

Suicidal ideation and suicide attempts are more prevalent among Latina youth than among White or African American adolescents (Price & Khubchandani, 2017). One in every seven Latina adolescents attempts suicide (Zayas & Pilat, 2008). Indeed, Romero, Edwards, Bauman, and Ritter (2014) called the Latina epidemic of suicide attempts *La Llorona* (crying female). Research has shown that U.S.-born Latina youth have a higher risk of suicide attempts than foreign-born Latinas (Romero et al., 2014). Numerous Latinx youth with immigrant parents tend to be depressed, engage in substance use, and attempt suicide (Peña et al., 2008). Likewise, suicidal Latina teens have higher lifetime use of cocaine, methamphetamine, and ecstasy (Granillo, Jones-Rodriguez, & Carvajal, 2005).

However, the psychological profiles of suicidal Latina adolescents and their suicide risk factors may not be that different from those of non-Latina suicidal adolescents (Zayas, Lester, Cabassa, & Fortuna, 2005). A portrait of suicidal Latina adolescents includes a combination of cultural and familial factors (e.g., *familismo*, acculturation, relatedness) with developmental, social, and individual factors (Zayas & Pilat, 2008). Sadly, social and peer group factors, cultural mores, bicultural challenges, and individual characteristics seem to collide with family dynamics. The developmental stage of autonomy and relatedness—a struggle between connection and separation from the family—seems to be at the center of Latina teens' suicide attempts. According to Zayas and Pilat (2008), Latina youths' autonomy-relatedness struggle, a discrepancy in acculturation between Latina adolescents and their parents, the scarcity of mentors for Latina teens, plus acculturative stress, appear to be related to suicidal attempts. Moreover, a perceived low mutuality between the suicidal girls and their mothers, coupled with periods of father absence, have been associated with suicidal girls, as opposed to nonsuicidal girls (Baumann, Kuhlberg, & Zayas, 2010). In summary, to properly address Latina youth suicidal behaviors, researchers recommend a focus on individual therapy, family treatment, and prevention (Baumann et al., 2010).

Eating Disorders

Eating disorders are prevalent among numerous Latina adolescents. The examination of eating disorders among Latina youth requires gendered, ethnic, and cultural attention (Lauer, 2017). The dominant U.S. society promotes an ideal female body type, weight, and shape. Unfortunately, the "ideal body type" represents a White, Anglo-Saxon cultural value. The pressure to conform to such body image is particularly painful for many Latina youth who have different body shapes. Consequently, many Latinas receive negative messages about their bodies, resulting in the embodiment of these damaging messages. Levy's (2009) stereotype embodiment theory can be used to examine how the dominant culture's negative stereotypes about Latina bodies result in their internalization of negative body images. Unfortunately, such embodiment often metamorphizes into eating disorders (Lauer, 2017). Indeed, Neumark-Sztainer and colleagues (2002) found that compared with White adolescents, Latina teens reported equal or greater eating-related concerns and behaviors. Latina adolescents in the study were most likely to report desiring a weight lower than their current weight, perceive themselves as currently being overweight, and indicate low body satisfaction. Moreover, the researchers found no significant differences between Cuban American,

Mexican American, and Puerto Rican female youth, suggesting that Latina teens are at risk of eating disorders regardless of their national background. In another study, Alegria and her colleagues (2007) found elevated rates of binge-eating behaviors and disorders in a U.S. epidemiological survey of Latinx households. The study revealed that those Latinx who had spent more than 70% of their lifetimes in the United States and thus had increased exposure to U.S. culture, reported greater rates of lifetime bulimia nervosa than those who spent more time in their home countries. This study's results are consistent with M. Perez, Ohrt, and Hoek's (2016) findings that binge-eating disorder is the most common eating disorder among Latinx individuals. In addition, eating disorders among Latina adolescents have been associated with substance use (Granillo et al., 2005). Although substance abuse among Latinx youth tends to be lower than other adolescents' abuse, increases in rates of marijuana use and prescription drugs have been noted among Latinx youth (Substance Abuse and Mental Health Services Administration, 2011).

Posttraumatic Stress Disorder

Most Latina youth have a legacy of historical, intergenerational, and community trauma. Although Latinx of Mexican ancestry have a historical trauma due to the repatriation of U.S. citizens of Mexican origin during 1939 (Rodriguez, 2003), Puerto Ricans have a perennial history of colonization. Moreover, many Latin Americans who immigrate from war-torn countries carry a history of war trauma. Along these lines, a study found that Latinx Vietnam veterans experienced more severe posttraumatic stress disorder (PTSD) symptoms than do other Vietnam veterans (Ortega & Rosenheck, 2000). Unfortunately, numerous Latinx experience contemporary trauma. Racism, unsafe neighborhoods, tense encounters with police, increased rates of incarceration, xenophobia, and a rise in hate crimes (Federal Bureau of Investigation, 2017) are a few of the stressful realities that many Latina youth encounter. In addition, 18.2% of Latinx students reported being bullied at school (Ramirez, Gallion, Aguilar, & Surette Dembeck, 2017). Moreover, numerous Latina adolescents may experience PTSD symptoms as a result of gendered racial ethnic discrimination (E. Flores et al., 2010).

Immigration can be traumatic (Foster, 2001) and thus contribute to the risk of Latina youths' mental health problems. Many Latinx immigrants experience chronic poverty, challenging living conditions, community violence, and political unrest in their countries of origin. Some immigrant families experience separation from relatives and leave young children behind for an undetermined time (Hurtado-de-Mendoza, Gonzales, Serrano, & Kaltman, 2014). Those who immigrate from war-torn countries are exposed to cumulative trauma.

When immigrant Latinas experience trauma, many can be identified as trauma survivors (Salas, Ayón, & Gurrola, 2013). Regrettably, the U.S. sociopolitical climate (after the 2016 presidential election) regarding undocumented immigrants, and Latinx immigration in general, creates anxiety among Latina youth (Cervantes & Walker, 2017). Moreover, if visible Latina youth seek mental health services, they could potentially trigger *political countertransference* (Chung, 2005) among some mental health practitioners. In its severe form, political countertransference can lead to a belief that all Latinx are undocumented and/or criminals. Moreover, if a Latina adolescent's parents are undocumented, she may experience vicarious trauma, relocation trauma, and PTSD. As previously suggested, the current political climate may nurture the suspicion that all visible Latinx are undocumented. Therefore, many Latina adolescents born and raised in the United States have been accused of being foreigners and thus exposed to microaggressions, such as being told to "go back to your country." In fact, numerous Latina teens have been victims of hate crimes (Cervantes & Walker, 2017).

BARRIERS TO TREATMENT

Latinx use of mental health treatment is low (López, Barrio, Kopelowicz, & Vega, 2012). This is not surprising because many psychological treatments are not gendered or culturally and linguistically informed (APA, 2017). The disadvantaged socioeconomic status of many Latinx, family immigration stressors, discrimination, and anti-Latinx sentiment constitute additional reasons for Latina youths' low use of mental health services. The following is a brief discussion of these factors.

Disadvantaged Socioeconomic Status

Lower socioeconomic status (SES) affects Latina youths' mental health. For instance, poverty exposes Latina youth to more stress and fewer coping styles to counter stress. Latina youth living in low socioeconomic areas are exposed to geographical stress, poor educational quality, dangerous neighborhoods (APA, 2017), and thus to traumatic experiences. Indeed, chronic exposure to poverty and community criminal activity increases Latina youths' risk of mental health problems (APA, 2017). Moreover, many Latinx immigrants have two or more full-time jobs and thus have limited opportunity to devote the necessary time to their daughters. According to Garcia and Lindgren (2009), Latina adolescents tend to have more intrafamilial stressors (family separation, parent–child conflicted relationship) compared with Latino adolescents, who tend to have more extrafamilial stressors, such as participation in gangs and law enforcement, among other problems. Consistent with disadvantaged SES, numerous Latina adolescents are exposed to health challenges. For example, living in noisy, overcrowded, inadequate housing can affect their health and well-being. Garcia, Zhang, Holt, Hardeman, and Peterson (2014) researched Latina adolescent sleep-mood relationships. They found that negative affect affected the adolescents' sleep quality. On the basis of these results, the researchers recommended public health interventions to encourage sleep-mood awareness among Latina youth.

Immigration and Acculturative Stress

Immigration contributes to the risk of Latina youth developing mental health problems. Latinx immigrants encounter significant stressors due to language barriers, cultural adaptation, and the process of immigration itself (Pérez Benítez, Sibrava, Zlotnick, Weisberg, & Keller, 2014). Latina adolescents are affected by immigration—their own and/or that of their families of origin. Depending on how recently Latinx have immigrated, the stressors include linguistic and acculturation processes and familial separation or reunification (Smokowski & Bacallao, 2011). As previously mentioned, acculturative stress has been associated with depression among Latinx teens. Certainly, immigrant Latina youth experience stressors related to both adaptation to life in the United States and to the developmental changes associated with adolescence. Latina adolescent depression is related to increased family acculturation; higher rates of depression are found among youth residing in more acculturated families. Yet, this depression–acculturation relationship is modified by family conflict, such that when conflict is present, rates of depression are high for Latinx youth irrespective of family acculturation levels (Gonzales et al., 2006). However, Latina adolescents whose parents are undocumented have added stress. They live in fear that their parents and other relatives will be deported, creating a continual state of fear and anxiety. Unfortunately, the potential threat of parents' deportation and relocation can result in vicarious trauma and PTSD (E. Flores et al., 2010). An anti-Latinx political sentiment exacerbates Latina adolescents' mental health problems.

Discrimination

Visible Latina adolescents are exposed to gendered racism and other types of discrimination. Being the victim of discrimination, such as experiencing racial microaggressions, produces anxiety and depression (Nadal, Griffin, Wong, Hamit, & Rasmus, 2014) and can result in trauma (Bryant-Davis & Ocampo,

2006; Helms, Nicolas, & Green, 2012). An operational definition of discrimination is Latinx's disproportionate rates of poverty, uninsured status, health
disparities, and incarceration. As previously noted, Latinx problems with
the police are increasing due to xenophobia, concerns about undocumented
status, racial profiling, and hate crimes (Nittle, 2018). Certainly, many Latina
adolescents experience vicarious trauma when members of their family
encounter problems with the police and are incarcerated and/or killed. Moreover, Spanish monolingual Latinx youth feel the pressure of the English-only
movement. Those speaking English with an accent can become victims of
linguistic terrorism. Conceived by Anzaldua (1987), *linguistic terrorism* entails
discrimination toward individuals who speak English with a subaltern accent
(such as Spanish), ranging from microaggressions to hate crimes.

Lack of Appropriately Informed Mental Health Treatment

Latina youth require a gendered, culturally, developmentally, and ecologically
informed mental health treatment. Latina youths' intersectional identities—
gender, ethnicity, skin color, sexual orientation, and socioeconomic class—
expose them to multiple oppressions. Unfortunately, there are not enough
mental health professionals who commit to continued learning and practicing
cultural competence for the rest of their lives (Comas-Díaz, 2012). Moreover,
when low-income Latina adolescents seek mental health services, they may
encounter psychologists who cognitively and behaviorally distance themselves from them due to their clients' poverty (Lott, 2012). Such distancing
interferes with the development of a positive therapeutic relationship. Therefore, effective mental health services for Latina youth require both prevention
and treatment modalities. The next section describes empowering community
programs that promote prevention as they help young Latinas to connect,
develop, and cultivate their strengths.

EMPOWERING COMMUNITY PROGRAMS

Traditional Latinx cultural values are embedded in collectivistic contexts.
Notably, the Latinx sense of self is grounded in a relational matrix. Belonging
to an ethnic community (an extended family) is central to the Latina sense
of identity. This is a cultural wealth resource that can be used to enhance
Latina youths' well-being. In this framework, community programs can help
empower Latina adolescents and promote their mental health. Given that
compared with other ethnic groups, many Latinx tend to endorse stigmatizing
beliefs and attitudes toward mental illness (Comas-Díaz, 2012), community

programs can be used as psychoeducation. The following is a discussion of several community-oriented programs, such as *promotoras*, school prevention programs, psychoeducation through media and technology, *Latinitas*, Latinx hip-hop, and emotional emancipation circles.

Promotoras

Promotoras are female community members who receive training to provide basic health education in the Latinx low-income community (Lujan, 2009). As members of the community they serve, *promotoras* communicate linguistically and culturally with Latinx individuals. Indeed, there is evidence that the use of *promotoras* has increased Latinx use of health services (Elder, Ayala, Parra-Medina, & Talavera, 2009). In addition to promoting health, *promotoras* act as mentors, educators, and advocates. In fact, the presence of female mentors is central to promoting Latina youth mental health. For instance, a study with a sample of inner-city Latina adolescent mothers found that Latinas with mentors had significantly lower levels of depression and anxiety than those without mentors, despite both groups being exposed to similar amounts of stress exposure (Rhodes, Contreras, & Mangelsdorf, 1994). In other words, *promotoras* teach, tutor, guide, mentor, and inspire Latina youth. In fact, the *promotora* model can be used to deliver preventive mental health services to Latina youth and their families. *Promotoras* could engage in psychoeducation after receiving basic mental health training. In addition, they can teach Latina youth how to develop healthy socioemotional coping. By teaching the importance of mutuality—a quality that many suicidal Latina teens need—*promotoras* could model a reciprocal exchange of warmth, respect, and admiration. Even more, *promotoras* could help Latina youth engage in emotional attunement to others and thus acquire perspective taking as a means of increasing effective communication with parents.

School Prevention Programs

Schools are in a great position to develop mental health prevention programs for Latina youth. For instance, they can provide bullying prevention programs, hire bilingual school counselors, conduct home visits, and teach educational sessions to reduce stress and anxiety. Moreover, they can offer psychoeducation programs for the whole family. Because Latina youth are less likely to be physically active and play fewer team sports than their White peers (Ramirez et al., 2017), schools can promote physical activities and sports among Latina teens. Moreover, they can provide mentors to Latina adolescents.

Community Psychoeducation: Media and Technology

Psychoeducation can take multiple forms to benefit Latina youth. To illustrate, media and technology can be useful because many young Latinx use these tools to communicate (Lopez & Livingston, 2010). For instance, research found positive responses to public health interventions through the use of a short messages service and social media among Latinx adolescents in Maryland (Vyas, Landry, Schnider, Rojas, & Wood, 2012). On the basis of the study's results, the researchers recommended the use of the messages service and social media to convey public health messages and to promote mental health.

Latinitas

Latinitas (see http://latinitasmagazine.org/about-us/) is an innovative program that uses a combination of technology, media, mentoring, and teaching. The program's purpose is to empower Latina girls and adolescents to validate their lived experiences. *Latinitas* aims to help Latina youth find their voice, learn about their culture, enhance self-esteem, and develop leadership qualities. The program was born out of the need to address the epidemic of suicide attempts among Latina youth. Consequently, *Latinitas* helps young Latinas improve their coping skills and prevent mental health problems. For instance, young Latinas learn socioemotional coping skills to increase their self-confidence and self-esteem and strengthen their cultural gender identity. Moreover, to promote positive Latina roles, *Latinitas* uses mentors and experts who teach, empower, and inspire Latina girls and adolescents. This community program fosters communication skills, critical consciousness, social justice advocacy, and community service among Latina youth.

Latinx Hip-Hop

Latinx hip-hop, such as spoken word (à la Nuyorican Poets Café; https://www.nuyorican.org/history-awards/) and other creative avenues (J. Flores, 2000), helps Latina teens express their problems and examine solutions. Indeed, the hip-hop culture gives voice to the voiceless (Drake-Burnette, Garrett-Akinsanya, & Bryant-Davis, 2016), especially to females of color. Within this context, Latinx hip-hop offers an empowering avenue for young Latinas. Indeed, females have a strong presence in the Latinx hip-hop culture (Hassan, 2015). These Latinas are strong feminists who model female empowerment for Latina adolescents (Reichard, 2015). Like African American hip-hop psychology, a Latinx hip-hop psychology could strengthen Latina youths' well-being, enhance coping, and promote thriving.

Emotional Emancipation Circles

Emotional emancipation circles can be helpful for Latina youth. Emotional emancipation circles (http://www.communityhealingnet.org/emotional-emancipation-circles/) were developed to support African Americans. In these programs, African Americans get together to tell their stories of racial trauma, combat internalized oppression, and create affirming narratives. A special focus is given to creating healthy, empowering, and supportive relationships. Moreover, African American hip-hop psychology is used to create and celebrate survival narratives. This program can be applied to Latina youth, making use of the Latinx hip-hop culture.

In summary, prevention helps young Latinas enhance their resilience. Because creativity is a healing and empowering medium for Latinas (Shapiro & Alcántara, 2016), psychotherapists can nurture their clients' creativity. In this regard, they can foster young Latinas' use of technology and social media (avenues endorsed by many Latinx) to express creativity through blogs, videos, and other means. Armed with the benefits of empowering community programs, psychologists can incorporate these approaches into their work. Castro-Olivo (2014) conducted a study using *Jóvenes Fuertes*, a cultural adaptation of the Strong Teens program with Latinx adolescents in school. Her results showed an increased social–emotional resilience among the program participants. In addition, psychologists can connect with community resources such as churches, clubs, and community leaders and workers such as *promotoras*. For example, I developed a collaborative professional relationship with a *promotora* expert on substance abuse recovery. Such collaboration resulted in the delivery of presentations on mental health and wellness to Latina teens in schools. Finally, psychotherapists can refer their young Latina clients to empowerment community programs as adjunct interventions to their treatment. The next section presents gendered and culturally relevant mental health treatments for Latina youth.

GENDERED AND CULTURALLY RELEVANT MENTAL HEALTH TREATMENT

Latina youth experiencing mental health problems need gendered, cultural, and developmentally informed counseling or therapy. Mental health treatment can help Latina youth change their negative embodied thoughts into empowerment and thriving. In fact, practitioners working with Latinx adolescents can enhance their clinical effectiveness when they (a) commit to cultural competence as a lifelong endeavor, (b) include a critical race theory orientation, and (c) ground treatment in a Latina lived experience.

Cultural Competence

Cultural competence—the awareness, attitude, knowledge, and skills that allow clinicians to understand, appreciate, and work with culturally diverse clients—is necessary when working with Latina youth (Comas-Díaz, 2012). Unfortunately, psychologists who are unaware of their implicit bias limit their cultural competence (APA, 2017). Some therapist implicit biases include the assumption that ethnic minority youth are less intelligent, more prone to use drugs and alcohol, more violent, and at more risk of treatment noncompliance (APA, 2017). Sadly, therapists' unawareness of their implicit bias can result in microaggressions during psychotherapy. To address implicit bias, psychologists can increase their self-awareness by completing a cultural self-assessment to examine the cultural differences between them and their clients (Comas-Díaz, 2012). In addition, therapists can conduct a power differential analysis (Worell & Remer, 2003), comparing their areas of privilege and oppression with those of their Latina clients.

An important component of cultural competence is *cultural humility*. Therapists committed to developing positive therapeutic alliances practice cultural humility (Tervalon & Murray-García, 1998). Rather than knowing facts, culturally humble practitioners focus on understanding significant processes that occur during therapeutic encounters. Indeed, research has documented that clients' perceptions of therapists' cultural humility were associated with a strong therapeutic alliance and an improvement in therapy (Hook, Davis, Owen, Worthington, & Utsey, 2013). Culturally informed therapists also aim to develop *cultural empathy*, a learned ability to understand their clients through an analysis of cultural data (Ridley & Lingle, 1996). Cultural empathy calls for therapists to "walk in the Latina teen's shoes" to enhance therapists' cultural understanding. This knowledge requires an awareness of Latinas' lived experiences, including the intersection of racism, sexism, and xenophobia.

Critical Race Theory

Psychologists working with visible Latina adolescents should include a critical race theory (CRT) perspective into mental health treatment. Proponents of CRT assert that because racism is normal in U.S. society (Delgado & Stefancic, 2012), Latinx adolescents can use their race and ethnicity to overcome racism and obtain power (Solórzano & Yosso, 2001). Indeed, psychologists can apply CRT to mental health treatment and prevention by adhering to Solórzano and Yosso's (2001) suggestions: (a) addressing race, racism, and intersectionality; (b) challenging dominant ideologies prevalent in mental health theory and practice; (c) recognizing the significance of Latina teens' experiential knowledge and using this knowledge in treatment; (d) using interdisciplinary perspectives; and (e) infusing treatment with a commitment to racial and social justice. Exponents of CRT argue that both understanding and analyzing racial inequality should be placed in contemporary and historical contexts. For example, CRT practitioners examine how, through one's race, a person constantly deals with racism but can resist and challenge racism and use one's race to overcome racism and obtain power (Delgado & Stefancic, 2012). Likewise, therapists can introduce the topic of race at the beginning of treatment, even if the client does not present it as a problem. By doing so, therapists communicate to their clients that racial material is appropriate and safe to discuss in treatment (Comas-Díaz, 2012). Infusing a CRT approach into therapy is essential for the development of interdisciplinary methods to address Latina youth lived experiences. As such, CRT aims to disrupt the apartheid of knowledge in academia (Perez Huber, 2009) and psychology.

Mental Health Interventions Grounded in Latina Lived Experience

The Latinx collectivistic value informs Latina adolescents' sense of self and others. Indeed, Latina youth inhabit a matrix of relationships. Therefore, family therapy approaches, including family therapy with one person, are congruent with this perspective. Certainly, family interventions can facilitate family members' communication skills, conflict resolution, and problem solving. Such an approach facilitates the Latina adolescent's family members sharing their concerns and participating in plans for the Latina teen's recovery. A review of the literature on mental health programs revealed that effective programs for Latinx children and adolescents included family and culturally infused interventions, in addition to Spanish-speaking facilitators to communicate with Spanish monolingual parents (Bandy & Moore, 2011).

Another collective treatment orientation is group psychotherapy. Specifically, group psychotherapy could be useful for Latina youth who experience PTSD. Although a cross-cultural study revealed similar distortions and disruptions in participants' autobiographical memories of PTSD, nonetheless Latinx teens experiencing PTSD benefit from a culturally relevant treatment. Latinx adolescents and their caregivers received a culturally adapted group psychotherapy, Positive Adaptations for Trauma and Healing (PATH; Hoskins, Duncan, Moskowitz, & Ordóñez, 2018). A manualized approach, PATH integrates a trauma model, positive psychology, resilience, and Latinx culture into treatment. The results of this pilot study showed a significant reduction in trauma symptoms and associated symptoms among a community-based Latinx sample composed of adolescents and their caretakers (Hoskins et al., 2018). Likewise, psychologists can use a holistic approach to trauma, including spirituality, CRT, art, social justice action, and holistic healing. Certainly, a significant aspect of grounding mental health treatment in a Latinx context requires addressing mind and body. Indeed, Cabrera, Villarruel, and Fitzgerald (2011) recommended physical activity to Latinx youth because this approach has proven to be effective in treating Latinx youth health problems (Ramirez et al., 2017). Therefore, Latina youth can practice sports, dance, yoga, stretching, and other movement activities. The remainder of this chapter offers a discussion of Latina youths' gendered and culturally informed treatments, followed by a case study.

Latina Feminist Therapy

Latina feminist therapy, a type of multicultural feminist therapy, is an approach consistent with Latina youths' lived experiences (Comas-Díaz & Vazquez, 2018). Because feminist therapy does not always reflect the lives and circumstances of all women (Brown, 1990), multicultural feminist therapy emerged to address the needs of women of color (Barrett et al., 2005). Womanist and *mujerista* psychologies are two forms of multicultural feminist therapy that address African American women's and Latinas' lived experiences, respectively (Bryant-Davis & Comas-Díaz, 2016). Both of these multicultural feminist psychologies differ from mainstream feminism in that they focus on racism, gendered racism, sexism, poverty, race, colorism, global solidarity, collective liberation, and of course, intersectional oppressions (Bryant-Davis & Comas-Díaz, 2016). In addition, *mujerista* psychology addresses immigration, coloniality, locality or place, borderlands, bi- or multiculturalism, linguistic issues, and transnationalism.

A Latina feminism emerges early in the lives of many Latinas. For example, a study on the conceptions of feminism among Latina adolescents showed that participants related their feminist identity to their sense of positive well-being (Manago, Brown, & Leaper, 2009). As noted earlier, living in the cultural borderlands is a Latina feminist construct related to transformation. Anzaldua's (1987) borderlands theory is an interdisciplinary approach integrating cultural studies, women's studies, art, Latin American indigenous religion and mythology, spirituality, and Jungian psychology. As such, it offers an integrative healing path for Latinas. Because coping with oppression can fracture the Latina's sense of self, alternatively, living in the borderlands imparts a border thinking as a reaction to the dominant cultural discourse (Mignolo, 2000), nurturing alternative possibilities and empowering Latinas to transform challenges into strengths. Living in *nepantla* (a Nahuatl word meaning "in between"), Latinas become painfully aware of their oppression. As Latinas acquire an awakening consciousness, they connect with ancestral knowledge and become empowered to integrate their fractured sense of self (Anzaldua, 1987). With this in mind, Latina feminist therapists foster Latina youths' gendered and cultural identity development by helping them connect with their ancestral legacy.

Latina feminist therapists use creativity to foment Latina youths' self-integration. To this end, Anzaldua (2002) recommended *testimonio* and *autohistoria*. A Latin American narrative, *testimonio* is a personal account of the Latina's experiences with marginalization, victimization, oppression, and trauma (Aron, 1992). Indeed, *testimonios* have been effective for Latina youth coping with microaggressions (Perez Huber & Cueva, 2012). As a form of life history, *testimonio* is a therapeutic approach that nurtures cultural survival, agency, and resilience (L. T. Smith, 2012). In addition, *autohistoria* (Latina self-history using multiple media) is a form of artivism that advances Latinas' self-integration. *Artivism*—art created to promote critical consciousness, engagement in social justice action, and social change (Sandoval & Latorre, 2008)—promotes healing and thriving. As artivists, Latina youth can use their creativity to represent their communities in their struggle against oppression and injustice. Multiple forms of artivism include spoken word, street art, indigenous murals, protesting, altar making (Sandoval & Latorre, 2008), and Latinx hip-hop. Along these lines, Anzaldua (2002) recognized the significant role of spirituality in the lives of most Latinas. She focused on the role of Latina feminists as spiritual activists to promote healing and social justice (Anzaldua, 2002). A specific Latina multicultural feminist healing based on psychospirituality is *mujerista* psychotherapy.

Mujerista Psychotherapy

Ada M. Isasi-Díaz (1994), a Latina feminist theologian, conceptualized the term *mujerismo* to denote a Latina liberation theology. The conceptual and political translation of *mujerismo* is "Latina womanism" (Comas-Díaz, 2016). Isasi-Díaz viewed *lo cotidiano* (everyday reality) as a central aspect of Latina lived experience. Moreover, she conceived *lo cotidiano* as an ethical space in which Latinas can enact their autonomy through decision making and action (Isasi-Díaz & Mendieta, 2011). A central aspect of *mujerista* psychology, *mujerista* psychotherapy is a Latina feminist healing approach with a psychospiritual base (Comas-Díaz, 2016). This approach is grounded in an integration of theology of liberation, psychology of liberation, Latina feminism, and mainstream psychotherapy. Therefore, *mujerista* psychotherapists focus on *lo cotidiano* to empower Latinas by nurturing their strengths, gifts, goals, and hopes.

Like other Latina feminists, *mujeristas* use narratives *testimonio*, artivism, and other creative expressions in therapy. In addition to promoting empowerment, *mujerista* psychologists foster *conscientizacion* (critical consciousness) among their clients. Following a CRT, *mujerista* psychologists help Latinas to challenge the dominant status quo that oppresses them. In this regard, *mujerista* psychotherapists promote decolonization within a liberation approach. To achieve this goal, they use strategies of resistance to oppose internalized colonization and neocolonization and foster the development of solidarity toward all oppressed groups (Comas-Díaz, 2016). *Mujerista* therapists encourage Latina adolescents to develop their ethnocultural identity because a strong ethnic identity has been associated with well-being among young populations of color (Smith & Silva, 2011).

Mujerista psychotherapy involves a holistic approach that includes mind, body, and spirit. As mentioned before, a central factor in *mujerista* therapy is the promotion of a connection with spirit (Comas-Díaz, 2016). Because many Latinas consider *la lucha* (the everyday struggle) to be an essential part of life, they embrace *la lucha* as a means of nurturing their spiritual resilience (Isasi-Díaz, 2004). The *dicho* (proverb) *Después de la lluvia, sale el sol* (After the rainstorm, the sun will shine) is an example of a Latinx spiritual resilience (Vidales, 2010). Indeed, such spiritual orientation seems consistent with the biological research findings of spirituality's positive association with the serotonin system (Borg, Andrée, Soderstrom, & Farde, 2003). In other words, because low serotonin has been associated with depression, spiritual activities can act as a mood stabilizer by increasing serotonin. Consequently, a *mujerista* psychospirituality promotes hope, self-integration, and self-healing. Indeed, many Latinx use spirituality as an adjunct healing approach to mainstream therapies (Reyes-Ortiz, Rodriguez, & Markides, 2009). As numerous Latina adolescents are exposed to traumatic experiences, *mujerista* psychologists explore their clients' trauma history and, if needed, practice trauma-informed psychotherapy in a psychospiritual framework. To accomplish these goals, *mujerista* psychotherapists endorse a holistic paradigm, grounded in indigenous healing. Coincidentally, a report on the racial and ethnic disparities in children's mental health recommended the inclusion of non-Western healing approaches in the mental health treatment of youth of color (Holm-Hansen, 2006). Illustrations of this approach include the combination of evidence-based trauma treatment with yoga for trauma (van der Kolk et al., 2014), a race-informed trauma therapy (Bryant-Davis & Ocampo, 2006), and cultivating creativity.

To help Latina youth thrive, *mujerista* therapists nurture their clients' relationship with spirituality. *Mujerista* psychologists define spirituality in a secular context as a transpersonal sense of connection. Therefore, *mujerista* therapists cultivate Latina adolescents' psychospiritual development. Psycho-spirituality helps Latina youth to connect with their gendered and cultural resilience. The *dicho El(la) que no sufre no avanza* (She or he who does not suffer does not progress) captures a Latinx positive reframing of the negative effects of adversity. Ultimately, a psychospiritual perspective helps Latina adolescents begin to view themselves as thriving. With this awareness, young Latinas see themselves in a different light and reformulate their identity to include their newfound strength, empowerment, and wisdom. The following is a case study illustrating the application of a *mujerista* therapy with a young Latina experiencing depression in the contexts of intergenerational, gender, cultural, and developmental conflicts.

CASE STUDY: A PILLAR OF STRENGTH

Pilar,[1] a 17-year-old Latina, attempted suicide with an overdose of over-the-counter medications and alcohol. The oldest of two children, Pilar was a mixed-race Latina with a Puerto Rican mother and a Dominican father. The emergency room physician referred Pilar to a Latina psychologist. Accompanied by Paz, her mother, Pilar saw Dr. Consuelo Buenvivir. After greeting mother and daughter, Dr. Buenvivir invited Pilar to her office. Dressed in casual clothes and wearing a blank expression on her face, Pilar sat on a chair and lowered her head. After a few minutes, Dr. Buenvivir asked, "What happened to you?" Pilar raised her eyes and tears ran down her cheeks. Dr. Buenvivir handed her a box of tissues. She then said, "*Caras vemos corazones no sabemos* [We can see the faces, but we do not know the hearts]." Pilar dried her tears and stared at Dr. Buenvivir.

After a long pause, Pilar said, "My dear *abuela* Esperanza used to say that *dicho*." "What did your *abuela* mean by this proverb?" Dr. Buenvivir asked. "That we don't know what is deep in the heart of the other person," Pilar replied. "Your *abuela* was a wise woman." In response, Pilar smiled at Dr. Buenvivir. The therapist moved forward in her chair and said, "I don't know what is in your heart. Can you tell me?" In a soft voice, Pilar said, "I'm in limbo."

The initial therapy session is extremely important for most clients of color (Comas-Díaz, 2012). Numerous Latinx clients expect therapists to earn their trust and to demonstrate cultural credibility. To earn Pilar's trust, Dr. Buenvivir used her *facultad*—the Latina feminist intuition nurtured by living between cultures. She quoted a *dicho* as an ethnic therapy to communicate her ignorance about Pilar's situation. This approach was a culturally appropriate way of inviting Pilar to share her story. Specifically, it helped Dr. Buenvivir to express

---

[1] Client descriptions have been anonymized to protect confidentiality.

cultural humility and thus earn cultural credibility. In short, this approach helped the therapist gain Pilar's trust. In addition to showing cognitive and affective empathy, Dr. Buenvivir exhibited cultural empathy by acknowledging Pilar's *abuela's* wisdom.

After developing rapport, Dr. Buenvivir explored Pilar's explanatory model of distress (Kleinman, 1980). This tool examines clients' distress experience and feelings of being sick, as well as their expectations from both clinician and treatment. During this assessment, Pilar said, "Depression runs in my maternal family." However, Pilar stated that she did not intend to kill herself. Instead, she labeled her suicide attempt as an act of impotence. The examination revealed Pilar's cultural conflict in navigating her adolescent developmental stage of autonomy and relatedness. Specifically, Pilar attempted suicide because her parents did not approve of her dating. Unable to date, Pilar was abandoned by her peers. "I feel like a pariah," she said. At that moment, Dr. Buenvivir asked, "What are your gifts?" Pilar straightened her back and said, "I do spoken word." At the completion of the assessment, both Pilar and Dr. Buenvivir collaborated on a treatment plan, one that included individual and family therapy.

The individual therapy focused on Pilar's sense of self. Indeed, the integration of ethnic psychotherapy into a feminist (*mujerista*) approach helped Pilar to validate the gendered, ethnic, and racial components of her cultural identity. Dr. Buenvivir incorporated mind, body, and spirit approaches into the treatment. Pilar responded well to this approach. Pilar nurtured her *facultad* and became empowered through her connection with her *abuela's* indigenous wisdom. "I honor my name—Pilar—I am a pillar of strength," she declared. Moreover, as a mixed-race teen, Pilar used a critical race lens to identified herself as Afro Latina. With this new understanding, Pilar examined her parents' strict female gender roles. She became critically conscious of her parents' differential gendered treatment. Whereas her younger brother was allowed to be independent, she was restricted under the aegis of protection.

Pilar remained in individual therapy for 9 months. During that period, she learned to identify her suicidality's triggers and manage them. Dr. Buenvivir explored Pilar's substance use (alcohol intake) and concluded that it was not a significant problem. Moreover, Pilar mastered effective communication skills—including being culturally assertive (Comas-Díaz & Duncan, 1985) with her parents. In addition, Pilar engaged in family therapy sessions. These sessions dealt with the cultural and gender conflicts that led Pilar to her suicide attempt. During a family session, Paz, Pilar's mother, said, "I don't want Pilar to go through what I went through." Paz then revealed that she had been sexually assaulted by a family friend when she was an adolescent. Family therapy addressed Paz's trauma and its effects on Pilar. Moreover, several family sessions were devoted to psychoeducation about trauma, depression, and suicidality. Dr. Buenvivir invited Pilar to compose her *testimonio*. After completing it, Pilar said, "It is like an extended spoken word." She read her *testimonio* during a family session. To Pilar's surprise, her parents responded with love, understanding, and compassion. Pilar's mood improved, and Dr. Buenvivir recommended physical activity as an adjunct therapy. Pilar followed her advice and began Afro Latinx dancing lessons. In summary, *mujerista* therapy helped Pilar to empower and name herself. She healed her gendered cultural dispute with her parents, improved her family relationships, and nurtured her creativity. At the end of therapy, Pilar told Dr. Buenvivir, "I'm not in limbo anymore." With a twinkle in her eyes, she said, "I recently performed at the Nuyorican Poets Cafe. My family was in the audience. It was so cool!"

CONCLUSION

We don't see things as they are, we see them as we are.

—Anaïs Nin
(Angela Anaïs Juana Antolina Rosa Edelmira Nin Y Culmell)

As Anaïs Nin suggested, we can change our reality by changing the way we see ourselves. Most Latina youth living in the cultural borderlands see themselves in a fractured mirror. Because of discrimination, intersectional oppression, immigration, acculturative stress, socioeconomic challenges, sociopolitical issues, and other psychosocial stressors, visible Latina youth are exposed to a series of mental health challenges. The most prevalent problems include depression, suicidal attempts, eating disorders, and PTSD. Latina adolescents require family, group, individual, and community mental health interventions. Community programs such as *promotoras*, *Latinitas*, emotional emancipation circles, media and technology activities, psychoeducation, and Latinx hip-hop can be used for the prevention of psychological problems. Unfortunately, numerous Latina youth need mental health treatment. However, effective healing approaches for Latina adolescents have to be gendered and culturally informed. When psychologists ground their mental health treatment in Latina youths' lived experiences, they can tap into their clients' gendered cultural strengths to promote healing, transformation, and thriving. As a result, young Latinas are able to repair their fractured mirror. When they see themselves in a different way, they can transform their ruptured sense of self. In this way, they are empowered to engage in social justice action. What is more, Latina adolescents' gendered ethnic resilience, cultural wealth, and psychospiritual gifts become fountains for blossoming. As they come into their own, thriving Latina adolescents will contribute to the well-being of their ethnic community, as well as to the welfare of the global village.

REFERENCES

Alegria, M., Woo, M., Cao, Z., Torres, M., Meng, X. L., & Striegel-Moore, R. (2007). Prevalence and correlates of eating disorders in Latinos in the United States. *International Journal of Eating Disorders, 40*, S15–S21. http://dx.doi.org/10.1002/eat.20406

American Psychological Association. (2017). *Addressing the mental health needs of racial and ethnic minority youth: A guide for practitioners.* Washington, DC: Author.

American Psychological Association, Task Force on the Sexualization of Girls. (2007). *Report of the APA Task Force on the Sexualization of Girls.* Retrieved from http://www.apa.org/pi/women/programs/girls/report-full.pdf

Anzaldua, G. (1987). *Borderlands/La Frontera: The new Mestiza.* San Francisco, CA: Spinster/Aunt Lute.

Anzaldua, G. (2002). Now let us shift . . . the path of conocimiento . . . inner work, public acts. In G. E. Anzaldua & A. L. Keating (Eds.), *This bridge we call home: Radical visions for transformation* (pp. 540–570). New York, NY: Routledge.

Aron, A. (1992). *Testimonio*, a bridge between psychotherapy and sociotherapy. *Women & Therapy, 13*, 173–189. http://dx.doi.org/10.1300/J015v13N03_01

Ayón, C., & Aisenberg, E. (2010). Negotiating cultural values and expectations within the public child welfare system: A look at *familismo* and *personalismo. Child & Family Social Work, 15*, 335–344. http://dx.doi.org/10.1111/j.1365-2206.2010.00682.x

Bandy, T., & Moore, K. A. (2011, February). *What works for Latino/Hispanic children and adolescents: Lessons learned from experimental evaluations of programs and interventions.* Retrieved from http://www.childtrends.org/wp-content/uploads/2011/02/Child_Trends-2011_02_01_RB_WW4LatinoChildren.pdf

Barrett, S. E., Chin, J. L., Díaz, L. C., Espin, O., Greene, B., & McGoldrick, M. (2005). Multicultural feminist therapy: Theory in context. *Women & Therapy, 28*, 27–61. http://dx.doi.org/10.1300/J015v28n03_03

Baumann, A. A., Kuhlberg, J. A., & Zayas, L. H. (2010). Familism, mother–daughter mutuality, and suicide attempts of adolescent Latinas. *Journal of Family Psychology, 24*, 616–624. http://dx.doi.org/10.1037/a0020584

Berger Cardoso, J., & Thompson, S. (2010). Understanding the concept of resilience in the Latino immigrant families. *Families in Society, 9*, 257–265.

Bermudez, J. M., & Mancini, J. A. (2013). *Familias fuertes*: Family resilience among Latinos. In D. S. Becvar (Ed.), *Handbook of family resilience* (pp. 215–227). New York, NY: Springer. http://dx.doi.org/10.1007/978-1-4614-3917-2_13

Bonanno, G. A. (2004). Loss, trauma, and human resilience: Have we underestimated the human capacity to thrive after extremely aversive events? *American Psychologist, 59*, 20–28. http://dx.doi.org/10.1037/0003-066X.59.1.20

Borg, J., Andrée, B., Soderstrom, H., & Farde, L. (2003). The serotonin system and spiritual experiences. *The American Journal of Psychiatry, 160*, 1965–1969. http://dx.doi.org/10.1176/appi.ajp.160.11.1965

Brown, L. (1990). The meaning of multicultural perspective for theory-building in feminist therapy. *Women & Therapy, 9*, 1–22. http://dx.doi.org/10.1300/J015v09n01_01

Bryant-Davis, T., & Comas-Díaz, L. (2016a). Introduction: Womanist and *mujerista* psychologies. In T. Bryant-Davis & L. Comas-Díaz (Eds.), *Womanist and* mujerista *psychologies: Voices of fire, acts of courage* (pp. 3–25). Washington, DC: American Psychological Association.

Bryant-Davis, T., & Comas-Díaz, L. (Eds.). (2016b). *Womanist and* mujerista *psychologies: Voices of fire, acts of courage*. Washington, DC: American Psychological Association. http://dx.doi.org/10.1037/14937-000

Bryant-Davis, T., & Ocampo, C. (2006). A therapeutic approach to the treatment of racist incident-based trauma. *Journal of Emotional Abuse, 6*(4), 1–22. http://dx.doi.org/10.1300/J135v06n04_01

Cabrera, N. J., Villarruel, F. A., & Fitzgerald, H. E. (Eds.). (2011). *Latina and Latino children's mental health* (Vols. 1–2). New York, NY: Praeger.

Cardemil, E. V., Kim, S., Pinedo, T. M., & Miller, I. W. (2005). Developing a culturally appropriate depression prevention program: The family coping skills program. *Cultural Diversity and Ethnic Minority Psychology, 11*, 99–112. http://dx.doi.org/10.1037/1099-9809.11.2.99

Castro-Olivo, S. M. (2014). Promoting social–emotional learning in adolescent Latino ELLs: A study of the culturally adapted Strong Teens program. *School Psychology Quarterly, 29*, 567–577. http://dx.doi.org/10.1037/spq0000055

Ceja, M. (2004). Chicana college aspirations and the role of parents: Developing educational resiliency. *Journal of Hispanic Higher Education, 3*, 338–362. http://dx.doi.org/10.1177/1538192704268428

Cervantes, W., & Walker, C. (2017). *Five reasons Trump's immigration orders harm children*. Retrieved from http://www.clasp.org/resources-and-publications/publication-1/Five-Reasons-Immigration-Enforcement-Orders-Harm-Children.pdf

Céspedes, Y. M., & Huey, S. J., Jr. (2008). Depression in Latino adolescents: A cultural discrepancy perspective. *Cultural Diversity and Ethnic Minority Psychology, 14*, 168–172. http://dx.doi.org/10.1037/1099-9809.14.2.168

Chesin, M. G., & Jeglic, E. L. (2012). Suicidal behavior among Latina college students. *Hispanic Journal of Behavioral Sciences, 34*, 421–436. http://dx.doi.org/10.1177/0739986312445271

Chung, R. C.-Y. (2005). Women, human rights, and counseling: Crossing international boundaries. *Journal of Counseling & Development, 83*, 262–268. http://dx.doi.org/10.1002/j.1556-6678.2005.tb00341.x

Collins, P. H. (1986). Learning from the outsider within status: The sociological significance of Black feminist thought. *Social Problems, 33*, s14–s32. http://dx.doi.org/10.2307/800672

Comas-Díaz, L. (1994). LatiNegra: Mental health issues of African Latinas. *Journal of Feminist Family Therapy, 5*, 35–74. http://dx.doi.org/10.1300/J086v05n03_03

Comas-Díaz, L. (2012). *Multicultural care: A clinician's guide to cultural competence*. Washington, DC: American Psychological Association. http://dx.doi.org/10.1037/13491-000

Comas-Díaz, L. (2013). *Comadres*: The healing power of a female bond. *Women & Therapy, 36*, 62–75. http://dx.doi.org/10.1080/02703149.2012.720213

Comas-Díaz, L (2016). *Mujerista* psychospirituality. In T. Bryant-Davis & L. Comas-Díaz (Eds.) *Womanist and* mujerista *psychologies: Voices of fire, acts of courage* (pp. 149–169). Washington, DC: American Psychological Association.

Comas-Díaz, L., & Duncan, J. W. (1985). The cultural context: A factor in assertiveness training with mainland Puerto Rican women. *Psychology of Women Quarterly*, *9*, 463–476. http://dx.doi.org/10.1111/j.1471-6402.1985.tb00896.x

Comas-Díaz, L., & Vazquez, C. I. (Eds.). (2018). *Latina psychologists: Thriving in the cultural borderlands*. New York, NY: Routledge.

Delgado, R., & Stefancic, J. (2012). *Critical race theory: An introduction* (2nd ed.). New York, NY: New York University Press.

Drake-Burnette, D., Garrett-Akinsanya, B., & Bryant Davis, T. (2016). Womanism, creativity, and resistance: Making a way out of "no way." In T. Bryant-Davis & L. Comas-Díaz (Eds.), *Womanist and* mujerista *psychologies: Voices of fire, acts of courage* (pp. 173–193). Washington, DC: American Psychological Association. http://dx.doi.org/10.1037/14937-008

Elder, J. P., Ayala, G. X., Parra-Medina, D., & Talavera, G. A. (2009). Health communication in the Latino community: Issues and approaches. *Annual Review of Public Health*, *30*, 227–251. http://dx.doi.org/10.1146/annurev.publhealth.031308.100300

Elsass, P. (1992). *Strategies for survival: The psychology of cultural resilience in ethnic minorities*. New York, NY: New York University Press.

Epstein, R., Blake, J. J., & González, T. (2017). *Girlhood interrupted: The erasure of Black girls' childhood*. Retrieved from http://hdl.handle.net/11212/3414

Federal Bureau of Investigation. (2017). *EEO complaint data*. Retrieved from https://justice.gov/jmd/federal-bureau-investigation-2017-fbi

Flores, A. (2017, September 18). *Facts on U.S. Latinos, 2015*. Retrieved from http://www.pewhispanic.org/2017/09/18/facts-on-u-s-latinos/

Flores, E., Tschann, J. M., Dimas, J. M., Pasch, L. A., & de Groat, C. L. (2010). Perceived racial/ethnic discrimination, posttraumatic stress symptoms, and health risk behaviors among Mexican American adolescents. *Journal of Counseling Psychology*, *57*, 264–273. http://dx.doi.org/10.1037/a0020026

Flores, J. (2000). *From bomba to hip hop: Puerto Rican culture and Latino identity*. New York, NY: Columbia University Press.

Foster, R. P. (2001). When immigration is trauma: Guidelines for the individual and family clinician. *American Journal of Orthopsychiatry*, *71*, 153–170. http://dx.doi.org/10.1037/0002-9432.71.2.153

Fry, R., & Taylor, P. (2013, May 9). *Hispanic high school graduates pass whites in rate of college enrollment: High school drop-out rate at record low*. Retrieved from http://www.pewhispanic.org/2013/05/09/hispanic-high-school-graduates-pass-whites-in-rate-of-college-enrollment/

Garcia, C., & Lindgren, S. (2009). "Life grows between the rocks": Latino adolescents' and parents' perspectives on mental health stressors. *Research in Nursing & Health*, *32*, 148–162. http://dx.doi.org/10.1002/nur.20317

Garcia, C., Skay, C., Sieving, R., Naughton, S., & Bearinger, L. H. (2008). Family and racial factors associated with suicide and emotional distress among Latino students. *The Journal of School Health*, *78*, 487–495. http://dx.doi.org/10.1111/j.1746-1561.2008.00334.x

Garcia, C., Zhang, L., Holt, K., Hardeman, R., & Peterson, B. (2014). Latina adolescent sleep and mood: An ecological momentary assessment pilot study. *Journal of Child and Adolescent Psychiatric Nursing, 27,* 132–141. http://dx.doi.org/10.1111/jcap.12082

Gómez, C. A., Villaseñor, E., Mann, E. S., Mandic, C. G., Valladares, C. S., Mercado, V., ... Cardona, V. (2014). The new majority: How will Latino youth succeed in the context of low educational expectations and assumptions of sexual irresponsibility? *Sexuality Research & Social Policy, 11,* 348–362. http://dx.doi.org/10.1007/s13178-014-0165-6

Gonzales, N. A., Deardorff, J., Formoso, D., Barr, A., & Barrera, M., Jr. (2006). Family mediators of the relation between acculturation and adolescent mental health. *Family Relations, 55,* 318–330. http://dx.doi.org/10.1111/j.1741-3729.2006.00405.x

Gonzalez, L. M., Stein, G. L., & Huq, N. (2013). The influence of cultural identity and perceived barriers on college-going beliefs and aspirations of Latino youth in emerging immigrant communities. *Hispanic Journal of Behavioral Sciences, 35,* 103–120. http://dx.doi.org/10.1177/0739986312463002

Gort, M. (2012). Code-switching patterns in the writing-related talk of young emergent bilinguals. *Journal of Literacy Research, 44,* 45–75. http://dx.doi.org/10.1177/1086296X11431626

Granillo, T., Jones-Rodriguez, G., & Carvajal, S. C. (2005, March). Prevalence of eating disorders in Latina adolescents: Associations with substance use and other correlates. *Journal of Adolescent Health, 36,* 214–220. http://dx.doi.org/10.1016/j.jadohealth.2004.01.015

Hassan, M. (2015). *13 women in hip-hop you need to know.* Retrieved from http://remezcla.com/lists/music/13-women-in-hip-hop-you-need-to-know/

Helms, J. E., Nicolas, G., & Green, E. (2012). Racism and ethnoviolence as trauma: Enhancing professional and research training. *Traumatology, 18,* 65–74. http://dx.doi.org/10.1177/1534765610396728

Holleran, L. K., & Waller, M. A. (2003). Sources of resilience among Chicano/a youth: Forging identities in the borderlands. *Child & Adolescent Social Work Journal, 20,* 335–350. http://dx.doi.org/10.1023/A:1026043828866

Holm-Hansen, C. (2006). *Racial and ethnic disparities in children's mental health.* Retrieved from https://www.wilder.org/sites/default/files/imports/TroubledYouth_10-06.pdf

Hook, J. N., Davis, D. E., Owen, J., Worthington, E. L., & Utsey, S. O. (2013). Cultural humility: Measuring openness to culturally diverse clients. *Journal of Counseling Psychology, 60,* 353–366. http://dx.doi.org/10.1037/a0032595

Hoskins, D., Duncan, L. G., Moskowitz, J. T., & Ordóñez, A. E. (2018). Positive adaptations for trauma and healing (PATH), a pilot study of group therapy with Latino youth. *Psychological Trauma: Theory, Research, Practice and Policy, 10,* 163–172. http://dx.doi.org/10.1037/tra0000285

Hunter-Hernández, M., Costas-Muñíz, R., & Gany, F. (2015). Missed opportunity: Spirituality as a bridge to resilience in Latinos with cancer. *Journal of Religion and Health, 54,* 2367–2375. http://dx.doi.org/10.1007/s10943-015-0020-y

Hurtado-de-Mendoza, A., Gonzales, F. A., Serrano, A., & Kaltman, S. (2014). *Me mandó a traer:* Weak "strong ties" in Latina immigrants' social networks. *Journal of Community Psychology, 42,* 479–494. http://dx.doi.org/10.1002/jcop.21623

Isasi-Díaz, A. M. (1994). *Mujeristas*: A name of our own. Sisters struggling in the spirit. In N. B. Lewis (Ed.), *A women of color theological anthology* (pp. 126–138). Louisville, KY: Women's Ministries Program, Presbyterian Church.

Isasi-Díaz, A. M. (2004). La lucha *continues:* Mujerista *theology*. Maryknoll, NY: Orbis Books.

Isasi-Díaz, A. M., & Mendieta, E. (2011). *Decolonizing epistemologies: Latina/o theology and philosophy*. New York, NY: Fordham University Press. http://dx.doi.org/10.5422/fordham/9780823241354.001.0001

Jurkowski, J. M., Kurlanska, C., & Ramos, B. M. (2010). Latino women's spiritual beliefs related to health. *American Journal of Health Promotion, 25*, 19–25. http://dx.doi.org/10.4278/ajhp.080923-QUAL-211

Kanagala, V., Rendón, L., & Nora, A. (2016). A framework for understanding Latino/a cultural wealth. *Diversity & Democracy, 19*(1). Retrieved from https://aacu.org/diversitydemocracy/2016/winter/kanagala

Kapke, T. L., Grace, M. A., Gerdes, A. L., & Lawton, K. E. (2017). Latino early adolescent mental health: Examining the impact of family functioning, familism, and global self-worth. *Journal of Latina/o Psychology, 5*, 27–44. http://dx.doi.org/10.1037/lat0000057

Kleinman, A. (1980). *Patients and healers in the context of culture: An exploration of the borderland between anthropology, medicine, and psychiatry.* Berkeley: University of California Press.

Krogstad, J. M. (2016a). 5 facts about Latinos and education. Retrieved from http://www.pewresearch.org/fact-tank/2016/07/28/5-facts-about-latinos-and-education/

Krogstad, J. M. (2016b). *Key facts about how the Hispanic population is changing.* Retrieved from http://www.pewresearch.org/fact-tank/2016/09/08/key-facts-about-how-the-u-s-hispanic-population-is-changing/

Kuperminc, G. P., Darnell, A. J., & Alvarez-Jimenez, A. (2008). Parent involvement in the academic adjustment of Latino middle and high school youth: Teacher expectations and school belonging as mediators. *Journal of Adolescence, 31*, 469–483. http://dx.doi.org/10.1016/j.adolescence.2007.09.003

Lauer, M. (2017). Identifying eating disorders in Latinas: Racial and ethnic bias in care. *Psychotherapy Bulletin, 52*, 41–48.

Levy, B. (2009). Stereotype embodiment: A psychosocial approach to aging. *Current Directions in Psychological Science, 18*, 332–336. http://dx.doi.org/10.1111/j.1467-8721.2009.01662.x

Lopez, M. H., & Livingston, G. (2010). *How young Latinos communicate with friends in the digital age.* Retrieved from http://www.pewresearch.org/wp-content/uploads/sites/5/reports/124.pdf

López, S. R., Barrio, C., Kopelowicz, A., & Vega, W. A. (2012). From documenting to eliminating disparities in mental health care for Latinos. *American Psychologist, 67*, 511–523. http://dx.doi.org/10.1037/a0029737

Lott, B. (2012). The social psychology of class and classism. *American Psychologist, 67*, 650–658. http://dx.doi.org/10.1037/a0029369

Lujan, J. (2009). Got Hispanic clients? Get *a promotora? The Internet Journal of Allied Health Sciences and Practice, 7*(3). Retrieved from https://nsuworks.nova.edu/ijahsp/vol7/iss3/4/

Manago, A. M., Brown, C. S., & Leaper, C. (2009). Feminist identity among Latina adolescents. *Journal of Adolescent Research, 24,* 750–776. http://dx.doi.org/10.1177/0743558409341079

Markoe, L. (2016, April 21). Shalom, Amigo! New study sheds light on Latino Jews in U.S. *The New York Jewish Week.* Retrieved from http://jewishweek.timesofisrael.com/shalom-amigo-new-study-sheds-light-on-latino-jews-in-us/

Martin, R. (2006, September 24). Latinas choosing Islam over Catholicism. *NPR.* Retrieved from https://www.npr.org/templates/story/story.php?storyId=6133579

McAlister, J. F. (2016). Making feminist, queer, Latinx, and #BlackVotesMatter. *Women's Studies in Communication, 39,* 353–356. http://dx.doi.org/10.1080/07491409.2016.1230988

Mignolo, W. (2000). *Global histories/global designs: Coloniality, subaltern knowledges, and border thinking.* Princeton, NJ: Princeton University Press.

Morales, L. S., Lara, M., Kington, R. S., Valdez, R. O., & Escarce, J. J. (2002). Socioeconomic, cultural, and behavioral factors affecting Hispanic health outcomes. *Journal of Health Care for the Poor and Underserved, 13,* 477–503. http://dx.doi.org/10.1353/hpu.2010.0630

Nadal, K. L., Griffin, K. E., Wong, Y., Hamit, S., & Rasmus, M. (2014). The impact of racial microaggressions on mental health: Counseling implications for clients of color. *Journal of Counseling & Development, 92,* 57–66. http://dx.doi.org/10.1002/j.1556-6676.2014.00130.x

Neumark-Sztainer, D., Croll, J., Story, M., Hannan, P. J., French, S. A., & Perry, C. (2002). Ethnic/racial differences in weight-related concerns and behaviors among adolescent girls and boys: Findings from Project EAT. *Journal of Psychosomatic Research, 53,* 963–974. http://dx.doi.org/10.1016/S0022-3999(02)00486-5

Nittle, N. K. (2018, February 20). *Racial profiling and police brutality.* Retrieved from https://www.thoughtco.com/racial-profiling-police-brutality-against-hispanics-2834820

Ortega, A. N., & Rosenheck, R. (2000). Posttraumatic stress disorder among Hispanic Vietnam veterans. *The American Journal of Psychiatry, 157,* 615–619. http://dx.doi.org/10.1176/appi.ajp.157.4.615

Padgett, T. (2013, October 9). *Why so many Latinos are becoming Muslims.* http://wlrn.org/post/why-so-many-latinos-are-becoming-muslims

Parra-Cardona, J. R., Bulock, L. A., Imig, D. R., Villaruel, F. A., & Gold, S. (2006). "*Trabajando duro todos los dias*": Learning from the life experiences of Mexican-origin migrant families. *Family Relations, 55,* 361–375.

Peña, J. B., Wyman, P. A., Brown, C. H., Matthieu, M. M., Olivares, T. E., Hartel, D., & Zayas, L. H. (2008). Immigration generation status and its association with suicide attempts, substance use, and depressive symptoms among Latino adolescents in the USA. *Prevention Science, 9,* 299–310. http://dx.doi.org/10.1007/s11121-008-0105-x

Perez, M., Ohrt, T. K., & Hoek, H. W. (2016). Prevalence and treatment of eating disorders among Hispanics/Latino Americans in the United States. *Current Opinion in Psychiatry, 29,* 378–382. http://dx.doi.org/10.1097/YCO.0000000000000277

Perez, W., Espinoza, R., Ramos, K., Coronado, H. M., & Cortes, R. (2009). Academic resilience among undocumented Latino students. *Hispanic Journal of Behavioral Sciences, 31,* 149–181. http://dx.doi.org/10.1177/0739986309333020

Pérez Benítez, C. I., Sibrava, N. J., Zlotnick, C., Weisberg, R., & Keller, M. B. (2014). Differences between Latino individuals with posttraumatic stress disorder and those with other anxiety disorders. *Psychological Trauma: Theory, Research, Practice, and Policy*, 6, 345–352. http://dx.doi.org/10.1037/a0034328

Perez Huber, L. (2009). Disrupting apartheid of knowledge: *Testimonio* as methodology in Latina/o critical race research in education. *International Journal of Qualitative Studies in Education*, 45, 392–410.

Perez Huber, L., & Cueva, B. M. (2012). Chicana/Latina *Testimonios* on effects and responses to microaggressions. *Equity & Excellence in Education*, 45, 392–410. http://dx.doi.org/10.1080/10665684.2012.698193

Pew Research Center. (2014, October 29). *2014 National Survey of Latinos details.* Retrieved from http://www.pewhispanic.org/2014/10/29/latino-support-for-democrats-falls-but-democratic-advantage-remains/ph_2014-10-29_nsl-politics-elections-35/

Pew Research Center. (2017, July 26). *Demographic portrait of Muslim Americans.* Retrieved from http://www.pewforum.org/2017/07/26/demographic-portrait-of-muslim-americans/

Price, J. H., & Khubchandani, J. (2017). Latina adolescents health risk behaviors and suicidal ideation and suicide attempts; Results from the National Youth Risk Behavior Survey 2001–2013. *Journal of Immigrant and Minority Health*, 19, 533–542. http://dx.doi.org/10.1007/s10903-016-0445-8

Ramirez, A. G., Gallion, K. J., Aguilar, R., & Surette Dembeck, E. (2017, September 12). *Mental health and Latino kids: A research review.* Retrieved from https://salud-america.org/healthy-minds-research/

Reichard, R. (2015, March 19). 8 Latina rappers whose music you have to hear. *Cosmopolitan.* Retrieved from https://www.cosmopolitan.com/entertainment/music/news/a37940/8-latina-rappers-who-are-killing-it/

Reyes-Ortiz, C. A., Rodriguez, M., & Markides, K. S. (2009). The role of spirituality healing with perceptions of the medical encounter among Latinos. *Journal of General Internal Medicine*, 24, 542–547. http://dx.doi.org/10.1007/s11606-009-1067-9

Rhodes, J. E., Contreras, J. M., & Mangelsdorf, S. C. (1994). Natural mentor relationships among Latina adolescent mothers: Psychological adjustment, moderating processes, and the role of early parental acceptance. *American Journal of Community Psychology*, 22, 211–227. http://dx.doi.org/10.1007/BF02506863

Ridley, C., & Lingle, D. W. (1996). Cultural empathy in multicultural counseling: A multidimensional process model. In P. B. Pedersen, J. G. Draguns, W. J. Lonner, & J. E. Trimble (Eds.), *Counseling across cultures* (4th ed., pp. 21–46). Thousand Oaks, CA: Sage.

Rivas-Drake, D., Syed, M., Umaña-Taylor, A., Markstrom, C., French, S., Schwartz, S. J., & Lee, R. (2014). Feeling good, happy, and proud: A meta-analysis of positive ethnic-racial affect and adjustment. *Child Development*, 85, 77–102. http://dx.doi.org/10.1111/cdev.12175

Rodriguez, R. (2003). *Brown: The last discovery of America.* New York, NY: Penguin Books.

Romero, A., Edwards, L., Bauman, S., & Ritter, M. (2014). *Preventing adolescent depression and suicide among Latinas: Resilience research and theory.* New York, NY: Springer. http://dx.doi.org/10.1007/978-3-319-01381-7

Romero-Marin, M., & Garcia Vázquez, E. (2012, July). *The intersection of family and community resilience to enhance mental health among Latino children, adolescents, and families*. Retrieved from http://www.apa.org/pi/families/resources/newsletter/ 2012/07/family-community.aspx

Ruiz, V. L., & Sanchez Korrol, V. (Eds.). (2006). *Latinas in the United States: A historical encyclopedia*. Bloomington: Indiana University Press.

Salas, L. M., Ayón, C., & Gurrola, M. (2013). *Estamos Traumados*: The impact of anti-immigrant sentiment and polices on the mental health of immigrant families. *Journal of Community Psychology, 41*, 1005–1020. http://dx.doi.org/10.1002/ jcop.21589

Sandoval, C., & Latorre, G. (2008). Chicana/o artivism: Judy Baca's digital work with youth of color. In A. Everett (Ed.), *Learning, race, and ethnicity: Youth and digital media* (pp. 81–108). Cambridge, MA: MIT Press.

Santos, C. E. (2017). The history, struggle, and potential of the term Latinx. *Latina/o Psychology Today, 4*, 7–14.

Shapiro, E., & Alcántara, D. (2016). *Mujerista* creativity: Latin@ sacred arts as life-course developmental resources. In T. Bryant-Davis & L. Comas-Díaz (Eds.), *Womanist and mujerista psychologies: Voices of fire, acts of courage* (pp. 195–216). Washington, DC: American Psychological Association. http://dx.doi.org/10.1037/14937-009

Smith, L. T. (2012). *Decolonizing methodologies: Research and indigenous people* (2nd ed.). New York, NY: Zed Books.

Smith, T. B., & Silva, L. (2011). Ethnic identity and personal well-being of people of color: A meta-analysis. *Journal of Counseling Psychology, 58*, 42–60. http:// dx.doi.org/10.1037/a0021528

Smokowski, P. R., & Bacallao, M. (2011). *Becoming bicultural: Risk, resilience, and Latino youth*. New York: New York University Press.

Solórzano, D. G., & Yosso, T. J. (2001). Critical race and LatCrit theory and method: Counter-storytelling. *International Journal of Qualitative Studies in Education, 14*, 371–395. http://dx.doi.org/10.1080/09518390110063365

Substance Abuse and Mental Health Services Administration. (2011). *The NSDUH report: Substance use among Hispanic adolescents*. Retrieved from https://www. samhsa.gov/data/sites/default/files/WEB_SR_007/WEB_SR_007/Subs_Use_ Hispanic_Adlscnts.pdf

Tacón, A. M., & Caldera, Y. M. (2001). Attachment and parental correlates in late adolescent Mexican American women. *Hispanic Journal of Behavioral Sciences, 23*, 71–87. http://dx.doi.org/10.1177/0739986301231005

Telzer, E. H., & Vazquez-Garcia, H. A. (2009). Skin color and self-perceptions of immigrant and U.S.-born Latinas. *Hispanic Journal of Behavioral Sciences, 31*, 357–374. http://dx.doi.org/10.1177/0739986309336913

Tervalon, M., & Murray-García, J. (1998). Cultural humility versus cultural competence: A critical distinction in defining physician training outcomes in multicultural education. *Journal of Health Care for the Poor and Underserved, 9*, 117–125. http:// dx.doi.org/10.1353/hpu.2010.0233

Todorova, I. L., Falcón, L. M., Lincoln, A. K., & Price, L. L. (2010). Perceived discrimination, psychological distress and health. *Sociology of Health & Illness, 32*, 843–861. http://dx.doi.org/10.1111/j.1467-9566.2010.01257.x

Torres, L. (2010). Predicting levels of Latino depression: Acculturation, acculturative stress, and coping. *Cultural Diversity and Ethnic Minority Psychology, 16*, 256–263. http://dx.doi.org/10.1037/a0017357

Umaña-Taylor, A. J., & Updegraff, K. A. (2007). Latino adolescents' mental health: Exploring the interrelations among discrimination, ethnic identity, cultural orientation, self-esteem, and depressive symptoms. *Journal of Adolescence, 30*, 549–567. http://dx.doi.org/10.1016/j.adolescence.2006.08.002

U.S. Census Bureau. (2017, August 31). *Facts for features: Hispanic heritage month 2017*. Retrieved from https://www.census.gov/newsroom/facts-for-features/2017/hispanic-heritage.html

van der Kolk, B. A., Stone, L., West, J., Rhodes, A., Emerson, D., Suvak, M., & Spinazzola, J. (2014). Yoga as an adjunctive treatment for posttraumatic stress disorder: A randomized controlled trial. *The Journal of Clinical Psychiatry, 75*, e559–e565. http://dx.doi.org/10.4088/JCP.13m08561

Vidales, G. T. (2010). Arrested justice: The multifaceted plight of immigrant Latinas who face domestic violence. *Journal of Family Violence, 25*, 533–544. http://dx.doi.org/10.1007/s10896-010-9309-5

Vyas, A. N., Landry, M., Schnider, M., Rojas, A. M., & Wood, S. F. (2012). Public health interventions: Reaching Latin adolescents via short message service and social media. *Journal of Medical Internet Research, 14*(4). Retrieved from https://www.ncbi.nlm.nih.gov/pmc/articles/PMC3409615/

Worell, J., & Remer, P. (2003). *Feminist perspectives in therapy* (2nd ed.). New York, NY: Wiley.

Yosso, T. J. (2005). Whose culture has capital: A critical race theory discussion of community cultural wealth. *Ethnography and Education, 8*, 69–91.

Yosso, T. J. (2006). *Critical race counterstories along the Chicana/Chicano educational pipeline*. New York, NY: Routledge Taylor & Francis.

Zayas, L. H., Lester, R. J., Cabassa, L. J., & Fortuna, L. R. (2005). Why do so many Latina teens attempt suicide? A conceptual model for research. *American Journal of Orthopsychiatry, 75*, 275–287. http://dx.doi.org/10.1037/0002-9432.75.2.275

Zayas, L. H., & Pilat, A. M. (2008). Suicidal behavior in Latinas: Explanatory cultural factors and implications for intervention. *Suicide and Life-Threatening Behavior, 38*, 334–342. http://dx.doi.org/10.1521/suli.2008.38.3.334

6

NEXT STEPS

An Integrated Model for Conducting Multicultural Feminist Therapy

THEMA BRYANT-DAVIS AND INDHUSHREE RAJAN

The template proposed in this chapter for a 6-week therapeutic empowerment group intervention is based on an integration of the themes in the previous chapters. This group can include girls of the same race or ethnicity or be used with diverse girls of color, and it can run 90 minutes to 2 hours. The therapist should prepare by educating herself on the historical and contemporary challenges and strengths of the cultures represented in the potential group. In addition, self-reflection guided by cultural humility is a key component of preparation for the intervention, particularly with historically marginalized community members. The 6 weeks are organized by the acronym THRIVE. The group, consisting of six to 10 girls, meets in a well-ventilated, culturally decorated space, with seats arranged in a circle. The group may also meet outdoors if the area is conducive for confidential dialogue. For the first session and the last session, the therapist invites the adolescent to bring one or two family members, guardians, or mentors. If the funding is sufficient, groups should have water, fruit, or a healthy snack available.

http://dx.doi.org/10.1037/0000140-007

Multicultural Feminist Therapy: Helping Adolescent Girls of Color to Thrive,
T. Bryant-Davis (Editor)

WEEK 1: TOUCHSTONES

Setting the Atmosphere

The therapist will have different scents, from oils or leaves, available for the girls to take some mindful breaths and calm anxieties they may have about starting the group. The girls can choose none, one, or all of the scents. Some potential scents are sage, lavender, peppermint, lemon, and frankincense.

Introduction

The facilitator or facilitators (preferably two) will welcome the girls and their support persons to the group, acknowledging the elders in the room and appreciating the girls for being willing to attend. Then the facilitators will introduce the rationale for the group, which is exploring and building on strengths, recognizing and coping with challenges, healing wounds from the past, planning for the future, and empowering one's self to resist the negative while creating the positive. Next, the facilitators will introduce themselves, including the personal reasons that motivate them to work with the girls. Finally, the facilitators should establish the ground rules by first describing confidentiality, including when confidentiality has to be broken, and then asking the attendees to list other rules they believe are important. On the list be sure to include respectful communication, freedom to choose how much they want to share, and acknowledgment that people have different experiences and views, so there is no need to debate or pressure people to agree. The facilitators should express the importance of the girls attending every session and notifying the facilitators if they are unable to attend a session.

Bringing Voices Into the Space

The facilitators will remind participants that they can pass whenever they do not wish to speak. The introduction question for Week 1 is, "Please share your name and one thing you are hoping to learn or gain from this group or one thing you are hoping the girl you are supporting will learn or gain from the group." The facilitators should answer first to model disclosure and engagement. Depending on the composition and preference of the group, the girls can pass a feather, talking stick, drum, or beads to the person who is speaking as a reminder of not interrupting and as a way of honoring the person who is speaking with attention.

Psychoeducation

The facilitators should provide information about the meaning and protective factors associated with healthy social support (family and friends), cultural identity, and spirituality. The therapist will describe these as touchstones—aspects of ourselves that can ground, support, inspire, and strengthen.

Group Response

Adolescents and their guest(s) are invited to share (a) someone who is an important part of their social support and why they are important; (b) something about their heritage they take pride in; or (c) something about their spirituality, religion, or faith that encourages them when they are feeling down.

Expressive Art

The attendees will complete a fill-in-the-blank poem that is recited aloud to avoid any literacy issues among attendees and honor the oral tradition of the girls. The two sentences the attendees will complete are "My roots are . . ." and "My branches are . . ."

In doing expressive arts work as related to trauma, healing, or connecting to deeper aspects of the emotional, intuitive self, poetry highlights the associative and redemptive power of language.

> Through language, we remember and try to reconstruct what we know. . . .
> Poetry is by nature associative—one word leads to another, one sound calls to another, one image relates to another, and in this way a poem can be the wave you ride, allowing your controlling mind to step aside and follow what your intuitive understanding knows you know. . . (McKim, 1999, pp. 211–212)

Sacred Pause

The facilitators will have everyone in the circle stand and direct them in the "breath of many and one." The facilitators will explain to the girls that their presence in this group is at once an expression of many and one: They are individuals and a part of the group community. The deep breath—inhale, hold, and exhale—that the group takes together ritualistically honors the truth of the many and the one, so as they leave group and go into their week, they will know that their community goes with them. The facilitators will then introduce the group to the *sacred pause*: 1 minute of silence for prayer, meditation, mindfulness, or reflection.

Closing Declaration

The girls will receive affirmation and encouragement from the support persons they invited. The girls will sit in the center of the circle. The person(s) they invited will individually say to the girl that they are accompanying, "May you have . . ." They may choose peace, confidence, joy, love, healing, health, good friends, or any positive phrase. After the girls receive their blessing or affirmation, the facilitators will encourage each girl to speak a word or phrase that they would each like to give back to the circle, as an intention for the group space: "May we have . . . (e.g., community, friendship, support, understanding, belonging)." By holding this refrain, this closing exercise also simultaneously affirms the value of the individual and of belonging to a community—the many and the one.

Closing

The facilitators will thank everyone for coming, share the theme for the next week, and give the girls the homework assignment to find a woman from their family and/or cultural heritage who overcame a difficulty and come prepared to tell the group about how she survived.

WEEK 2: HEALING HEARTS

Setting the Atmosphere and Introduction

Welcome the participants, remind them of rules, and follow as outlined in Week 1.

Bringing Voice Into the Space and Group Sharing of the Topic

After again sharing their names, each girl will tell the group about a woman from her family or culture who overcame difficulties (the homework assignment from the previous week).

Psychoeducation

The facilitators should provide information about the meaning and effects of stress and traumatic stress. Psychoeducation should include the potential physical, emotional, cognitive, relational, behavioral, and spiritual effects of stress and trauma. Stressors may include financial stress, family conflict, school pressures, rejection, and discrimination. Effects may include depression, generalized anxiety, distrust, somatic complaints, and anger.

Group Response

The facilitators invite the girls to share from their personal experience a stressor and its effects.

Psychoeducation

The facilitators will provide information on healthy versus unhealthy coping strategies, including talking to a support system, praying, attending therapy, journaling, and creating expressive art, as well as unhealthy strategies such as emotional eating, substance dependence, and initiating fights.

Group Response

Girls will share one healthy and one unhealthy strategy they have used in the past. The facilitators should highlight the various strategies that were mentioned and encourage the girls to try a healthy coping strategy that was mentioned by another participant.

Expressive Art

The attendees will be led in movement, stretching, and/or cultural dance with therapeutic and empowering music from the cultures represented. If the facilitators have this skill set, they can lead it, or they can invite an outside guest to lead the movement component.

As an addition to or in place of the Expressive Art exercise, the facilitators may lead the girls in the *Authentic Share and Witness integrative exercise*, which helps to locate emotional experience in the body. In this exercise, each girl pairs off with a partner, and the two take turns sharing a hope or fear story related to their experiences with stress or trauma, while assuming an authentic physical pose (e.g., sitting cross-legged, bending to the side, standing facing the opposite direction, or whatever pose intuitively appeals to the person who is sharing). Once the sharer finishes, her partner mirrors the shared story back to her, while assuming the same physical pose the sharer did so that the sharer can be fully held and honored in their experience. The process is then repeated so that the original sharer may now assume the role of witness. The integration of voice and body position in this exercise allows for a fuller experience of vulnerability, risk, and trust. The girls are then invited to process their internal responses and impressions of the exercise with their partners and then with the larger group. Guiding questions may include: Was I worried about how I would be physically perceived by my partner? How did having to hold my physical pose impact my being able to share my story? Was I concerned about being taken seriously? Did I feel seen and understood during the exercise? After the exercise? Was there any part of the mirroring portion of the exercise (being mirrored or mirroring) that was impactful for me?

In that these questions evoke aspects of acceptance, belonging, being seen and understood, and dealing with the new and unexpected, the girls are given an integrative and reflective experience of their stress, as well as the experience of accepting and being accepted by another group member while vulnerable. The integrated expressive and receptive aspects of this exercise serve to encourage the girls to embrace authenticity in self and other. "Usually we act and live as if our bodies, feelings, and minds are separate. We live in a house divided" (Halprin, 2000, p. 134). To hide our feelings away in the liminal spaces of such a house will only cause us to "lose our body language, which makes the creative response impossible" (Highwater, 1987, p. 1).

Sacred Pause

Follow as outlined in the previous week.

Closing Declaration

The girls will make a positive declaration over themselves using the phrase "May my heart . . ." They may choose words or phrases such as "begin to heal," "grow stronger," "release the pain," or "feel love."

Closing

The facilitators will thank everyone for coming, share the theme for the next week, and give the girls the homework assignment to discuss with an elder in their family or community one goal they have for 5 years from now and one goal they have for 10 years from now. The adolescent should ask the elder for their thoughts about the goals.

WEEK 3: ROAD TO THE FUTURE

Setting the Atmosphere and Introduction

Follow as outlined in previous weeks.

Bringing Voices Into the Space and Group Sharing of the Topic

The introduction question for Week 3 is, "Please share your goals and the response of your elder" (the homework assignment). If any of the girls did not receive positive support, the facilitators should be prepared to acknowledge the ways it can be difficult to work toward a goal that others do not value or see as attainable.

Psychoeducation

The facilitators should provide information about the importance of goals, academically, vocationally, socially, and personally (emotional growth). The facilitators will then discuss some of the barriers to goal attainment as well as some strategies for addressing these barriers. Barriers may include lack of role models, discouragement, lack of knowledge, limited resources (finances), and the priority of immediate needs over long-term goals. Strategies can include ways of accessing information, identifying and approaching a potential mentor, progressing on a budget (e.g., scholarships), seeking sources of inspiration, not internalizing the voices of discouragement even if they are family or teachers, and identifying the traps of devaluing delayed gratification.

Group Response

The facilitators invite the girls to share a barrier they have faced or anticipate facing on the path to goal attainment and how they have tried to cope with it in the past or how they plan to address it in the future.

Group facilitators may alternatively, or as an addition to the Group Response discussion prompt, implement an acting exercise to emphasize healthy engagement with discouragement. By externalizing their internal, emotional experiences, the girls have the opportunity to separate themselves from emotion and create room for self-dialogue within the space of dramatic role-play. "There is always another to whom the Self is telling his or her story, even if . . . this takes the form of an internal dialogue" (Holmes, 2001, p. 85). Each girl takes 10 minutes to express what discouragement looks like and says on a sheet of paper, using markers and colored pencils. A chair is placed at the center of the circle, a mirror is placed across from it, and each girl takes a turn in the circle to dialogue with her representation of discouragement.

For example, when it is her turn, a girl goes into the center of the circle, places her expression of discouragement on the chair, and while standing next to the mirror, looks at discouragement and says why she has a hard time talking to discouragement. She might say, "When I am with discouragement, I feel like a failure" or "When discouragement finds me, I feel like I will never reach my goals." Once she does this portion of the exercise, the girl walks and stands next to the chair and now faces the mirror. While looking at her reflection in the mirror, the girl affirms why the things she felt when interacting with discouragement are not true. For example, she might say, "Even though I didn't reach my goal this time, I choose to believe that I am not a failure. I believe that I can try again and be successful." Or she might say, "Even though others may tell me that I am not good enough to achieve my goal, I choose to believe that I am strong, smart and good enough," and so forth.

The experience of externalizing discouragement and reframing its message in a positive, proactive way encourages participants to differentiate between positive and negative self-talk. It also helps them to actively experience the power of personal agency in choosing focused thought (affirmation) over feelings, illustrating that pervasive feelings, even if expressed or supported by respected and trusted family members, teachers, or other role models, are not necessarily true and do not have to herald failure or negative self-perceptions.

Psychoeducation

The therapist will discuss the need to move from long-term goals to short-term goals. The girls will be encouraged to consider steps they can take now to build the road to their future. If they want a college degree, a particular career, healthy family life, economic stability, or emotional wellness in their future, they have to think about concrete steps that are important for their present.

Group Response

Girls are invited to share one thing they need to work on changing or continuing this year to prepare for the future.

Expressive Art

The attendees will create a collage about their future or a vision board using words and images from magazines that centralize girls and women from their cultural heritage.

Sacred Pause

Follow as outlined in previous weeks.

Closing Declaration

The girls will make a positive declaration to the girl to their right using the phrase "May you . . ." They may choose words or phrases such as "have the courage to follow your dreams," "have the support to reach your goals," and "have the faith to be what you want to be."

Closing

The facilitators will thank everyone for coming, share the theme for next week, and give the girls the homework assignment to journal about the qualities that make a friendship or dating relationship healthy.

WEEK 4: INTIMATE ISSUES

Setting the Atmosphere and Introduction

Follow as outlined in previous weeks.

Bringing Voices Into the Space and Group Sharing of the Topic

The introduction question for Week 4 is, "What are three qualities of a healthy friendship or relationship, and why do you think they are important?" (the homework assignment).

Psychoeducation

The facilitators will discuss the importance of self-acceptance and the ways insecurities can create difficulties in friendships and romantic relationships. Facilitators will then explore the power and control wheel, as well as the wheel for healthy relationships, connecting the information to both friendship and dating. The facilitators will then share a number of experiences that may have affected the girls' confidence and self-acceptance. These should include trauma; beauty myths related to their race or ethnicity, phenotype, or body image; only seeing unhealthy relationships; disappointment; or rejection. Traumas may include assault, partner abuse (experiencing or witnessing), child abuse, hate crimes, and traumatic losses.

Group Response

The facilitators invite the girls to share how a negative experience made them feel about themselves.

As an addition to the Group Response discussion prompt, group facilitators may implement an Expressive Arts exercise to illustrate the creation of the "false self" and its connection to trauma. "The child puts themselves away. . . . And develops a self that will get acknowledgement and love . . . a false self" (Winnicott, 1952/1987, p. 587).

In the first stage of this exercise, the girls are allowed 20 minutes to create masks. They may choose either a human or animal-shaped mask (facilitators provide blank, white cardboard, precut masks). Using markers and colored pencils, the girls write one of two core messages across the front of the masks: "Please love me" or "Please don't hurt me," whichever message has most resonated for them when they have been criticized, ridiculed, or abused. They then color and decorate the masks however they wish.

Once the girls finish their masks, they reform the circle, and the facilitators talk about the idea of a "false self" that can completely take away, hide, or cover up whatever problem is causing the abuse. For example, the false self can act sweet and pretend nothing is wrong to cover up fear so that "Mom will stop yelling and love me again." Or the false self can go on a strict diet and pretend that everything is fine to hide pain and fear of rejection, so "my boyfriend will think I'm pretty and not criticize me anymore." The girls then share about an experience in which they have pulled out their false selves to mask how they felt or what they wanted to do, to finally be loved, or to keep from getting hurt or rejected. Follow-up process questions might include: Did it work? Were you able to avoid the pain or get the love you wanted? How does masking your actual feelings make you feel about yourself? (Sajnani & Read Johnson, 2014).

Psychoeducation

The facilitators should provide the girls with ways to build or rebuild their self-esteem, self-compassion, and self-worth. These can include doing activities they enjoy, building friendships with positive people, learning to communicate and advocate for themselves, engaging in therapy and self-care, recognizing and appreciating their strengths, recognizing negative thoughts and working to replace them, and learning about the beauty and strength of their culture.

Group Response

The facilitators should invite the girls to share one thing that helps them feel better about themselves. If there is nothing, they can name one thing they are willing to try to build their self-esteem.

Expressive Art Closing Exercise[1]

The facilitators will provide the girls with colored pencils and a sheet of paper. Facilitators will then instruct them to use the pencils to divide the paper into three sections. In the first section, they will use words or images to depict how they saw themselves before the most negative event happened, the middle panel is to show how they felt about themselves during the upsetting event, and the last panel is for how they would like to see themselves in the future. The girls will then share their artwork. They do not have to explain but can let the art speak for itself.

Sacred Pause

Follow as outlined in previous weeks.

Closing Declaration

Together, girls will read the lyrics to a song about friendship, such as "Lean on Me" by Bill Withers.

Closing

The facilitators will thank everyone for coming, share the theme for next week, and give the homework assignment for the girls to spend a few minutes each day listening to a song that helps them feel more positive about themselves. Facilitators should ask them to bring the lyrics to the song for the next group.

---

[1] The Expressive Arts exercises may be interchanged or used in sequence of sharing and closing as desired.

WEEK 5: VOICE

Setting the Atmosphere and Introduction

Follow as outlined in previous weeks.

Bringing Voices Into the Space and Group Sharing of the Topic

The introduction question for Week 5 is, "Please share a section (potentially one stanza and the chorus) of the lyrics from the song that inspires or encourages you" (the homework assignment).

Psychoeducation

The facilitators will explore the difference between shame and guilt and then discuss the ways shame can silence us. The facilitators will also describe ways family, cultural community, media, and even school or religious settings can discourage girls and women from fully speaking up.

Group Response

The facilitators invite the girls to share a time when they felt unable to or uncomfortable about speaking up for themselves or others or about a particular issue.

Psychoeducation

The facilitators will discuss the contributions that girls and women have made and can continue to make. Psychoeducation should focus on confidence, courage, communication skills, assertiveness versus aggression, and humility as a value versus oppressive silencing.

Group Response

Facilitators should invite the girls to share a time they saw someone speak up that they found admirable; it could be a personal example or a public figure.

Expressive Art

The therapist will invite the girls to practice role-playing, speaking up about something important to them. It may be something they wish they said to a person in the past, or it may be speaking up in the future.

Sacred Pause

Follow as outlined in previous weeks.

Closing Declaration

The girls will complete a spoken word exercise about their voice. They can either write freely or use the following template: My voice sounds like . . . My voice feels like . . . My voice looks like . . . My voice tastes like . . . When I speak . . .

Closing

The facilitators will thank everyone for coming, share the theme for the next week, and give the homework assignment for the girls to find information about an issue they believe is having a negative effect on adolescent girls. Examples may include toxins in the environment, racism, sexism, poverty, addiction, dating violence, sex trafficking, or mass incarceration. They should come to the final session along with their support persons prepared to talk about their issue. Facilitators should encourage them to talk from the heart instead of reading verbatim from a piece of paper. They can be prepared to share what the issue is, the negative effects it is having, and why it is important for the community to address it. (The facilitators should schedule a 20-minute call with each girl during the week to allow her to practice sharing her information because the closing week will include her guests.)

WEEK 6: EMPOWERMENT

Setting the Atmosphere and Introduction

Follow as outlined in previous weeks.

Bringing Voices Into the Space and Group Sharing of the Topic

The introduction question for Week 6 is, "Please share the issue that you chose to highlight that has a significant impact on adolescent girls" (the homework assignment). Support persons will have the opportunity to respond to the girls' presentations. They can be prompted with such comments as, "Please share with the girls one thing you found important about their presentation" or "Please share with the girls why you find it valuable for them to use their voices to speak up for what is right."

Psychoeducation

The facilitators will discuss three components of empowerment: awareness, resistance, and activism or advocacy. The discussion of *awareness* should bring attention to how racism, sexism, and other forms of oppression affect the girls and their families. Psychoeducation regarding *resistance* will focus on working against internalized oppression—not accepting or passing on to your daughters, nieces, granddaughters, or mentees the negative self-beliefs that oppression teaches us. *Activism* should explore the various ways people can combat oppression, such as participating in marches, creating artwork, supporting leaders who work to address their issues, volunteering in community care or social justice organizations, and raising awareness of others (Bryant-Davis & Adams, 2016). The facilitators can also share that self-care and self-love as well as love and care for others can be radical acts to combat the intention of oppression, which is to dehumanize.

Group Response

The facilitators invite the girls and their support persons to share one incidence or story of oppression and discrimination that has affected their lives or the lives of persons in their social support network. Facilitators will then invite them to share one way in which they have already, or in the future, would like to work against injustice.

Expressive Art

The girls will each present one of their creative expressions from past weeks that they are comfortable sharing with the group: a collage or vision board, spoken word, part of the lyrics to an inspiring song, movement (cultural dance), and so forth.

Sacred Pause

Follow as outlined in past weeks.

Closing Declaration

The girls will declare a blessing over their elders or support persons to bring the group full circle. They have received, and they have something to share. They will declare to their support person, "May you . . ." If for any reason, a girl's support person is not able to attend, the facilitators will ask whether the girl is willing to allow a facilitator to stand in for their elder.

Closing

The facilitators will thank everyone for coming and present each girl with a journal to continue her journey.

This group is a proposed model based on an integration of the material from the prior chapters. Facilitators may evaluate the group using either a weekly post-group brief survey or a single survey at the end of the 6 weeks that assesses both knowledge acquisition and subjective report of changes in levels of traumatic stress symptoms, substance use, anxiety, and depression. A qualitative question may also provide important insights regarding the most enjoyed aspect and what, if anything, they would like to change about the group. These groups may serve as standalone interventions, as well as complementary interventions to accompany individual psychotherapy.

ISSUES TO CONSIDER IN THE IMPLEMENTATION OF A THRIVE GROUP

Cultural Sensitivity and Awareness

In cocreating a safe and proactive group container with culturally diverse participants, it is critical that facilitators be sensitive to stereotyping and diagnostic overshadowing in their work. Toward this end, implementing facilitator pre- and postprocessing groups to bookend sessions with THRIVE participants would encourage facilitators to share their personal experiences in leading groups and provide feedback and support to one another about holding group space in cultural sensitivity.

In addition to group process about specific issues arising for facilitators in their respective groups, therapists could also engage in activities, such as thematized role-play, personal sharing, and authentic movement exercises, to address the ways personal and/or sociocultural triggers inform work with culturally diverse participants. For example, therapists could engage in the Authentic Share and Witness exercise, as outlined in the proposed group model. The processing portion of the activity, in that the guiding questions evoke aspects of acceptance, belonging, being seen and understood, and dealing with the new and unexpected, may help facilitators gain insights into what sharing or participating in new or unfamiliar activities may feel like for THRIVE participants. The vulnerability, risk, and self-consciousness commonly evoked by this exercise can more specifically serve as a good opening to discuss topics such as self-esteem, body shaming, and racial discrimination, allowing facilitators to face and process their own biases and blind spots as they relate to these issues.

Group Safety and Cohesiveness

Another important aspect of the THRIVE model is safety and boundaries. Participants need to feel safe in the context of what they will be expected to do in the program and how their feelings, needs, and concerns will be met in the group process. Encouraging participants to share their perspectives, opinions, and concerns in the service of cocreating boundaries for the group is a vital way in which participants can feel empowered to advocate for their needs while working together to choose how they want to protect and support one another. Practically, cocreating group "agreements," or a mutually accepted code by which the group will function throughout the program, would be a good way to realize group safety needs and create group cohesiveness.

The Agreements Exercise

A talking stick is passed in turns around the circle, and each participant is allowed to share (or not share) a fear or concern she has about personal sharing and/or participating in group activities, and the therapist will write down and read back each concern, to ensure accuracy.

After this exercise, the therapist facilitates a group discussion about how these concerns may be addressed and supported in the group. The group then negotiates a set of agreements and boundaries. For example, to address someone being emotionally triggered, the group may decide to create free space at the other end of the room or in an adjacent room in which the participant may have some space to calm down and re-center herself. Or the group could choose to "press pause" on an activity and instead provide a community holding space for an emotionally triggered participant to witness, listen to, and encourage her. Once group agreements and boundaries are settled, the group can ritually recognize and close this process by taking turns holding the talking stick and speaking one word into the circle, meant to describe a value that they are upholding as a group community by creating these agreements (e.g., safety, honor, peace).

FUTURE RESEARCH AND CONCLUSION

Multicultural feminist therapists have to continue to document and evaluate the outcomes of their interventions, both quantitatively and qualitatively. This work should include traditional psychotherapy, cultural modifications of traditional interventions, and culturally emergent interventions. Although scholars have understudied treatment with American Indian, African American, Asian American, and Latina adolescent girls, there are additional ethnically diverse girls in the United States whose treatment needs further exploration in the clinical literature.

These adolescent girls include but are not limited to Middle Eastern, Arab American, African immigrant (American), Jewish, Muslim, Indian, and Caribbean. There is in addition much more attention needed to research focused on intersectional identities of adolescent girls of color, such as those who are same-gender loving, who are genderqueer, and who have disabilities. Although the contributors touch on these important issues, the available research on counseling these populations is underdeveloped (see Chapter 5, this volume).

Additional scholarship should attend to the intersection of multicultural feminist therapy with adolescent girls of color, indigenous psychology, and international psychology. The critical topics facing adolescent girls of color and the appropriate interventions vary across geographical lines. Such themes facing adolescent girls in various countries include domestic and international trafficking, HIV and AIDS, war, refugee status, limited access to education, female circumcision, coerced marriage, child labor, kidnapping, ethnic conflict, dispossession of family land, xenophobia, and severe intergenerational poverty. Counseling interventions for international multicultural feminist therapy mandate decolonization of the field of psychology that creates space for indigenous therapeutic practices, such as drumming, dancing, connecting with nature, connecting with ancestors, and group-based interventions.

Womanist and *mujerista* psychologies are born from womanist and *mujerista* theologies, which predate them and have significant bodies of work on the religious lives, challenges, and contributions of Black and Latina women. Psychologists can learn from these traditions as they seek to develop a more holistic, authentic psychology of girls and women of color.

Another area of this research that has to be further pursued entails better understanding intersectionality and identity for women and girls in India, in the context of a paradigm shift from Western issues of gender equality toward issues of feminine identity and empowerment, as unfolding within Indian society today. Rana Haq (2013) wrote,

> The challenges facing women [and girls] in India due to the intersectionality of gender and other forms of identities impacting on their lives by exploring the intersection of gender, colour, caste, ethnicity, religion, marital status, and class as sources of discrimination against women in Indian society. (p. 171)

The scholarship explored in this text highlights the needs, strengths, and potential healing pathways for adolescent girls of color (see Chapter 3, this volume). The contributors attend to the ecological context of development for the adolescents and their families (see Chapter 4).

Multicultural feminist therapists centralize the values of cultural humility and cultural competence, as well as the intersectional experiences of adolescent girls of color. Appreciation for cultural history, values, and resources, as well as the celebration of resistance and empowerment strategies, creates a pathway for adolescent girls of color to thrive (see Chapter 2 and Chapter 5). By decolonizing psychotherapy from culture-blind and culture-stereotypical models (Conwill, 2015), multicultural feminist therapists work to liberate adolescent girls of color from oppressive forces while empowering them to survive and thrive.

REFERENCES

Bryant-Davis, T., & Adams, T. (2016). A psychocultural exploration of womanism, activism, and social justice. In T. Bryant-Davis & L. Comas-Díaz (Eds.), *Womanist and mujerista psychologies: Voices of fire, acts of courage* (pp. 219–236). Washington, DC: American Psychological Association. http://dx.doi.org/10.1037/14937-010

Conwill, W. L. (2015). De-colonizing multicultural counseling and psychology: Addressing race through intersectionality. In R. D. Goodman & P. C. Gorski (Eds.), *Decolonizing "multicultural" counseling through social justice* (pp. 117–126). New York, NY: Springer Science + Business Media. http://dx.doi.org/10.1007/978-1-4939-1283-4_9

Halprin, D. (2000). Living artfully: Movement as an integrative process. In S. K. Levine & E. G. Levine (Eds.), *Foundations of expressive arts therapy: Theoretical and clinical perspectives* (pp. 133–149). London, England: Jessica Kingsley.

Haq, R. (2013). Intersectionality of gender and other forms of identity: Dilemmas and challenges facing women in India. *Gender in Management, 28,* 171–184. http://dx.doi.org/10.1108/GM-01-2013-0010

Highwater, J. (1987, November–December). The primal mind: Vision and reality in Indian America. *Creation Magazine, 3,* 5.

Holmes, J. (2001). *The search for the secure base: Attachment theory and psychotherapy.* Philadelphia, PA: Brunner-Routledge.

McKim, E. G. (1999). Poetry in the oral tradition: Serious play with words. In S. K. Levine & E. G. Levine (Eds.), *Foundations of expressive arts therapy:*

Theoretical and clinical perspectives (pp. 211–222). London, England: Jessica Kingsley.

Sajnani, N., & Read Johnson, D. (2014). *Trauma-informed drama therapy: Transforming clinics, classrooms, and communities.* Springfield, IL: Charles C Thomas.

Winnicott, D. W. (1987). *The spontaneous gesture: Selected letters of D. W. Winnicott.* London, England: Karnac Books. (Original work published 1952)

Index

About the Editor

Thema Bryant-Davis, PhD, is a professor of psychology and director of the Culture and Trauma Research Lab at Pepperdine University. She was the 2015 recipient of the California Psychological Association Distinguished Scientist Award, the 2013 recipient of the American Psychological Association (APA) Early Career Award for Distinguished Contributions to Psychology in the Public Interest, and the 2007 recipient of the APA Emerging Leader of Women in Psychology Award. She is also a past president of the Society for the Psychology of Women and a former APA representative to the United Nations.

Dr. Bryant-Davis has authored or coedited several books, including *Thriving in the Wake of Trauma: A Multicultural Guide*; *Surviving Sexual Violence: A Guide to Recovery and Empowerment*; *Religion and Spirituality for Diverse Women: Foundations of Strength and Resilience*; and *Womanist and* Mujerista *Psychologies: Voices of Fire, Acts of Courage*. Her research areas include trauma psychology, ethnic minority women, oppression, coping, and spirituality.

ESSENCE magazine named her among women who are shaping the world. Visit http://www.drthema.com and follow @drthema.